AFTERLIFE

★★★★★

"A chilling and intimidating subject that many avoid but that the authors of AFTERLIFE have met head-on with refreshingly sound theology."

— Dr. Thomas Horn, CEO SkyWatch TV

AFTERLIFE

Near Death Experiences, Neuroscience, Quantum Physics and the Increasing Evidence for

LIFE AFTER DEATH

DONNA HOWELL JOSH PECK ALLIE ANDERSON-HENSON

DEFENDER

CRANE, MO

Afterlife: Near Death Experiences, Neuroscience, Quantum Physics, and the Increasing Evidence for Life After Death
By Josh Peck, Donna Howell, & Allie Anderson-Henson

Printed in the United States of America

Scripture taken from the King James Version unless otherwise noted.

Cover design by Jeffrey Mardis

ISBN: 9781732547896

Dedications

This is dedicated to my son, Nathan, who beat cancer during the writing process of this book. I would also like to dedicate this to three talented researchers and friends who passed away during the same time period: Joseph "Doc" Marquis, Richard Shaw, and Joe Hagmann: I'll see you on the other side, brothers!

—Josh Peck

To my beloved husband, James, and my two wonderful children, Joe E and Althia.

—Donna Howell

To Randy, John, Karol, Gwyneth, Kat, Reagan, and Ian. May you follow the Lord always, continually placing your hope in eternity with Him.

—Allie Anderson-Henson

Contents

Introduction

Where do we go when we die? For a Christian, the quick answer may *seem* as simple as "Heaven" or "Hell," yet there are many within the Church who shy away from touching on the subject in-depth because it is so hard to answer related questions with a sense of authority. Even for those who look to Scripture for information on such matters, a certain vagueness seems to envelope the concepts of the afterlife and death, provoking even many who feel secure in finding an eternity in Heaven with God to evade the subject.

Many people find such questions as "What is it like to physically die?" hard to answer; tougher still are such questions as "Why does God send people to Hell?" and "Where is God when His followers are being martyred?"

Beyond the theological difficulty related to such inquiries is the well-founded caution many have toward ideas such as communication with the dead, the existence of ghosts, the phenomenon of hauntings, and near-death or out-of-body experiences.

What does the Bible say about such matters? Is there a balanced perspective that upholds Scripture while addressing such perplexing spiritual issues? For many Christians, the lack of resources for addressing such topics often means (1) avoiding the topic, or (2) engaging in secular (worldly or extrabiblical) study. However, when believers need clear, scripturally founded answers, neither of these approaches will suffice.

In the pages of this book, Josh Peck, Donna Howell, and I (Allie Anderson-Henson) attempt to unravel the mysteries of such confusing, modern phenomena while offering a biblical foundation. It is our hope that this work will bring you peace about *your own* afterlife, encourage you to secure your own eternity with Jesus, and offer a scriptural perspective regarding matters that the world has distorted.

PART ONE

NEAR-DEATH EXPERIENCES, OUT-OF-BODY EXPERIENCES, AND REAL-LIFE OCCURRENCES

chapter one

NDE and OBE Science and Testimonies

Difficulty of Subjective Supernatural Experiences

It can be difficult to know what to do when someone shares with you a supernatural experience. By nature, these types of experiences tend to be completely subjective; in fact, it's rare to have physical or objective proof of something supernatural or miraculous. Yet, many people have either had (or know someone who claims to have had) a supernatural experience.

One of the most profound experiences reported falls in the realm of OBEs (out-of-body experiences), which can include NDEs (near-death experiences). OBEs can consist of activity that has nothing to do with a physical threat, such as supernatural visions causing one to be "caught up" or taken out of the body. NDEs are a *type* of OBE in which there is a threat to the physical body, hence the "near-death" label. Typically, this occurs when a person has suffered an almost-fatal accident or a severe medical condition, yet has managed to survive, retaining enough memory to tell others what the NDE was like. Generally speaking, one can have an OBE that is not an NDE, but one can't have an NDE that is not an OBE.

As stated, when someone relates a personal, supernatural experience, it's difficult to know how to react, because generally there is very little to no physical proof. Because of this, we tend to give more credence to accounts from people we know, those who have a proven history of credibility. Apart from that, when we hear the stories from people we don't know, we must do a great deal of research in order to verify as many of the details as possible.

In this chapter, you will see examples of NDEs and non-NDE OBEs from personal acquaintances of the authors as well as from people we don't know, but whose well-researched accounts contain compelling evidence. The topics of these narratives are vast in scope and include everything from subjective experiences, objective evidence, and scientific research to theological interpretations and all manner of opinions. Even more, each of these categories relies on the other for the whole to make any kind of sense. Due to this, it would be very difficult, perhaps even impossible, to separate each of these topics within OBEs/ NDEs into separate chapters. Therefore, we (Donna, Allie, and Josh) have decided to deal with OBEs/NDEs at length right at the beginning. In this chapter, you'll read some personal accounts, current scientific research, evidence supporting OBE/NDE claims, theological interpretations, personal opinions, and much more.

Moment-after-Death Research

More than a hundred years ago, a debate began in the medical and scientific realm that has permeated speculation in the spiritual/philosophical forum. In 1907, reputable physician of Haverhill, Massachusetts, Dr. Duncan MacDougall, set out to measure the weight/mass of a human soul by conducting an experiment whereupon six dying patients were

SOUL HAS WEIGHT, PHYSICIAN THINKS

Dr. Macdougall of Haverhill Tells of Experiments at Death.

LOSS TO BODY RECORDED

Scales Showed an Ounce Gone in One Case, He Says—Four Other Doctors Present.

Special to The New York Times.

BOSTON, March 10.—That the human soul has a definite weight, which can be determined when it passes from the body, is the belief of Dr. Duncan Macdougall, a reputable physician of Haverhill. He is at the head of a Research Society which for six years has been experimenting in this field. With him, he says, have been associated four other physicians.

Headline from the *New York Times*, March 11, 1907

placed on a specially made scale just before their death.[1] The declining patient was counter-measured by an exact weight that made the scale sensitive to a variation of as little as a tenth of an ounce. The *New York Times* reported: "In every case after death the platform opposite the one in which lay the subject of the test fell suddenly, Dr. MacDougall says."[2] MacDougall's claims of the person's weight loss ranging between a half to a full ounce at the time of death were said to have been corroborated by four medical associates—other physicians involved in the experiment who were said to have witnessed the startling evidence as one subject died of tuberculosis: "The instant life ceased the opposite scale pan fell with a suddenness that was astonishing—as if something had been suddenly lifted from the body. Immediately all the usual deductions were made for physical loss of weight, and it was discovered that there was still a full ounce of weight unaccounted for."[3] MacDougall, in his account of the experiment, commented that one of the strangest things he and his comrades noticed surrounded the death of the third patient, whose manner was "phlegmatic"[4] and "slow of thought and action,"[5] was that, upon dying, the patient showed no variation of weight for up to a full minute after death. Then, one minute after death, the patient showed the same "sudden" decrease in weight as the previous patients had shown. MacDougall attributes this delay in weight loss to the man's demeanor, stating that he believed "the soul remained suspended in the body after death, during the minute that elapsed before it came to the consciousness of its freedom.... And it is what might be expected to happen in a man of the subject's temperament."[6] MacDougall reported weight changes before expiration and upon time of death to each of the subjects of this experiment, factoring in such elements as sweat, urine, oxygen, and nitrogen.[7] His goal was to prove that the human soul had mass/weight. If so, this would demonstrate that the soul exists and is measurable. Because there are 28.34 grams in an ounce, and the patients each lost between a half and a full ounce, this experiment suggests that the average human soul weighs 21 grams (roughly three-fourths of an ounce). This is where the popular belief that the soul weighs 21 grams derives.

Critics of MacDougall included Dr. Augustus P. Clarke, who reminded members of the scientific community of a possible explanation for the missing 21 grams by stating that "at the moment of death, the lungs stop cooling the blood, causing the body's temperature to rise slightly, which makes the skin sweat—accounting for Dr. MacDougall's missing 21 grams."[8] MacDougall's response included the fact that the halt in circulation that accompanies death would prevent the skin's temperature from rising as a result of an occurrence isolated to the lungs.[9] Subsequent arguments mounted in both fervency and followers, and this experiment has become the subject of much debate in ensuing decades.

Interestingly, it is said that Dr. MacDougall, in an effort to rule out natural elements explaining the variation in weight upon death (thus confirming the existence of a measurable human soul), conducted subsequent experiments on fifteen dogs, which rendered no change in weight upon death. Thus, he concluded that humans have a measurable soul that weighs about 21 grams—and animals do not have souls.[10] Many in the scientific and medical communities criticized MacDougall's experiment on several levels, including: 1) the ethical aspect of how these subjects spent their final moments, 2) the questionability of the scale's accuracy, 3) the lack of corroboration of peer physicians whom MacDougall claimed attended the experiment with him, and 4) the inconsistency of weight diminution in an inadequately small test group. However, the boldness of the doctor's assertion endowed his theory with resiliency, and the idea that the human souls weigh 21 grams is still alive and well in modern culture.

After this experiment, MacDougall's focus shifted to attempts at photographing the soul. Despite his claims of having captured a light in these photographs, which he described as "resembling that of the interstellar ether," no photographic evidence of a soul was ever seized by the man, who died in 1920.[11]

Understanding Death

Death is a vast topic with many aspects. For psychologists, a healthy view of death is broken into five concepts: nonfunctionality (all processes—including thought, sensation, and bodily functions—halt); finality (one who has passed cannot be brought back); universality (everything dies; no living beings can escape death); applicability (death can only happen to beings who are living); and causation (either a gradual breakdown or a sudden event causes bodily functions to cease.)[12] When an individual understands these elements, he or she understands what death is. However, as shown throughout this book, there is much more to death than these elements, and questions abound regarding the issue that, for many, causes terrible fear.

While plenty of information is available on the grieving process and the psychological aspects of dealing with death, the physiological science surrounding the moment of death is a point of research growing in popularity. Considering the debate of soul weight (argued by Dr. MacDougall) vs. mortuary changes (the position held by Dr. Augustus Clarke), it is helpful to understand the process the body endures immediately after death, since these physical elements are often called into question to explain certain, possibly supernatural, phenomena (just as the debate between MacDougall and Clarke has shown).

Physical Changes at the Moment of Death

Before modern medical innovations such as defibrillators, life-support machinery, or cardiopulmonary resuscitation (CPR) progressed to the point that life-saving intervention could be used to halt or even reverse the onset of death, many doctors were obligated to accept a vaguer definition of death than modern circumstances allow.[13] Whereas decades ago, the decline of vital signs and eventual stopping of critical functions such as breathing were enough to indicate death, the availability of modern interventions (and when and how they can be applied) have provided a means by which the actual moment of medical/clinical death is more ambiguous. The result is the need for a more pinpointed, technical understanding of the physical aspects of death, which Dr. Sam Parnia, assistant professor of critical care medicine and director of resuscitation research at the University of New York at Stony Brooke, provides:

> Physiologically, the immediate cessation of blood that follows the heart stopping leads to the instant cessation of respiration and brainstem activity as well as whole-brain function, owing to the immediate cessation of oxygen delivery to vital organs. As the functions of the heart, lung, and brainstem are exquisitely linked together, a process that leads one organ to stop functioning will inevitably lead to the cessation of activity and functioning in the other…organs (with a resultant loss of all vital signs of life and life processes) and death.[14]

Physical changes that take place at the moment of death and throughout the first several hours postmortem cause the appearance of an individual's remains to immediately change. A condition called "primary flaccidity" sets in; that is the ultimate relaxation of muscles throughout the body.[15] Facial features, including eyelids and the jaw, slacken, and pupils dilate. The skin begins to sag and limbs hang loosely. Because the heart no longer beats to circulate blood throughout the smaller veins of the skin, the skin takes on a grayish tone, known as "pallor mortis."[16] Eventually, this lack of circulation causes blood to pool at the lowest points of the body's position, a phase known as "livor mortis."[17] Next, a condition called "algor mortis"[18] begins to take place, wherein the body begins to cool to the temperature of its environment. Next, the muscles stiffen, resulting in "rigor mortis."[19] This becomes more profound over a period of hours, then dissipates about forty-eight hours after death. Between twelve and forty-eight hours past death, the skin shrinks, causing hair and nails to appear longer than they did at the moment of death.

While previously, it was believed that the brain activity stopped at the moment of death, scientific studies are now revealing that brain activity continues for about ten minutes after physical death takes place,[20] suggesting that an individual may be aware of the process of his or her own death. (More on this later.)

The Near-Death Phenomenon

Dr. Jeffrey Long, a physician who practices radiation oncology, initially developed an interest in studying near-death experiences when he read about them in a medical journal. Because he worked in the medical industry, he began to hear additional stories from people who had experienced NDEs. As his curiosity grew, his research gained momentum, causing him to found the NDERF (Near Death Experience Research Foundation). Since 1984, this respected physician has studied more than 1,300 near-death experiences, more than 600 of which he scrutinized at great length in a study known as the NDERF Survey. This study renders findings that serve as tools for quantifying common criteria experienced in NDE occurrences and presents statistics for each.

While many are curious about the spiritual or psychological aspects of an NDE, Dr. Long's medical training caused him to approach the subject from a scientific angle. His subsequent research has been founded upon information that is medically confirmable, while using statistics alongside observational and correlational studies to collect data. As Dr. Long himself stated, "What is real is consistently seen among many different observations."[21]

Dr. Long has likewise compiled a list of criteria for validating a claim of NDE: First, the person has to be medically near death or even clinically dead; his or her condition must be "so physically compromised that [he or she] would die if there condition did not improve…[and he or she must be] generally unconscious…with the absence of heartbeat and breathing."[22] Furthermore, the NDE must have taken place *while* the individual was near death or dead, and the experience had to be coherent, meaning that it must have defined a cohesive event or series of events. Reports of fragmented memories or disorganized flashes are not included in Dr. Long's list.

For individuals claiming to have had NDEs, more than 95 percent are certain their incident was "definitely real,"[23] while nearly the entire remaining 5 percent rated their episode as "probably real."[24] Within Dr. Long's study, not one participant rated his or her experience as "definitely not real."[25] The doctor likewise explains that people report NDEs to be life-changing moments. For many, their lives are transformed forever, and they return from such an occurrence with the knowledge of and belief in a higher power—one who embodies the purest peace and love they've ever experienced, love so strong that those who attempt to explain it say the right words do not exist. Dr. Long elaborates on this euphoria: "Imagine that—[the peace and love felt by the individual during an NDE]—an experience that begins with the sheer terror of a life-threatening event and evolves into an event of wonder and mystery!"[26]

Dr. Long presents the NDERF survey, a series of sixteen scaled questions regarding content of a claimed NDE considered by many in the medical/scientific field to be the best way to distinguish actual NDEs from those that are not. While no two NDEs are exactly the same, some commonalities make it nearly impossible to discredit the validity of an NDE. Likewise, the common factors usually occur in the same order. Vast studies exist on each of these common denominators, so we will offer a truncated description of each in the upcoming pages.

Barbara Bartolome's NDE

Barbara Bartolome of Santa Barbara, California, had an NDE after being injected with dye before she underwent a medical procedure.

The technician made a mistake and pressed the wrong button, apparently administering an incorrect amount of one of the chemicals to be injected. Bartolome remembers seeing the look of panic on the technician's face as he realized he had his hand on the wrong button. Immediately after that, Bartolome's eyes closed and she was out of her body across the room, watching the medical staff's frantic efforts to save her life. She later was able to describe in detail the procedures that were done in an effort to save her life, and she could even describe the equipment was used on her body—despite the fact that she had no medical training. During the NDE, she was enveloped in feelings of euphoria, and she was aware that God was with her. She began to speak to Him, even asking questions about what was being done to her body. At one point, she expressed curiosity about one of the pieces of equipment that had been brought into the hospital room while she was observing, and upon this inquiry, her vantage point changed: She found herself observing the action from a different angle, where she could get a better look at the machine she had shown interest in. Her recollection of details during the NDE included knowing the medical staff had doubted whether they could get a defibrillator into the room in time to save her life, so they resorted to manual chest compressions. When these compressions began, Bartolome was suddenly pulled back into her body, and her point of view shifted to that of being beneath the oxygen mask. Other details she remembered from the NDE included incriminating particulars about mistakes made during her medical care that contributed to her near-death state.[27]

The Out-of-Body Experience

Near-death and out-of-body experiences are often mistaken for the same thing, but, as stated earlier, they're not. Frequently, those who have an NDE encounter an out-of-body experience as well, but each can happen separately, for varying reasons. An out-of-body experience takes place when a person feels the distinct separation of the consciousness from the body.

More than 75 percent of people who experience NDEs claim that, simultaneously, they saw events as though they were a spectator (thus defining an out-of-body experience).[28] This factor makes argument more difficult for the skeptic, because the individual is often able to tell details they wouldn't otherwise know. Recent studies have alluded to the conclusion that the brain is active for up to ten minutes after the moment of death. This places a unique perspective on a near-death experiencer's capability of knowing such details: The notion that our minds are active throughout the transition between life and death adds credibility to NDE stories.

Those who report being outside the body as observers are often able to give details about what's happening (medical interventions, etc.), which proves that NDEs are more than hallucinations. At certain points in scientific history, some have speculated that NDEs are the result of a dream or hallucination induced by trauma, blood loss, semiconscious-ness following injury, or other fading vital systems of the dying body. But strange, yet accurate, details given by an individual after an NDE lends credibility to the experience.

For example, as we will read about in detail a bit later, after being crushed nearly in half by a fallen Peterbilt logging truck, Bruce Van Natta had an NDE in which he witnessed angels ministering to the injured area of his body while medical personnel worked on him. Bruce recalls watching one of the paramedics enter the building from a rear door, unlike all the other responders on that day. His knowledge of this information later validated the fact that he had *observed* the event. Details such as this often serve as evidence that, during the moments of death, individuals can be at a vantage point outside of the body. Interest-ingly, even Sigmund Freud said, "When we attempt to imagine death, we perceive ourselves as spectators."[29] Yet, the unknowable details Bruce (and others like him) are able to recount confirm that the occurrence is more than our own imagination of our death. Furthermore, specifics that near-death experiencers report are almost always accurate and realistic.

In addition to knowing some of the strange and accurate details on the part of a person who has experienced an NDE, there is the additional fact that the incapacitated person's ability to perceive the happenings around him or her during the unconscious/medically dead state can't be easily chalked up to coincidence or a "lucky guess." For example, in a recent interview, Dr. Jeffrey Long noted that individuals who have suffered a cardiac arrest have "no potential for interaction on a conscious level with the world around them."[30] One whose heartbeat has flatlined has no way to understand the happenings around his or her body that can be explained outside the phenomenon of an NDE. In addition to this, there are those who encounter the near-death experience while anesthetized before the medical procedure. Like other NDEers, these individuals are often able to describe medical equipment or procedures that they have no other way of being familiar with, and yet, are medically covered "under a blanket of complete sleep,"[31] wherein they should be in no position to obtain details about the occurrences taking place in the earthly realm around them.

As stated earlier, all NDEs are OBEs, but not all OBEs are NDEs. There are people who have reported an out of-body experience without there being any discernible threat of death to the physical body. Next is one such example.

Josh Peck's OBE

I wasn't seeking a sign from the Lord. I wasn't chasing an experience. On this particular day, these things could not have been farther from my mind. I had recently been saved—not more than a few weeks earlier—and I was watching TV in bed, not really thinking about anything deep or profound. This day had started just like any other, and was seeming to end the same way. Even now, about six years after the fact, I can't remember anything else about that day. Yet, it would turn out to be one of the most profound moments in my Christian life and a big reason I wanted to participate in writing this book.

While I still have many questions about what happened to me, this was the first and strongest taste of eternity I've ever had. I learned a few key details on what the afterlife might be like for believers, but I also learned something deeper that goes beyond a focus on experiential details. To start, I am reminded of the apostle Paul's words in 2 Corinthians 12:3, because they seem to describe something similar to what I experienced:

> And I know that this man was caught up into paradise—whether
> in the body or out of the body I do not know, God knows.
> (2 Corinthians 12:3, ESV)

I write "similar," not "exactly," because I don't believe I died, as described in the above verse. I would say my experience falls in the realm of an OBE rather than an NDE. Neither do I know if I was "caught up into paradise," exactly. Yet, I had an experience that I cannot fully explain. I don't know if I was in the body or out of the body. Only God knows.

So, as I said earlier, I was lying in bed, watching a sermon on TV, when all of a sudden, I found myself in a large, brightly lit auditorium. I don't remember making a transition from one place to another. I was simply watching television one moment, then, seemingly with no time in between, I was someplace else entirely. Strangely enough, I wasn't taken by surprise by the abrupt shift in location. It felt completely natural and even expected that I should be there, even though I didn't know where I was or why I was there.

I found myself standing at what would be the front row of an auditorium (I don't remember seeing seats anywhere). I also quickly noticed that I was not alone. Standing with me were fifteen to twenty other people. As far as I knew, I'd never met these people—but again, it just seemed right that we were all there together; no part of me questioned what was going on, even though I knew nothing about it. I wasn't analyzing anything; I was only experiencing and enjoying the beauty of the auditorium and its light.

The other people and I were facing the front of the auditorium toward a large, wooden stage. A man walked out onstage, greeting us with a smile. He appeared to be elderly, yet seemed full of life. He was dressed in a suit, yet he also seemed completely relatable to me. I felt like I was waiting to learn from a personal mentor at his home rather than waiting for an unknown pastor to preach at a church I had never visited. I also got the sense that everyone around me felt the same way as we waited for the man to speak.

Without even introducing himself, the man began speaking about Adam and the Garden of Eden. He explained what the moment was like when God had to explain death to Adam. God, as the man told the story, was heartbroken over Adam's decision to sin, because it would mean he would have to die and, naturally, Adam didn't fully understand that concept, because he had never seen death before. Though God was disappointed with Adam, He still loved him, as any good father would love his son. The man told us how God decided to handle this situation: "God told Adam not to worry, because He would rather lay down and die with Adam than be eternally separated from him."

We all waited in great anticipation for what the man would say next.

"And that is exactly what He did on the cross!"

All of a sudden, I and everyone else in the group began praising God out loud, weeping with the most intense and personal joy I've ever known. In that moment, everything made so much sense. Nothing was complicated—this was just a simple, yet pure, truth about God's love for every single one of us.

As we were all praising God in thanksgiving over His absolute goodness, love, and sacrifice, I began to feel myself moving backwards, almost like I was falling into a tunnel—only it was horizontal rather than vertical. As I was moving backwards, the light diminished, my vision became blurry, and I felt myself becoming denser, or more solid. This "denseness" wasn't only physical, but it was emotional, too. I began losing the feeling of joy and happiness that, until then, had been flowing freely through my spirit. I was still joyful, but I was losing the ability to experience that sensation as intensely as before. It was as if the emotions were water and I was a sponge that was turning into a brick. I knew I would remember the details of the experience itself, but I would never be able to truly remember how it felt—only that it was incredible and indescribable by human terms. I've often wondered if this is what Paul meant when he wrote the verse following the one we looked at earlier:

And he heard things that cannot be told, which man may not utter. (2 Corinthians 12:4, ESV)

I stopped moving, my vision became clear again, and I found myself back in bed with the TV still on. I remember being acutely aware of my physicality for the first time ever. I reasoned that this was because, before this experience, I'd never had anything to compare with physical, solid existence. I still felt joy and happiness, but it was only a very small fraction of the degree to which I had felt those sensations just moments before.

I immediately spent some time in prayer, thanking God for the experience and asking Him why it happened. I still don't know the purpose of the experience or why that message was taught to me and the others in that specific way. I also often wonder how literally I should take what had happened. Were the other people with me real human beings around the world who were experiencing the same thing? Who was the elderly man? Was he a human, an angel, or something else entirely? Had I been in Heaven, or was this a dream or a vision in which God was using experiential metaphors to teach me a higher truth—specifically, to teach me more about His love for us?

While I still have these questions, sometimes I have to remind myself that analyzing the details is not nearly as important as what I learned about God's love that day. While I was having the experience, I didn't question or analyze anything. I only enjoyed it. It wasn't that I was a mindless drone at the time; it was more like I intrinsically understood that trying to make sense of the details wasn't important. To focus on them would have been a great waste of what I was involved in.

Therefore, even today, I have to remember not to get hung up on the details; the point isn't to dwell on the particulars of what happened and try to put them into human terms to be understood by a physical, human brain. Again, that would be a great waste. Instead, the point is to focus on what God sacrificed and how much He truly and personally loves each of us. It's up to us to accept His love and His gift of salvation, and to choose to live our physical lives with Him, then on into eternity. God loves you and me so much that He would rather die than be eternally separated from us—and that is exactly what He did on the cross!

Interpreting OBEs

Interpreting OBEs and their aftermath can be difficult. Unfortunately, there isn't much in the realm of Christian explanations of OBEs beyond a simple "it must be fake" or "I believe it's real, but I don't know what to do with it." Typically, this is because of the theological baggage that can come with some NDE claims. If a person has an NDE, then claims to have psychic abilities, for example, it is typically far easier for the Christian to say "it must be fake" or "it is a lie from Satan" rather than entertain the idea. As Christians, we tend to denounce psychics and their abilities. We understand that even if psychic abilities are legit to a certain extent, we shouldn't be practicing them, according to what we're taught in the Bible. However, what constitutes a legitimate psychic practice that dishonors God and pays homage to the devil? What would it mean if a

Bible-believing Christian suddenly received a glimpse of the future that turned out to be true? Would this be considered a gift from God or a psychic ability?

The Bible makes clear distinctions between gifts of the Holy Spirit and witchcraft or sorcery. The way it is generally understood within Christianity (at least by those who research such things) that God Himself will deliver gifts at certain times of His choosing; human beings are not to try to *cause* them to happen. Praying for gifts is acceptable; however, it is ultimately up to God whether He will deliver any gifts. Witchcraft and sorcery, however, involve the pursuit of acquiring gifts without God's help or permission. A person can create a spell, meditate, or use other means to try to gain supernatural powers, but this is strictly prohibited in the Bible; it is an attempt to go outside of God's wishes and fulfill human desires. However, this subject can get tricky. Some Christians who have never been taught theology fully believe God gave them psychic abilities. Could these people possibly have the gift of prophecy, yet be misinterpreting the gift? Is it possible that Satan is deceiving these people with a false gift in order to discredit Christianity? Is it possible that these folks are simply mistaken—and no such ability is present in the first place? We must ask these and many other questions, because there is much we simply don't know about the spirit realm. We must look at each instance of "psychic ability" case by case and consider all the available data before we can even attempt to draw any conclusions. Included in that data must be what the Bible has to say on the matter, if anything at all. Only after we do all the work can we form a possible interpretation—but even then, we must be willing to admit that, on certain subjects that fall outside of biblical explanation, our limited understanding can only take us so far.

Because there simply aren't many Christians researching NDEs in a scientific, objective way, we must rely on what information about the subject *is* available. Dr. Raymond Moody is a philosopher, psychologist, forensic psychiatrist, physician, and author who has dedicated his life to the study of the afterlife and NDEs; he even served as Chair in Consciousness at the University of Nevada in Las Vegas. While at times, Moody's science and theology have been the subject of criticism, he makes interesting observations worth noting. One is his claim that, on rare occasions, a bystander will share in the NDE of an individual. To describe this shared occurrence, Dr. Moody has coined the phrase "shared-death experience" (SDE). "In these experiences," he says, "bystanders who are close to a dying person experience many of the same elements of the NDE with the dying person, including leaving their bodies, meeting beings of light, and seeing the life review of the dying person. These bystanders are themselves healthy and not dying, yet seem to share these experiences."[32] For example, a parent or relative of the dying individual is suddenly pulled into some sort of spirit realm, wherein he or she claims to witness or share in the NDE. Furthermore, sometimes the individual sharing in the NDE isn't close to the dying person, which makes the phenomenon seem even more valid. While this possibility raises as many questions as it does answers, its authentication would certainly help refute the concept that NDEs are dreams or hallucinations induced by physical trauma. If the NDE is actually a *spiritual experience*, rather than a byproduct of physical depletion, then a bystander has a greater chance of sharing and later corroborating the entire occurrence.

Even more amazing, reports of incredible supernatural experiences are sometimes backed by equally incredible evidence that they actually happened. Many times, these events involve entities and actions commonly referred to as ghosts, psychic abilities, and premonitions, causing the Christian community to distance itself from them entirely. However, what if these occurrences are sometimes mislabeled? What happens when a Christian is given a premonition? What happens when a Christian accurately predicts the future? What happens when what looks like the ghost of a dead woman saves the life of a child?

"Ghost Saves Kid"[33]

Excerpted from *The Supernatural Worldview* by Cris Putnam

Paranormal Witness, a Syfy network documentary television series made by a British production company, is described as featuring eyewitness testimony from everyday people who claim to have experienced paranormal activity. The show is unique in the genre in that the cases are usually reported by reliable witnesses and supported with evidence that can be verified or dismissed through research.

One case in particular captured my attention, because it encapsulates in one story multiple instances of paranormal and, indeed, supernatural phenomena. That episode was called "Haunted Highway" (season 1, episode 102),[34] and originally aired on September 14, 2011, to an audience of 1.36 million viewers.[35]

Actually, the same case first ran on the February 21, 1997, episode of *Unsolved Mysteries,* and its reuse by *Paranormal Witness* testifies to its utterly unique combination of events and phenomena. It is an amazing case. The story centers on twenty-four-year-old Christine Skubish and her three-year-old son, Nick, who went missing off Highway 50 in the Sierra Nevada Mountains of California about fifteen miles outside of Placerville. A single mother, Christine had recently earned her paralegal certification and was moving to start a new career. She was also hopeful about marrying her son's father, who lived in that area. When she left her family's home near Sacramento on Sunday, June 5, 1994, her hopes were high.

According to the show's version of events, Dave Stautzenbach, Christine's stepfather, received a telephone call on Wednesday, June 8, from one of her friends, who said she had expected Christine to arrive in town on Monday—but it was now Wednesday morning. Worried, Stautzenbach called the police to make a missing-persons report, and he started checking with hospitals along the route Christine would have traveled.

Regrettably, his effort was to no avail. Deputy Rich Strasser told viewers, "There's people reported missing all the time, every day, throughout this country. There was nothing out of the ordinary. I thought it was just another, I hate to say it, routine missing-persons report."[36]

Of course, the vast majority of cases do turn out to be nonevents when the missing person shows up after an unplanned excursion. However, this case was anything but routine, and it qualifies as one of the most diverse paranormal cases in history.

I contacted Christine Skubish's aunt, Karen Nichols, whose story is also featured on "Haunted Highway." According to her, the report isn't very accurate. On the program, Karen calls Dave Stautzenbach and recounts a strange dream that included Christine and Nick, as well as the number "sixteen" repeated over and over. Karen told me that the TV version is mostly fiction, because the number "sixteen" was *not* part of her dream. Somehow, the details of her dream got mixed up with other details, and the show presented a falsehood. It's not clear whether the inaccuracy was intentional.

Perhaps this was because Karen refused to participate in either *Unsolved Mysteries* or *Paranormal Witness,* even though both programs offered her money. Why did Karen decline the monetary offers? She said she is a born-again Christian who felt it was wrong to sensationalize the tragedy. She wrote to me, "I declined their offer because I didn't see how this could in any way glorify the church. I didn't feel it in my spirit."[37]

Despite the errors, however, "Haunted Highway" did report at least a few details about Karen's dreams that were correct. For example, on the show, Stautzenbach commented concerning Karen's dream: "She had premonitions before, but this was so real, she knew that she was going to find him."[38] This is absolutely true; Karen has written in detail about her lifelong experiences with premonitions, visions, and precognitive dreams. In fact, she once warned a relative concerning cancer weeks before it was diagnosed and accurately predicted a close family member's demise.

It is important to note that having these dreams and premonitions is not something Karen tries to do. They just happen to her unexpectedly. She states that she repented from occult involvement by dedicating her life to Christ many years ago.

This is Karen's account of the first dream she had on the night of the accident:

> *Monday morning about 3 a.m., June 6, 1994, I had a dream of riding in the backseat of a car at night. I could see the silhouette of a child in the passenger seat and a girl driving. I could see the reflection of the headlights and the hood of the car. I could tell we were on a dark road because there were no streetlights, and outside it seemed to be mountainous.*
>
> *That morning, I spoke to my mother and my sister and asked if they had heard from Chrissy. They said, "No," but I knew she was going to stop by a friend's house in Carson City, Nevada. So, even though I felt a bit uneasy, I continued to push it out of my mind and told myself everything was OK.*[39]

The above dream probably occurred at the time of the accident or shortly afterward. Interestingly, it seems to transport Karen into the car with her niece and young Nick. The setting is correct: It was a dark mountain road.

That morning, Karen called her sister, Brenda, and asked if she had heard from Christine—the answer was no. The following night and into Tuesday morning, Karen had a similar dream:

> *That night when I went to sleep, I had the same dream, exactly as the night before, and I repeated the same activities as the day before, calling to check on Christine, with the same disappointing result. It*

was now Tuesday, June 7, and my concern grew stronger, and I felt very anxious. My heart felt heavy, and I had a sick feeling in my stomach. I knew that something was very wrong.

With no word from Christine on Tuesday, Karen was distraught. The character of the third dream might reflect this mental state, but the content suggests the supernatural: The spirit of Christine Skubish was contacting Karen in her dreams in order to save Nick, who was still in the woods.

Karen's third dream is much more disturbing (keep in mind that Karen calls Christine her "sister" because they were so close, but technically, she is Christine's aunt):

That night I had another dream that was different than the other two. This dream was more of a catastrophic nature. I was in my sister's house and there was a horrible wind. This wind had so much force that the trees were completely bent in half. I was standing in front of the window and looking out into the yard. It was a big yard, as my sister lived on sixteen acres with many tall pine trees. It was nighttime, and all of a sudden, the winds increased to hurricane-like winds. I could hear the sound of glass breaking and popping and metal scraping. I could see sparks.

I looked over in the yard and I could see Nicky standing in the middle of the yard. I also saw my sister trying to get to him. There was so much debris blowing around and glass shattering and metal that looked like it was curled up. I was trying to help my sister, but I couldn't find my shoes. I was barefooted, and I knew I wouldn't be able to make it to her because of all the glass that was on the ground. I finally found them, and when I opened the door, the wind stopped. I ran to her and she was just standing there with Nicky.

Nervously, I was laughing, and I turned her towards me and asked if she was all right. When I looked in her eyes, they were blank and there was no life in them. Her face was inexpressive. She looked like she was in a trance, because she didn't look at me but through me.

I asked if she was okay, and she said, "No."

I said, "Are you going to be okay?"

She looked at me with very haunting eyes and with a melancholy expression and again said, "No."

This dream seems to meet the definition of what experts call an after-death communication (ADC), because Christine is telling Karen that she (Christine) is deceased, but that Nick needs help. This was early on Wednesday morning, June 8, 1994, and nobody had any evidence about a car accident. However, Karen was now absolutely sure that something was amiss.

At this point, I woke up to hear a loud screaming sound and a pounding like a loud bang. I sat up. My heart was racing; I could hear the sound of my heart beating. It was hard to breathe. It felt like someone hit me hard in the pit of my stomach. It felt like all the blood had rushed to my head. It was brutal. It was the kind of dream that shakes you to the very core, and it wasn't going to go away. There was no shaking this dream. This was probably about the same time of night as the other two dreams I had previously.

Now this is Wednesday, June 8. I couldn't go back to sleep. I got ready for work and still my gut hurt. My heart felt heavy. My chest felt tight. My head felt swollen. I felt completely out of sorts. When I got to work, it was really hard to concentrate on my work. I told my coworker about the dream and how I couldn't shake it. I kept having a chill that ran down my back. I made it through the day, but I felt really tired.

When I got home, my daughter asked, "Mom, did you hear that Chrissy is missing?"

I said, "No," I hadn't heard, but I flippantly said, "Chris isn't missing. How can you miss Chris? She was too loud to miss."

As I said that, I took a couple of steps and stopped dead in my tracks. I knew that this was it. Chrissy was supposed to have arrived today, and I still hadn't heard from her.

The dream occurred the morning of Wednesday, June 8, and it was that evening when Deputy Strasser got the missing-persons report. Thursday came and went with no new developments. Karen was convinced that her entire immediate family should be scouring the roadside, but she had no car. She asked her husband to rent one.

Karen continued:

I was trying to convince my family that if she had been in a wreck, there was a good possibility that Nicky could have survived. I could feel him. I could feel that he was alive. I didn't feel Chrissy, but I did feel Nick. But still, no one would help. My sister did make fliers and hand them out and post them with a picture of Chris.

Increasingly concerned, the family printed up fliers and began distributing them along Highway 50. Karen, who lived five hundred miles away, was finally able to rent a car in order to start searching the roadside with her husband.

Karen described the search:

On Friday, June 10, I knew the window of opportunity was closing for Nicky. I was desperate. The car rental [company] called to tell me that the car we were to pick up had been returned vandalized and we would have to wait on another car to come in. Well, it finally came in, and by the time we picked up the car, it [was] around 8 to 9 p.m. We had about a seven-hour drive ahead of us, so on our way, we stopped and bought a spotlight so that we would be able to see if we arrived before sunup.

As we left on our journey, I was praying, and continued to pray all the way. We were probably about two hours into our drive, and I just couldn't find the words to pray. Then there was a groaning in my spirit, and I began to hear an utterance that I couldn't understand. I believe it was the Holy Spirit. I began to hear a man's voice; it was dynamic and forceful, and he was praying. He was demanding and he was rebuking. Even though it was strange, I understood every word.

He was covering Chrissy and Nicky with the blood of Jesus. He was sending God's angels to surround them. It sounded like heaven was being called down with all the glory and love and protection. I do not believe I ever experienced such power before. I felt like I was enveloped in peace and warmth. I heard this for what seemed the entire trip, but then, at one point, I couldn't feel Nicky any longer. I told my husband he could slow down...it was over. Nicky was gone. I could no longer feel him.

This sounds like a mystical experience of the spiritual warfare variety. Karen heard a male voice, enveloped in power, commanding angels to protect Christine and Nick. However, then something happened, and Nick dropped off the radar. Did Nick lose his grip on this world for a brief time? The extrasensory mechanism assuring her that Nick was alive no longer detected his life force. Karen believes that Nick actually died at this time—and there is some startling confirmation of that from Nick himself after his rescue.

The great miracle of this case is three-year-old Nick's unlikely survival. The serpentine highway winds its way through the Sierra Nevada Mountains from Sacramento to Lake Tahoe. Because there were no skid marks, the police hypothesize that Christine fell asleep just prior to reaching the corner known as Bullion Bend. Running off the road with no guardrails, the car plunged forty feet down an embankment, making it invisible to passing motorists. Of course, no one really knows what happened. However, if a third party ran her off the road, or even if an animal ran onto the highway, one would expect to find skid marks.

I was able to locate, contact, and interview Nick, who will be twenty-three by the time this book hits the street. He actually remembers quite a bit, considering that he was only three at the time of the tragedy. Of course, this accident was an extremely traumatic and life-altering event that affects his life to this day. With that in mind, I endeavored to maintain a degree of sensitivity with the questions I asked.

Cris: Nick, do you actually remember the accident?

Nick: Oh, the accident? Absolutely…but I don't remember anything before the accident, and I don't even remember the hospital at all, like recovering. But I remember the accident quite a bit actually.

Cris: Tell me what you remember.

Nick: I remember almost every night; I don't remember the days too much, but I remember the night we wrecked. I remember the car flipping. I remember hitting tree after tree after tree…. And I remember when the roof of the car got ripped off. I remember seeing my mom. I remember getting out of the car. I remember climbing up that forty-foot embankment and sliding down on pine needles. I remember seeing the lights. I remember every night, pretty much. I just don't remember the days at all. If anything, I feel like I was sleeping, but I don't remember the days at all.

Cris: Did you have any water or anything?

Nick: Not that I remember. I know we wrecked at two o'clock in the morning, June sixth, and they found us sometime in the afternoon on June eleventh.

Cris: So, a little over five days and six nights counting the night of the accident.

Nick: That sounds right.

Cris: That's a long time to go without food and water.

Nick: Yeah, I had a severe concussion; matter of fact, I still have a scar—I'd say a good three inches long on the side of my head, more of an indentation really, and I went through severe malnutrition and severe dehydration.[40]

Paranormal Witness titled this story "Haunted Highway" for a good reason. The second episode of the first season featured an interview with Deborah Hoyt, an unrelated traveler, who adds another paranormal element to the Skubish story. She describes awakening in the middle of night—the early morning hours of Saturday, June 11—with an overwhelming urgency to go home. Based on the vague but powerful premonition, she persuaded her husband to wake and drive up Highway 50. On the way home to Lake Tahoe, Deborah was astonished to see a naked, apparently deceased, young woman on the side of the road. She described the woman as young, dark-haired, attractive, and endowed with large breasts—features matching Christine Skubish. Because this was the age before cell phones, Deborah and her husband drove to the closest gas station to call 911. When an officer arrived, Deborah led him to Bullion Bend…but there was no sign of the ghostly white, nude woman.

Deborah related her disappointment: "[The police officer] had a big spotlight and he was looking, and then he came back down and told me they hadn't found anything and that we should go home. I told my husband that I didn't think they believed me and that they thought I was crazy and they would probably just stop the search."[41]

Apparently, the police were led back to Bullion Bend later that night, but that information has never been disclosed to the public—that is, until now. That will be explained shortly. For now, we return to Nick.

In the meantime, deep down the precipitous embankment, three-year-old Nick was in the car next to his deceased mother's broken body. After talking to the officer who responded to Deborah Hoyt, Deputy Strasser was increasingly convinced that the apparition and the Skubish disappearance were connected.

But there's more.

While thirsty and starving, Nick was strangely *not* alone.

Cris: Do you believe you saw angels at the scene of the accident?

Nick: Yes, only at night.

Cris: Can you describe them for me?

Nick: Sure. Take the silhouette of a person, just the form, if you will. And make that form an essence of light, just light radiating from the form, but no physical features, no hands, no clothes…just light.

Cris: So just a shape of a body glowing light?

Nick: Yes, exactly.

The Supernatural Worldview allows one to postulate that the spirit of Christine Skubish was desperately trying to save her child. In contrast, skeptics have suggested that perhaps the body on the side of the road was actually Nick. While it's hard to imagine a three-year-old boy being misidentified as a busty adult female, it offers a nonparanormal possibility. As a matter of fact, Nick remembers climbing up to the road, but after no cars came, not knowing what to do, he returned to the car and his mom.

Cris: You remember making it to the road?

Nick: Yes. I definitely got up to the road a couple times.

Cris: Is it possible the naked body people saw was you?

Nick: I don't know. Honestly, I don't ever remember laying up there, but anything is possible. I just remember what I remember, and other people saw what they say they saw.

Cris: Do you think the naked apparition seen at the road might have been your mother?

Nick: I would say...yeah. I think, if my Mom were playing a part in what happened, she might have to go about things in different ways with different people to get them to perceive what was actually going on. Maybe their mind would've told them it wasn't real. But a woman lying on the side of the road was a real possibility; therefore, Deborah Hoyt saw it when she did.

Cris: It seems like that was a big part of what saved you: People reported a naked woman's body on the side of the road. Deborah Hoyt definitely saw a female, and she seemed pretty sure about it. So it's hard to believe it was you, but I suppose a skeptic might say that, so I wanted to ask. Some people just do not want to believe in anything supernatural.

Nick: That is one thing I have found throughout the years. A lot of people I have met have a hard time believing in anything big at all. People think they do, but not everyone generally believes what they think they do, I have found.

Cris: That is what this book is about: how the presuppositions you hold, the things that you believe about reality, will mold your opinion about everything else. If you don't believe in the possibility of miracles or super-natural things, then you will always try to come up with an explanation that excludes them, no matter how fanciful. In this way, opinions are really a product of worldview as much as facts. People always interpret facts through their worldview. It's like the lens that you view the world through.

Nick: It is. You know what? I really like what you're talking about. I've read a lot of books on spiritual things; I read a lot. I am definitely inter-ested in this book that you are writing.

Ghost or no ghost, a naked woman lying on the side of the highway is hard to ignore. Nick believes his mom was doing what was necessary to get a reaction. His great aunt, Karen, also believes that the apparition was her niece's postmortem effort to save her son.

She offered:

Some say that to be absent from the body is to be present with the Lord. But if there was any possible way to make this happen, I know Chrissy could. She had such a great love for the Father and Jesus and she was so strong-willed and determined that nothing would stop her from making sure her baby was safe. She loved him so much. He was all she had in this world. He was her everything, and there were no boundaries where he was concerned. Her love remained even in death—even if it meant taking her clothes off to attract someone to the site of the wreck.

I asked Nick for more details about the angels that were with him at night. Perhaps they had something to do with apparition sightings? Interestingly, this led Nick back to Karen's dreams.

Cris: These beings of light that you saw, were they close to you? Were they only at a distance? Did you interact with them?

Nick: One of them was next to the car the whole time, and one of them was next to the road. I've been told by a lot of people that when I was in the hospital—and, like I said earlier, I don't remember the hospital, I don't remember the recovery at all—I was told by a lot of people that I told them I saw the angels. I told them a lot of other things, too. I told my aunt [Karen] a few things. I don't know what show you saw, but one that goes way back [*Unsolved Mysteries*] talks about my aunt having visions; that's the same aunt. She had multiple dreams, I guess, at the time it was going on. She has actually had quite a few paranormal experiences. A lot of people in my family have had paranormal experiences—on that side of the family at least.

Cris: Your aunt had a dream, and she reported it, and others saw a naked body by the road—and it was those things put together that helped them find you, correct?

Nick: My aunt's dreams never get focused on because she did not want to be involved in any of the television programs. So the next show that covered it [*Paranormal Witness*] was because my grandfather submitted it, and it was the first one I took part in since the accident.

An important idea developed in *The Supernatural Worldview* is that some folks, like Karen Nichols, are more inclined to perceive the spirit realm than others. This doesn't make them guilty of witchcraft or of practicing the occult arts. It isn't something Karen asked for or intentionally developed, but rather is an inherent ability. In her third dream, an after-death communication from Christine led Karen to conclude that her niece was deceased, but that Nick was in desperate need of rescue. The dream featured broken glass and tearing metal—details that are consistent with the actual mangled automobile. Karen's actions support her story as well. Desperate, she and her husband rented a car to drive five hundred miles as they scoured the roadside for any small sign. Karen described the journey and a remarkable event that was spiritually perceived and later confirmed:

> *I was praying as we left on our journey and continued to pray all the way. We were probably about two hours into our drive, and I just couldn't find the words to pray, and there came a groaning in my spirit, and I began to hear an utterance that I couldn't understand. I believe it was the Holy Spirit, and I began to hear a man's voice. It was dynamic and forceful, and he was praying, he was demanding, he was rebuking. I understood his every word; he was covering Chrissy and Nicky with the blood of Jesus. He was sending God's angels to surround them. It sounded like heaven was being sent down with all the glory and love and protection. I do not believe I have ever experienced such power before. I felt like I was enveloped in warmth and peace. I heard this for what seemed the entire trip, but then at one point I couldn't feel Nicky any longer, and I told my husband he could slow down. It was over; Nicky was gone...I couldn't feel him.*

Karen believes that Nick briefly departed this life. This odd detail is especially interesting in light of what she later learned at the hospital. For now, we return to the search as described by Karen:

> *I knew that there would be something of Chrissy's or Nicky's on the road or at a turn out that would let me know where they were. So I*

began looking on the side of the road. If I didn't have a clear view, I would have my husband stop so I could get out and physically look over the side. There was so much vegetation on Highway 50, a very mountainous highway that leads to Lake Tahoe.

The timing of the discovery is amazing, because it seems that Karen and Deputy Strasser arrived at the scene within minutes of each other. The Associated Press reported: "Strasser had spotted the boy's tennis shoe on the side of the highway Saturday, and then found the car. He believes the boy at some point climbed from the car to the highway, and then returned to the car. That is the only explanation for the shoe being on the road, Strasser said."[42] Just minutes after Deputy Strasser had followed the shoe to locate the car, Karen and her husband spotted Nick's shoe on the road and pulled up next to the patrol car.

Karen continues:

As we were looking, I saw a little tennis shoe lying on the side of the road and also noticed that the patrol car had stopped there. I told my husband, "She's here; stop the car!" I got out of the car and started to run, but the deputy stopped me and told me that I couldn't go down there. By "down there," I mean there was a drop-off about twenty feet down and I could see Chrissy' car. I was yelling Chrissy's name. The deputy said that Chrissy was gone. I remember it felt like my legs turned to rubber, and I and my husband hit the ground.

Nicky was alive, but barely. He looked like a little bird that had [fallen] out of a nest: His skin was dark and baggy, his little eyes [were] filled with muck. His lips were parched; he was marked and curled up in a fetal position next to Chris. When his name was called, he responded quietly. I left to go to Marshall Medical Center in Placerville to wait for the ambulance to bring Nicky there.

When I was finally able to see Nicky, he was alert but weak. I knew something miraculous had taken place, but at that time I wasn't sure what it was. Later that morning when they were able to stabilize him, they transferred him to UC Davis. His organs were shutting down. They said he only had thirty minutes, maybe less, of life left because his kidneys were shutting down and they still weren't sure if they would be able to reverse the damage. So we left Marshall Hospital and went to UC Davis in Sacramento.

When I walked in the hospital room, Nicky sat straight up and looked at me, his little eyes as big as saucers, and said, "Aunt Kiki, Aunt Kiki, my mommy died!"

I said, "Yes, Nicky she did."

Then he said, "I died too, but I wasn't afraid because I was with Jesus and His angels, but I couldn't stay. I had to come back here."

He also said that Jesus' angels were there with him in the car. I asked where they were, and he said, "There were three—there was two by the car and one on the road."

I didn't say anything. I couldn't speak. I just held him and thought back to the time when I couldn't feel him anymore, and said, "Well there it is."

I thought to myself, "He is only three and a half years old; how would he know these things?" He wasn't old enough to be influenced by anyone.

This corroboration from Nick suggests that when Karen could no longer feel Nick's life force, he actually had a near-death experience. This possibility brings the number of paranormal phenomena associated with this case to five: 1) Karen's extrasensory perception (ESP) dreams; 2) Christine's after-death communication to Karen; 3) The apparition on side of the road that was seen by multiple witnesses; 4) Nick's angels; and 5) Nick's NDE. Of course, the atheist fundamentalists and debunkers cannot allow a case this strong to stand uncontested.

According to the police, the female apparition matching Christine's description was undoubtedly what first led them to Bullion

Bend, where it was eventually discovered that the car ran off the road. This obviously isn't a coincidence, but skeptics can't accept the idea of supernatural intervention. One callous online cynic suggested that the apparition was invented by Deborah Hoyt in order to conceal the fact that she and her husband had run Christine off the road. To escape responsibility, the cynic asserted, she concocted the ghost as a way to alert the police to the location without incriminating herself or the driver. Such a libelous accusation offers the antisupernaturalist a plausible escape—a disparaging tactic common to paranormal debunkers. However, the absence of skid marks reveals that Christine never hit the brakes. Even more, the skeptical slander is controverted by evidence not included on the television shows. These are new details never reported before.

After Nick's rescue, a California highway patrolman, Jack Greenwood, gave Karen astonishing information not reported on any of the television programs. He even told her that "something supernatural took place." She recalled the conversation between her and her husband and Greenwood shortly after Nick's rescue:

We met with Jack, and when we first met, his eyes were big and he spoke very precisely. He began with a deep breath and started by saying, "I'm not a religious man. I'm not a Christian man."

Then he said, "I am Catholic, but I'm not religious. I have to tell you something happened here that I can't explain."

He was on duty the night before Christine was found, and there had been not one but actually three calls. The first call was about a woman lying on the side of the road. They reported she was naked, had dark brown hair, was petite with big breasts, and her skin looked real white, like she had been in the cold for a long time.

[Greenwood] said he went out to the area to investigate and found nothing. Later that night, he received another report of a woman lying on the side of the road with the same description in the

same area. Again, he went to investigate and found nothing. Later that morning, he received another call with the same report of a naked woman of the same description. He said he told the caller that he had been out twice and there was nothing there.

The man replied, "The hell there isn't!" He told Jack that he was sitting on the side of the road with his cell phone watching her from his rearview mirror and that she was running frantically back and forth like she looking for something. He said, "I'm watching her as we speak."

Again, [Greenwood] found nothing. He went on to say that later that morning, he was still on duty and received the call on the accident and he was the one that responded.

Greenwood reported that *three different people* had reported seeing a naked woman by the side of the road. In fact, one witness had seen her pacing back and forth! This unprecedented information substantially changes the case in favor of a supernatural worldview. Karen continued with her recollection of the conversation:

He went on to say that he had been a highway patrolman for over twenty-eight years and had seen a lot of accidents where people had been in the elements for days. He said that when the body deteriorates, the abdomen will usually swell and burst, and that is what he expected to find. The days all that week had been very hot, about 106 degrees in the daytime. He was the CHiP officer who went to the site of the accident. It was a wilderness area. He said the insects were awful. They were being bitten by mosquitoes and other bugs. There were lots of varmints and wild animals in that area, but the strange thing was that when they got to the car, it was as though a tent or a veil had been placed over the car. He said there wasn't one insect bite, no blowfly larva, no animal bites, no sign of anything.

Nicky's clothes had been folded and placed on the hood of the car. There were signs that Nicky had been out of the car, and when he was picked up and put on the gurney, he had been sitting on a book of Bible stories, and you could see the imprint of his little bottom on it. [Greenwood] then said that he was the one that took Christine out of the car, and her tummy was just as flat as if she had just died. There was no sign of deterioration or decay; she only had a little trickle of blood from her nose. [Greenwood said] that she had probably died at impact; it was obvious that she had broken her neck from the protrusion of the cervical spine. He said that there was only one tiny spot on her elbow that showed any sign of deterioration. He said that when he took her out and looked at her, she fit the total description of the girl that had been reported.

He said, "I don't know what happened, but something supernatural took place here, folks." He said we should report to Unsolved Mysteries.

These details have also never previously been revealed. Of course, Greenwood's final piece of advice came to pass, and the case premiered on *Unsolved Mysteries* (season 9, episode 16) as: "Highway 50 Phantom" on February 21, 1997. But what about the other unreported details? It seems unlikely that a toddler bothered to fold his clothes after he stripped them off in the sweltering summer heat. Did the angels fold his clothes, or did his mother's ghost do it? I suppose we'll never know. What about Christine's body? If we count its (and Nick's) unexpected preservation, we have seven paranormal phenomena.

1. Karen had ESP dreams (view from inside the car).
2. Christine and Karen experienced after-death communication with one another.
3. At least three witnesses reported an apparition pointing to the scene of the accident. Deborah Hoyt's account is on record; the accounts of two others were verified by officer Jack Greenwood.

4. Angels (figures of light) were seen near the car and by the road at night.
5. Nick had a possible near-death experience.
6. Christine Skubish's body was inexplicably preserved.
7. Nick was able to survive without food and water for five days in temperatures over 100 degrees.

According to Karen Nichols, Christine had her challenges, but was a Christian who loved the Lord. While recovering in the hospital, Nick said he was briefly with Jesus and His angels in heaven. Officer Greenwood related that Nick was discovered sitting on a book of Bible stories in the torturously wrecked car. Without food or water, Nick was miraculously preserved through scorching heat. Despite the loss, God's hand of provision can be seen throughout the tragedy.

How can evangelical Christians respond to a story like this? All too often, it ends up being "demonize first, ask questions later" (that is, if ever). It seems disingenuous and inconsistent coming from folks whose central message involves the resurrection of the dead. In this case, it appears that God allowed a departed mother's spirit to intercede with passing motorists and to communicate in the dreams of her aunt. Why should this stretch plausibility for those with a biblical worldview? I don't believe it should, but it often appears that way. If Karen hadn't been informed by dreams, and if the apparition hadn't been reported, Nick would not have been found in time. At least one ghost story has yielded good fruit.

During the process of interviewing Nick Skubish in 2013, I suggested to him that God must have an important plan for his life. We all know that many young children are killed in car accidents. The odds for the toddler's survival in the wilderness for five days were exceedingly low. Nick quickly agreed, and told me he is still experiencing unusual events to this day. I shared my personal testimony and asked Nick to read the Gospel of John.

After he read it, I asked for his reaction. Nick responded, "I thought it was a good example of how consuming sin really is. Seems like the people's pride in their own opinion or religious views prevented them from seeing who He was and why He was even here."

Needless to say, I was very impressed with his answer, since this was his first reading of the book of John.

I did my best to explain why his response about the consuming nature of sin was so accurate: "We need saving because God's judgment against sin is real. But the really cool thing He did was to provide a way for imperfect sinners like you and me to make it. He took the punishment we deserve. The really important passage is: 'For God so loved the world, that he gave his only Son, that whoever believes in him should not perish but have eternal life. For God did not send his Son into the world to condemn the world, but in order that the world might be saved through him. Whoever believes in him is not condemned, but whoever does not believe is condemned already, because he has not believed in the name of the only Son of God'" (John 3:16–18).

I asked, "So do you know that you have experienced that rebirth that Jesus was telling Nicodemus about?" Nick responded that he has never really experienced it. We prayed together, and Nick accepted the gospel over the phone. Nick has moved from "paranormal witness" to "gospel witness." He has a challenging path before him. Please pray for Nick.

End of excerpt from *The Supernatural Worldview* by Cris Putnam

Amplified Sensations

After an NDE, experiencers often have difficulty explaining what they have seen and felt within the afterlife realm. Those who attempt description often resort to phrases like "there are no words" or "there's no earthly comparison." Common features of this realm, however, involve descriptions of colors more vivid than anything that exists in the earthly realm.

Light is more brilliant. Clarity is heightened, both in features observed and in emotional and intellectual sensation. In general, the realm entered by an individual experiencing an NDE is reported to be more conscious, alert, and intense than anything experienced in the earthly realm. Even stranger, some have reported being able to see all sides of an object at once, signifying that this could be an experience existing outside of our physical three dimensions of space and one of time (we will get into more of this later).

Feelings of Love, Happiness, or Peace

While experiencers seem to have the greatest difficulty putting this part of the experience into human words, common remarks include words and phrases such as "unconditional, all-encompassing love, compassion, peace, warmth, safety, belonging, understanding, overwhelming sense of being home, and joy."[43] Reports unanimously detail a lack of fear—despite facing death.

The Tunnel

Nearly 35 percent of those recounting an NDE speak of a tunnel described as being filled with light.[44] Often, the individual is given the option to or even begins to travel through this tunnel, and each person seems to be filled with the innate knowledge that his or her final destination is on the other side. Nearly every time the tunnel is reported, the individual describes it with feelings of love such as he or she never experienced here on earth. As mentioned before, an ultimate peace and sense of belonging are found in this tunnel. Many people report seeing beings of light within this setting, and some have even reported seeing deceased family members who wait for them with some sort of message. In a few cases, individuals have been greeted by people they did not recognize, but later identified in old family photographs, realizing that even though they didn't recognize the dead ancestor who had come to greet them, this is precisely what happened.

A Pure and Brilliant Light

Two-thirds of NDEers report encountering a light so brilliant and pure that not only is there no equivalent of it on earth, there are likewise no words in the human language that capture its description.[45] Many accounts include a glow so brilliant that a person is only capable of feeling positive emotion. This luminescence seems to engulf a person; yet, it doesn't hurt the eyes to look at the light. Many who report this light attach personhood to it, believing it is the presence of God. Some even report seeing other, smaller light-beings within the larger, more all-encompassing light, alluding to the concept that lesser beings have merged or become one with God's presence in this realm. Some who report seeing these smaller lights believe them to be angels, while others say they are human souls who have already passed and are likewise embraced by the presence of God.

Interestingly, experts who have studied NDEs explain that this experience with such a light is universal, regardless of religious affiliation. Neuropsychiatrist Peter Fenwick elaborates: "Atheists will have exactly the same experience [of seeing light beings or angels during NDE]."[46] He later stated: "The fact that you don't believe anything is going to happen [regarding spiritual beings during an NDE] doesn't stop it happening."[47]

Reuniting with Loved Ones

As mentioned previously regarding reports of a tunnel, many people who have reported a near-death experience claim it included some sort of reunion with loved ones. While the majority of the 57 percent reporting interaction with the dearly departed claimed to have encountered actual relatives, some said they reunited with friends.[48] Being met by these others increased the NDE experiencers' feelings of love, joy, peace, and general euphoria. Some have claimed that relatives were visible, while others say they only heard the loved ones' voices.[49] Still others noted that those who had died at an elderly age appeared to be young in this realm, while those who had died as children seemed to be young adults. Some folks didn't directly recognize the individuals greeting them, but they did feel a sense of familiarity. In some such cases, family photographs later revealed that those relatives had died two decades before the birth of the NDE experiencer.[50]

The phenomenon of seeing deceased loved ones or relatives as one moves closer to death is so prevalent that many who work in the medical field even acknowledge this experience as a sign regarding one's readiness to pass. Some, who call this type of occurrence an "apparitional experience,"[51] consider this a sign not to be ignored by attending medical staff. Hospice worker Diane Arcangel reported in the documentary film *Seeing the Unseen* by David Hinshaw and Dr. Raymond Moody: "I've never worked with a dying patient who did *not* have an apparitional experience...it's 100%: you can write this in stone. If a person is terminally ill... they're going to have an apparitional experience. In fact...in hospice, if a person has had an apparitional experience or...a reunion [with a deceased loved one], that person becomes top priority, because we know death is imminent...once a person has...[an] apparitional experience...we know [that apparitional individual is there to escort] them to the other side."[52]

Disconnection from Time and Space

For a person experiencing an NDE, it can seem as though the experience has covered a vast amount of time. However, those within the earthly realm typically report that the individual was only unconscious or even medically dead for a very short period of time. Furthermore, more than 60 percent of NDE experiencers said they felt that time and space were altered from the earthly realm,[53] while nearly 35 percent claimed a general disconnect from time as we know it altogether, as "everything seemed to be happening all at once."[54]

Entering a Beautiful Otherworld

More than 40 percent of those who have experienced an NDE claim that they entered an afterlife dimension that is beautiful, full of colors, and luminescent.[55] In this realm, an indescribable life seems to glow from within all of the surroundings. As previously mentioned, colors are reportedly more vivid than anything seen here on earth. The captivating splendor of this world, however, is not only found in the visual elements encountered by the NDEer, but in the enveloping senses of love, peace, and joy that embrace a person upon crossing over. Some claim to see flowers, light beings, and even luminescent cities on the horizon. Furthermore, some attempt to describe breathtaking music that seems to play in the background.

Dean Braxton Exclusive Interview[56]

Dean Braxton, author of *In Heaven!,* a licensed minister who has been in ministry for more than twenty years, has openly shared his testimony of being dead for an hour and forty-five minutes, during which time he claims to have experienced Heaven. In this occurrence, Jesus informed Dean that it was not his time to die; he would have to go back. After his NDE, Dean found out that his wife, Marilyn, had been praying for him to return to life. Their testimony about this experience has been widely received in the Christian community, and Dean was kind enough to offer his time for an interview to be included in this book.

Allie: Let's start from the beginning. Tell us a little about yourself.

Dean: I've got probably all the titles you can have for a minister but I don't use them. I just say Dean Braxton. I'm married and we have six children and nine grandchildren. We live in Virginia now. Two of our children live in Virginia and they're not that far from us. I have four grandchildren here. The rest? Texas, California, Arizona.

Allie: Do you get to see your family often?

Dean: We don't get to see them all at the same time, because they're all over the place. We get to travel. I get to see them that way.

Allie: Tell your story that you'd like us to hear.

Dean: Well, one of the things that's unique about this story is that we have the medical records. They proved that my heart stopped for one hour, forty-five minutes, and I was considered clinically dead. So I'll start off at that point right there, because most people don't have all the evidence like we do.

The name of the critical care doctor who was actually in the room when I ended up on life support is Dr. Iregui, a physician out of Washington State. It is impressive that he was the one who was able to witness my experience. He is a very reputable doctor in the sense that he received a number of awards from Washington State for his practice. And it was by chance that he was the doctor who observed all this. We have his testimony two times on two shows: one that was done by a Christian organization called the 700 Club. The other one was done by *Beyond and Back*, a program that used to talk about near-death experiences. It was on television for a few years. In both of these programs, when Dr. Iregui says that I was dead, I was, in fact, clinically dead…for a long time…. That's what the medical records say…[it's] documented in the actual medical transcripts….

I had a kidney stone that got stuck on the right side trying to pass through, and it blocked the ureter, which caused the kidney infection. The doctor did what you are supposed to do, and this wasn't Dr. Iregui to begin with, it was another doctor. I don't mention his name because I just don't want people to go after him. I never have mentioned his name to people over the many years. He made a mistake. That's the bottom line. What he made a mistake in isn't that he gave me the wrong medicine or antibiotics to kill the kidney infection. It was that the antibiotic didn't work on me and he didn't notice.

I had gone into the hospital on a Thursday.... There was a mobile kidney machine that goes from hospital to hospital, and it happened to be coming to that hospital the next day. So…[this doctor] decided to keep me overnight and, in the meantime, gave me an antibiotic to fight this infection. Then in the morning, he would do a routine lithotripsy blast (a common procedure for kidney stones) to break the stone up. Then I should pass it and I should have been okay. That's what was supposed to happen, but what actually happened was that I was resistant to the antibiotics that he gave me. The antibiotic was effective for 99.9 percent of the people. But I was one of that 0.1 percent of the people for whom it isn't effective. So I was a rarity in the sense that the antibiotics were not working on me.… He never went back to check to make sure it that it [the antibiotic] had worked, and that's where his mistake was… he just assumed, "It's going to be taken care of when he passes the stone." Apparently, he didn't think anything more about me.

The next morning, my wife, because she worked in the medical field, had taken my temperature just before the procedure. And it was 104°. Yet when we informed [the doctor]…he told her…[it was normal to have a high temperature under such circumstances]. But the reality of it is…[that] he should have never even gone through with the procedure. Nevertheless, he…[did]. He told me later…that when he blasted the stone, it "opened up" the whole area…[pushing] the infection…into my bloodstream, and I became septic…everything in my body started slowing down…[but] no one knew that was happening.

So, after the procedure, I was in the recovery room…getting worse and worse and worse, instead of getting better and better and better, considering that this was a really easy procedure. It was getting harder for me to breathe every moment. It seemed like I wasn't getting enough air into my lungs. I didn't think that much of it, nor did my wife or anybody else. I thought maybe it was because I was excited; maybe I was hyperventilating.…

They…switched from giving me oxygen through a nasal canula to a mask. But I still didn't think that much of it, and I must have fallen asleep during recovery. Then the next thing I know, I'm on this gurney and they're wheeling me down the hallway really quickly. And that's when it really hit me that something seriously is going wrong here…and I couldn't really figure…out [what was happening].… But I knew it was harder for me to breathe. I was having a harder time grasping air…[it occurred to me] that, "I am dying."

I don't know why it came into my mind like that, I was kind of confused in a way, because I was thinking, "Wait a minute. I don't remember getting hit by a car. I don't remember falling off a building. I don't remember anything that says that I should be in this type of situation." The last thing I remember is that I was having an operation for a kidney stone. For me, it was an oddity due to the fact that I had a kidney stone four years earlier and I didn't go through all this then. So why would I be going through it now? But the thing that was really amazing to me is, because [I'm born again, I'm a Christian] I didn't freak out. I thought that was kind of odd at the time, because I always thought that when I come to that moment of knowing that I was dying, I would be having a lot of fear.… But, all of sudden, what rose up on the inside of me were these words, "I'm going home." All of a sudden, I had peace, joy and comfort hit me like you wouldn't believe.…

I was so peaceful, so calm about the whole situation. That was amazing to me.… Because it was my…[most dreaded way to die]—that is, by suffocation. But that is exactly what was happening…my lungs, because of the infection, were shutting down…literally being put out of commission.… The explanation for why it was the…[most dreaded way to die] is because I almost drowned as a little kid. I remember the trauma of that experience of almost drowning. I used to think, "If I'm going to die, I don't want to suffocate."… Yet here I…[was], suffocating and having the complete opposite experience of…[the fear I would have anticipated while] dying.

They did finally get me to ICU. A new critical care doctor, Dr. Iregui, took over the case.... But the other doctor had not informed him of the temperature I had prior to the procedure or anything else…the communication did not happen. So Doctor Iregui…[wasn't aware of] my previous problems with the antibiotics. So, he… [administered more] antibiotics, but by the time he started…[the additional medications], I was still deteriorating. They were going to intubate me and put me on life support, but they didn't get…[these measures into place] in time. (And this is all hearsay, because by this time, I wasn't conscious.) By the time they…[got life-support procedures set up to implement], I had died. Then he [Dr. Iregui] was working on me. He worked on me for an hour [and] forty-five minutes.

In one of the interviews, when the interviewers asked him, "Why did he work on me that long?" he said, "I really don't know. There was just a sign that I knew I had to keep working." He said his norm to really work on a person is only about thirty minutes, then he pronounces them dead.... But for whatever reason, he went thirty minutes, then another thirty minutes, and another thirty minutes, and then, finally, fifteen minutes working on me. I really believe it was because others were praying…maybe he was being urged spiritually, being encouraged by God to keep working on me, and so he did. But to this day, if you ask him, "Why did you keep working on this man?" he really doesn't know.

[Once during an interview regarding this event], when Dr. Iregui brought out the EKG from his records…[and upon being reminded of] how long I was flatlined.... Tears…[started]coming to his eyes and he said, "It's a miracle."

There's no way I should be back on this planet…from a medical or scientific standpoint, because I lost oxygen to my brain for one hour and forty-five minutes.... Then…[my physical body became] biologically dead: …after seventeen minutes, usually…[the body of the deceased] starts deteriorating because there is no oxygenated blood in it.

Allie: Had the deterioration process actually started at that point?

Dean: The deterioration process had begun in that my toes had died. They had no life in them. That's a miracle in itself. Because [later] they were healed…and I didn't lose a toe. But I found out from some nurses that the plan was to release me to go home, let me get strong enough and then bring me back in the hospital to amputate all my toes. That didn't happen because my toes literally were healed.…

[Later,] when we look at the medical records…with a couple of medical people, they pointed out about twenty-nine different things that went wrong with this body. I can't pronounce a lot of the technical terms or even tell you some of the things that went wrong from a layman's point of view. But all twenty-nine issues were healed.

Allie: Were there no marks on your skin from the defibrillator? Or the effects of the chest compressions or the electric defibrillator, anything like that?

Dean: None of those things showed up. It's like it never happened. It was amazing to them [the medical personnel who were later consulted regarding the event] that I didn't have any ill effects from any of it. They thought I should have some cracked ribs [from the CPR].… After all this, one doctor did a couple of tests. He said, "Man, it's like, according to the medical records, your heart exploded." That's the way he put it. Yet there's nothing in the follow-up tests that shows that my heart exploded. We know that all the medical pieces are factual and no one can really explain what happened to me. Because we have both the testimony of the doctor and the actual records, it would be hard to say that it didn't happen… [A person] could say I didn't go to heaven or I left my body and went to another place, but they *can't* say I didn't die. Those are the facts, right there, from a medical point of view and the records.

I always tell people I went *somewhere,* because I wasn't in my body.… I was considered clinically dead. I found out just recently by someone reading the records that they were in the process of signing the death

certificate papers [when]...I came back into my body all of a sudden....
[This was after] the [medical] team had stopped working on me for
anywhere from fifteen to thirty minutes. Then I came back to my body
and, of course, they went into action again....

Sometimes [describing this event is] like I'm talking to people about
[an occurrence that happened to] someone else. Yet, I know that it was
me that went through it. And so I [am a little disconnected from] the
medical aspect of it. Even when I first came back, I had no discomfort;
no pain. I wasn't suffering or anything like that. The only problem was
my toes, but those were healed in a few days. I didn't have an appetite
and I made myself eat. And I had a hard time sleeping at night....

I said all that just to get you to understand that whole medical aspect
of it, and all twenty-nine different things I was healed of. They brought
me in for tests for the next three months...because sepsis is one of the
leading causes of death in the hospital. If they could figure out how to
stop sepsis from happening with a person, then there would be a lot of
people's lives that could be saved.... [But after all the testing, medical
personnel were unable to figure out how I survived.]

Now [while I was clinically dead], I left my body; that is, *spiritually* I
left my body...[which] stayed here on the planet and I went to Heaven.
When I entered Heaven, what got my attention was that everything was
right. There was nothing wrong. It was past peace. I say that because
there was nothing to be peaceful *from*. There was no strife to get away
from. I don't know how to...[help people] grasp that. There is a Scripture that says you can really experience peace "past all understanding,"
and that would be the best way to say it: It's past all understanding...
nothing [was] wrong, and everything was right. The other thing that
got me when I entered Heaven was that I *fit*. It was like I was supposed
to be there, and I fit like a square peg that fits inside a square hole perfectly. That would be the best way to describe it. And I wasn't at a place:
It wasn't like I got there and said, "Oh man, I made it to Heaven."... I
knew this is where I was supposed to be....

[I didn't question]…anything there. Most of the questioning took place when I got back on the planet and I was processing things in my own head. That was mainly done in the hospital the next few days. But the reality of it is that it was simpler than I thought it would be: It wasn't as complicated as we make it out to be. It was very, very simple. The other thing that got me in those first few moments was that everything there was glad I was there, like I was welcome to be there. I didn't feel out of place. If you have ever been in a place where you you've been out of place, you'll understand how uncomfortable that is. But that isn't what happened…. In Heaven, it was different [than a setting where you know you don't belong]. I fit in and everything there was glad I was there. You could feel the joy of everything there that [rejoiced because] you were there. You are very much welcome to be there. That really was something for me to see: the simplicity in their welcoming of me. I have grandchildren. And whenever I see them, it doesn't matter what they've done or what they look like. I'm glad to see them. Whatever they've done doesn't matter anymore. I'm glad that they're here.

But…despite how great…the welcoming…[feeling was], I… wanted to be with Jesus. I wanted to see *Him*. My desire even [in a setting as beautiful as Heaven]…was to be where He is and to see Him. So I walked through this place. I say "walked," but this is hard to describe, because it was different than walking like we do on the planet. If you've ever been on those people-movers in the airport, [the way that] they just move you, this is the closest I can come to [describing] it, although I'm not saying this is really what was going on, either. Even though you're walking, it seemed that…[an unseen force propelled] you faster.

So that's what it was like for me when I was going to where Jesus was. There were trees before me, but they moved out of the way and made a path, and it seemed like everything around me…[made] the statement: "He's going to see the King." Don't ask me why they were making a statement. I don't know. I didn't have the mindset to even pay that much attention to the statement, but for whatever reason, I was drawn to be where He was.…

I remember coming out into a meadow and the trees were behind me when I came out, and He was in the meadow. He was addressing all these creations before him. Some of them were angels and some of them were people who had been on the planet and gone to be in Heaven. The way He was addressing them wasn't like He was speaking with…[an audible] voice speaking out. It was thought-to-thought. So even though His mouth was not opening, He was saying things. It was like somebody is in an auditorium…but it was more real…because it was so personal… [the way that He spoke with each creature individually].

I remember when I first saw Him, I couldn't stand. It wasn't that I was shaking, and for *that* reason I had to go down on my hands and knees: I wanted to…bow down on my face and put my hands out before me and my face in my hands. Then I…looked at His feet…and I made a statement: "You did this for me"…because I… [knew] at that moment, the only reason I was there was because of what He had done. It was such a reality to me that my good works didn't get me in nor did my bad works keep me out. I was there because I accepted *Him*. And because I accepted Him, it was that simple. You need to know that: Prior to going to Heaven, that was not my belief system.

I laugh about it now. But it was not the way I [had previously] believed. When I figured out how simple it was, I wasn't amazed… because you're not amazed there. But later on, back in my room in the hospital, I was thinking about it, [contrasting between] how simple it really was and how complex we make it.… I came to understand that my good works, all the good things that I do, is Him working through me, so He gets the credit for those good works. It wasn't that I didn't initiate it…I opened [the opportunity by saying] "if you want to use me in this way, I'm willing to be used this way." Then, regarding my bad works, I came to understand that whatever they were, if I asked Him to forgive me, He not only forgave me, He forgot it. Most people don't think about the forgetting part of it. They get the part where He forgives you. But really, He forgot it. So when you present yourself before Him, it's as if you never did anything wrong in your entire existence.

So clearly, you see that He was the One who got me there. That was really outside of my thinking, so a lot of the things I had thought were a certain way…[were different than I had once imagined] with the Father and Jesus in heaven. [Later, when I would] read my Bible [I would see a passage that registered differently for me after the NDE experience, and I would appreciate the new revelation].

There are two verses I use. One is in Colossians, where it says, "if we do everything, let us do it as unto the Lord."[57] So any…[good works] that we do, let it be Him working through us. Then with the bad stuff, I found in Hebrews, the eighth and tenth chapter that says that "when He forgives you, He forgets it."[58] I didn't know that before, yet, they have always been in those Scriptures.

So all this…[in Heaven] really hit me hard. The welcoming, the acceptance, and the pureness of everything towards me was something that I was supposed to experience. That's the best way to put it. And I didn't earn it…because even the Bible says in Ephesians… "not by works," yet we try to work for it a lot. Now…[that] doesn't mean you go out and do everything wrong.… If you are a Christian…you are a new creation in Christ Jesus, so you need to act like it. That's what the Scriptures say. And so that, again, is very simple. Either you are a Christian and you're going to act like it, or you're not a Christian and you're not going to act like it.

That doesn't mean a person isn't going to mess up or isn't going to do some things wrong. But the Bible talks about those who practice these things [being a Christian].… So let's say you do something, but you mess up. If you truly regret it, that's forgivable. But if you are constantly doing these things that are wrong, then that's a problem. [If you're] not practicing being a Christian…[then] it hasn't become a part of your daily routine.…

But after I said…[to Jesus], "You did this for me," then I…looked up. And this really impressed me. He looked at me like I've never been looked at before. That look was overwhelming. I didn't know that would happen—I just didn't know. Then, after that, I just thanked Him.

It was almost as if everything that He [had ever done for me in my entire life], that I…[hadn't recognized], was playing over for me. I don't mean like a movie screen; I just *knew* it. And I realized…[toward Jesus], "You were in this moment," or "You were in that moment," "And that moment…." And there were all these moments that I didn't even know He was there. But He *was* there, so all I could do was…[look at His feet and] thank Him.

I didn't need to see another portion of His being: I didn't need to see His face…His head…anything, because I was experiencing…the fullness of the love of God…coming through the feet of Jesus. (This love got me for a long time while I was in my hospital room, because [of the way that] He loved only me…. I knew He loved others. But looking at those feet… [I felt a love so specific that it was almost as if] He only loved me. And I wrestled with it for a while, just because of what I did for a living at the time, which was working with people. And I cared for people so much. The best way I could explain it was, He only loved me, yet I know He loved others.)

Allie: Did you see, and are you willing to describe, Jesus' face?

Dean: I did see His face, very clearly. In the book I wrote, I said, "Every moment He looks different to me." So the moment I saw His face, the first time it looked different than the next moment, and [then it] looked different than the next. Does it look like a human face? Yes, it does. It's more beautiful than you could ever imagine. And the beauty isn't so much the outward appearance as much as the essence of who *He* is.

Remember, He has a physical form. We know that He came to this planet in a physical form. But where we are spirit, soul, and body, three put together, He is no longer spirit, soul, and body. He is all one: His Body, His Spirit, and His Soul are all one. That's one of the reasons He could move through walls and move really quickly. Our flesh is not spiritual, so it can't move through physical things that are of this world. But Jesus' flesh is spiritual now…everything…[is] fused together: …spirit… soul, [and]…body is no longer three-in-one. It's just *one*.

People always want to know about His hair, its color, all of that. Colorwise, it's more of a rainbow color. I say that only because He was changing colors for me as I'm looking at Him. People say, "Well, what color was His skin?" But because of the brightness of the light that was shining out of Him, it's hard to tell you. You know, in the Bible, John said He looked like the sun. But he [John] could look at Him.

So look at [how] John…described Jesus in Revelation…[to me], His feet looked like "metals mixed together." That was my term when I first came back…John said His feet looked like "bronze."…I found out later on that to make bronze you have mix…[metals] together…. So John describes him pretty well…. I'm going to tell you the truth: He's more beautiful than you can ever imagine.…

Allie: What else did you experience while you were with Jesus?

Dean: [I realized that when]…you were…created by God Almighty, [He]…created love [specifically] for you that no one else could receive but you. It's not a blanket love or a mass-produced love, it's a tailor-made love that is just for *you*. What I was receiving was the love that was created for *me*. If you are there [in Heaven with Him], you're going to receive your specially created love. If somebody else is…there though, it's…all going to be different [specifically made for *them*]. You can see this…[in] Scripture…[when you observe] how God reacted to [different] people. Everything's personal, nothing is just a "group" thing. We [human beings] do the same type of thing. We don't (and can't) love our children all exactly the same. What we do is based on their different talents…ways of doing things…[and] thinking…we tailor-make our love for each child, based on all these…things. Even as they become adults, each one has a…[unique]personality, they may live in different towns…[and have varying] kinds of jobs. We tailor-make our love just for that person based on all these different factors. That's just the way we do it. And God Almighty does the same for us.

Then I could accept…that everything about Him loved me. He didn't have to say, "I love you." When I looked at another part of His being, He loved me. I looked at His hands. They loved me. There's no way I could *not* experience the love He had for me being in His presence. It was like I couldn't get away from it—not that I was trying to! I'm just saying that I couldn't get away. And I remember looking in His eyes…remember that communication there is mostly thought-to-thought. And…all of a sudden, I would think about someone else…. And I could see…[that same tailor-made] love [that He had] for them…. I thought about a few [specific] people and I could see the [tailor-made] love [that He had] for them…. And [it suddenly hit me, what Scripture has said all along: and] I said…to Him…[:] "You really *do* want everybody here."

Up to that moment, I assumed it and I probably even taught it when I was on the planet before this experience. But the reality of how much He really…[*does*] want everyone there really hit me at that moment….

[I began to think of people who had committed the most vulgar, atrocious, and grievous sins: those for whom, at times, I had wondered if forgiveness could be achieved with the same *simplicity* as other people.] And I'm down at His feet on my hands and knees, but by this time I am looking at His head [He was still communicating with the multitude before Him, yet simultaneously began communicating with me]…and He says this to me: "When you put a person in jail, they get out. They either get out because their time's up or they get out because they die, but they get out. But when we put a person in Hell, they are there for eternity."… And then…He turned and He looked down at me. And [in response to the thought I had about those who commit heinous crimes] He said, "Who are you to nullify what I have done?" Some people [have since] said, "Well, He rebuked you." But He said all of that in love. I did not feel any fear. I didn't feel any discomfort. In fact, I felt, if anything, freedom.... He paid the price for *everyone*, no matter who they are, *what* they've done. And if they come to Him and ask Him to forgive them, and accept Him, He's going to do it, because He's already paid the price.

[Later]…I found that…in Scripture…in Hebrews…[where] it talks about how when Jesus Christ died, He died for everyone. And literally, it tells you that He went through the physical portion of dying for people. So He didn't only die their *spiritual* death, He died their *physical* death, and I experienced that when I died because I didn't go through any other physical discomfort…[meaning that we will not experience the] actual discomfort [of dying] that we *should* feel, because Christ already died for us and took that discomfort....

[Also, something that struck me] is that, all of a sudden, I saw things that I didn't see before. Think about how He was beaten. The Bible says that He was turned over to the court or Roman court. Now, the Roman court is made up of five hundred men, and the Bible said they beat Him. So in reality, five hundred men beat Him. It wasn't just two or three soldiers, like we usually think.... And that makes sense, because the Bible says in Isaiah, the fifty-third chapter, that He was beaten in such a manner that He was unrecognizable as a human being.... So when He said [to me], "Who are you to nullify what I have done?"… [He was reminding me that] He's the one who paid the price for it all, and I had no right to nullify or put any criteria on top of it [other] than what was already there.

[Another]…thing that was amazing was that my family came to greet me…I mean anybody who was connected to me in any manner of three ways. One was to be biologically connected. That means I came through that family DNA-wise. Another was being adopted. If that family member was adopted into my family or my family members were adopted into that family, they would come to greet me. Then the last one was to be stepparents on either side. We all became family, those three groups. The last two I didn't know were possible until I found out we could be grafted into a family. (And again, [later, as] I was reading my Bible...all of a sudden [could] I see it. Where it was pointed out to me...was when Jesus Christ was on the cross, and He looked at John, the Beloved, and said to him that Mary (who was His mother) would now be John's mother, and John now would be her son. The Bible says that from that day, Mary, moved in with John. So you could be grafted into a family and become a part of that family. That's...helped...[a lot of] adopted [people whom I've shared my story with] over the years. They're always wondering, "Man, who's going to come to greet me?" I tell them, "Well, you're going to have both groups. You're going to have your adoptive family *and* your biological family."

[It]...was amazing to me that my family was there, because that was not my belief system beforehand. I did not think it really mattered if your family was there or not...because we are all the family of God, so [I thought] it doesn't really matter. But when...my family literally came...to greet me...it was amazing to me...because my grandmother, Mary, to whom I give the credit for praying me into the Kingdom of God...stood out in front of all these people. Everybody else was behind her—maybe about two or three feet—and she was in the front....

The other thing that I noticed is that it [the family greeting] was generation after generation after generation...[not just those I knew from my own life] like grandparents, uncles, aunts, and cousins. It was the previous generation, and the...[one] before that, and the...[one] before that.

Allie: Were these people who were on the earth before you were even alive? But somehow you recognized them? Or were these people you knew about beforehand?

Dean: No, these were people who existed before I was on the earth. I always tell people that 99 percent of everything I experienced, I can... [validate from within] the Word. So the [correlating] Word that comes from [my] memory is when Jesus was on the Mount of Transfiguration and Elijah and Moses showed up. If you think about it, that was generations before Peter, James, and John, the apostles who were with Him, [but they] saw them and recognized them. How did they recognize them? It couldn't...[have been] visual...because there were no pictures of them. So they had to know spiritually or from their heart that these people were part of their family, and that's how you recognize people in heaven. You see them, [and] the primary way of connecting with them is through your heart. The closest I could come to...[explaining] this is like most mamas. They have a child...[who] could be in another room. But if that child's crying, and there could be a lot of babies crying, they'll recognize [the sound of] their own baby. They'll know it.... But, *how* do they know it? There's this...spiritual connection, I believe, that we can't describe. So in reality, when I got to heaven, all my family members [greeted me; I recognized them in this way].

And you see them visually...[but it's hard to describe a person who isn't within the realm of time]. I know people say they look "young." But even using that word...[falls] short, because that's a "time" word, and they're no longer in time. I've heard people...[try to describe it before, but any word we can use comes from within the realm of time, which makes our words fail to describe the existence of beings which dwell outside of this realm].

[As]...I was leaving my body and going to be...in Heaven...these lights...passed me by [which] I knew...were prayers. I knew they were prayers for me and others. But I was moving fast...and yet, the prayers... were really moving faster than I was. Well, one of the things I always talk about with these prayers [is that] they don't have a shelf life.... Most people don't realize...[that] prayers don't expire. They're [always] up there, and God is acting off of them.... [I believe the family greeting for me] was because of…[my family's] prayers…for generations after them. And I'm one of those results.…

One of the most amazing things about that was that there were people there…who I didn't even think would be there…[one in particular that] I thought…would be in Hell[:]…my Aunt Barbara. And it wasn't that I didn't love my Aunt Barbara or care for her, but I didn't… [know] she had made a commitment to God.… I don't know when she accepted Jesus, but I know the only way you get in [to Heaven] is to receive Christ as Lord and Savior…so I know she had to accept Him.

And the third thing that hit me really hard was learning that family's important to God. I didn't really take it that way before. I distanced myself from my family because I was a Christian and they weren't. Yet… [this experience showed me that how] important…[family is] to God. So…when I was being told, "No, it's not your time, go back," [my grandmother Mary, who stood in front of the other family members who greeted me] communicated to me to bring as many of our family members back with me as I can. What that meant was to pray for them, to talk to them about Jesus, to find a way to communicate into their lives about God and how to get there [to Heaven].… I [was able to] understand her [Grandmother Mary's] desire, after wanting Jesus and the Father, was that all of her family members would be with her [in Heaven] forever. So that was amazing to me, then, the significance of how important family is to God.… Family was created to be together forever.

Sometimes when I say that…[people respond], "Man, you don't know my family, I don't want to be with them." But in Heaven, everything is right. You're right, they're right. You get along with them and they get along with you. We get to experience family the way God really meant for us. I really think that's to give hope to a lot of people who even come from families that are not the most loving Hope that if those people end up in Heaven, you'll be the most loving family you could ever experience. Those three things about family were really significant.

Then usually I talked about what it was like to be told, "No, it's not your time, go back." I really was told that three times. The first time I… [thought to myself], okay, I could accept this. Then, my body wasn't ready for me to come back. The next time I was told to go back after I traveled through Heaven…[and then Jesus told me I could not stay], He said, "No, it's not your time, go back."

I remember that I didn't really want to go back. I did not want to leave that place at all. And I remember getting to what I call the edge of Heaven…. I remember getting ready to leave and I knew my body was ready. I was so happy in Heaven, because I wanted to stay. So I… traveled through Heaven again, and then went back to Jesus. Finally, He said, "No, it's not your time, go back." Anytime He said those things, He spoke it to me [audibly]. He didn't do that thought-to-thought. And when He spoke it to me, it was like everything around me got out of the way…[as if to say], "He's not talking to me, He's talking to you." …I remember leaving and how sad I felt…like a baby crying. As I was going back, I remember seeing the prayers go in the opposite direction that I was going in. I remember entering back into the hospital room and set-tling into my body. And next thing I remember was…being transferred from one hospital to another.

Allie: I understand it took quite a while for anyone to come forward to validate your story.

Dean: Yes. I did write a number of books, like *In Heaven! Before the Throne of God*. That one is kind of like an overview. I call it my "flyby." And I put the medical records in there. The first five years, no doctor would come forward or say anything, mainly because the hospital was afraid that I was getting the information to be a part of litigation at the time. But Dr. Ire-gui finally came forward after five years, so all the television programs… [featuring him took place after] five years…. I put the transcripts, [and] medical records in the books…. I just put them in there to show what was going on with me…every medical person I've ever shown …[the medical records] to looked at the records and said, "Man, if you didn't die of that, you should have died of this."… [Some people have even speculated that] they messed up the records or they gave me somebody else's records. But in reality, they didn't [as Dr. Iregui has verified].

Allie: Was there a specific moment when you felt yourself cross from life to death? Did you have an out-of-body experience? What was that transition like?

Dean: You know, that's a good question. For years, it was hard for me to really describe it. Because it wasn't like I thought it was going to be. I'll tell you what it was like, then I'll tell you where it is in the Scriptures. I left my body, and *then* my body died. I always thought it was [that] my body…[would die] and *then* I would leave my body. But it was the other way around. That was confusing for me for a long time, because I believed that you die, and then your spirit leaves. Then one day, I was reading in the Bible. James, the second chapter, says, "Faith without works is dead." I thought, just like the body is dead without the spirit… so then I thought about it. Well, how did man become a living soul? The Bible says in Genesis, the second chapter, that God breathed into man, which means He put a spirit into man, and *then* he became a living soul. So the body was there, but it wasn't alive until the spirit came in.

When people say "you transfer over" [into another realm], it… [wasn't that way for me]. It wasn't like one moment, I was in this realm, and then the next moment, I was in that realm. I had always been in that other realm because I had eternal life. When Jesus said that you have eternal life, it starts when you're born again. It doesn't start when you leave your body and go to Heaven. It starts when [you make the decision for Christ and are]…born again. So most people don't realize you're not going to feel a transference like you think. When I entered Heaven, there was a difference. But leaving the body, there was none. Paul says,

"Whether I was in the body, I cannot tell you or out of the body, I cannot tell you." I have no conscience of leaving the body....

Now, where I probably have a consciousness is coming back into the body. When I came back in, it was like, "Okay, I'm limited again," because I was unlimited there. All of a sudden, I'm limited again... there were certain things I couldn't...because of my body.... I came to understand that when you become born again, you are eternal, whether you realize that or not. Your body isn't.... Your body dies, but you never die.

Allie: Did you feel yourself stepping out of your body? You do hear of out-of-body experiences. Did you have that? Where was the first place you realized you were?

Dean: [In leaving the body, I felt] a pull on me...or the sense that I was going home. If you were to have that experience right now, being born again, I'm telling you something...you're not looking back. You're going home. I tell people sometimes, if you would have come in the room, trying to pray for me to stay alive on this planet, I would have been fighting, because I was going home. It was so strong. It was like a magnet, drawing metal towards it.... And that's what I felt like leaving the body.... [It says in] Hebrews, second chapter, verses 14 and 15: "He did it so that you will not fear death." You don't die; your body does. So when you say "transformation," well, you've been *transformed* already, whether you realize it or not.

[But in returning to my body]...I was never being pulled back to this planet. I was told to go back to the planet [and was *sent*] back to the planet.... That's a whole different thing.

Allie: A lot of people who have said they've had a near-death experience describe a handful of key elements over and over that are visual. I don't want to put words in your mouth. But it kind of sounds like, with you, the vision was more, I don't want to use the word "psychic," but within your psyche, rather than visual.... I'm not hearing you talk about the tunnel of light and things like that, that so many people talk about. It sounds like, for you, was it more of a mental thing?

Dean: No, I did see the light. I didn't say that earlier, but I always say it looked like a window, not like a tunnel [filled with] light. I knew it was happening. I thought the moment I was leaving my body, I was going to be with the Father and Jesus.... I believe I was inside my body when I saw the light, and left to go toward it. I just didn't look back. I went through the ceilings...through the atmosphere...through outer space, and into what I call outer darkness in getting to that light. It's just that I didn't die—my body did.... When you get to Heaven, you're not going to think about how your fleshly body is doing on the planet. You come to realize how spiritual you really are. You are a spirit with a body—you're not a body with a spirit...the only reason I could put it in these words is because the Bible says it the best way: When you become born again, you have eternal life; you don't die. That means your body dies. It doesn't go anywhere. It stays right here on the planet and dissolves back into the ground.

Allie: When you were going away and you were in the light, is that the moment when you said the little lights that were prayers were passing you? Is that when that was happening?

Dean: Really, they were passing me as soon as I got into outer space. But I didn't pay that much attention to where the planets, like Jupiter and Uranus, Venus, and all those things are, in our universe. I left our universe and entered that dark area where you heard people say they felt a light at the end of the tunnel...there's the light that they see before them, which I said looks like a window. That's the closest I can describe it. I noticed the other things passing me by: the prayers... They weren't shooting stars, but that's the best way I could describe it.... And really what I was seeing was not so much the beginning of them. I was noticing the end of them, the tail. [1 Peter 3 tells us that]...the Lord is... attentive to our prayers, and He's anticipating us talking to Him.... When man was created, he was given a voice and a mouth. It wasn't to talk to animals; it was to talk to God. Most people don't realize that you were created to talk to God, and then [you were] given ears to hear from God....

I saw those prayers leave what I call the dark area going past me. When I entered Heaven...the prayers still went on...to the Father, and they entered *into* the Father...that was even amazing to me. I didn't know our prayers enter *into* Him.... In Psalms, the eighteenth chapter...David says his prayers entered *into* God. Then...[in] Revelation... it talks about the prayers that arose like incense. Incense is a smell. So God...[breathes in] your prayers.

Allie: What are you doing currently?

Dean: Well, one of the things I am doing is...writing things out now. I'm putting together a ten-book series called *Moments in Heaven*.... This goes deeper into some of the areas that I experienced when I was there. One of the things I didn't talk to you about when I was there was worship, and what that worship was like for me in Heaven. I'm describing it in the book that I put out called *Worship in Heaven*, and trying to...[present] the most visual experience I can of what it was like to be in Heaven worshiping with everything. Then I just got done with a book called *What It Feels Like to Die*. I feel like I learned a lot about the subject by dying.

Life Flashes Before One's Eyes

More than 22 percent of people who have experienced NDEs claim to have completely relived every important moment in their life, both the good and bad.[59] Many recall moments they hadn't thought of in years, and some were able to observe events that would've taken place when they were too young to remember, such as bonding moments with parents as infants. A smaller percentage report seeing visions of the future, such as flashes of events to come, wherein their future work makes a difference in the lives of others here on earth. For these people, it is common to return from an NDE with a new perspective on the rest of their lives: They return with a mission or a purpose. An important element to note regarding the life review during a near-death experience is the fact that one's earthly or material gains are never the focus. Rather, people become more aware of the kind of person they've been, the way they have influenced the lives of people around them, and their own capacity to love and be loved. Furthermore, the details are rarely the type of memory a person would think to discuss if asked to highlight significant life moments.

It's important to remember that these experiences are *near* death and not *full* death. From full death, there is no return. For Christians, there should be an understanding that, in every near-death experience, there was an intent by God for the person to survive. Therefore, it wouldn't be wise to jump to the conclusion that life reviews are the same as God's judgment as described in the Bible. Even more, we learn that God's ultimate judgment occurs at the resurrection of the dead, which is generally understood to happen sometime after the return of Jesus Christ to earth. There have been attempts to equate a type of life review with God's judgment, such as in the chick track entitled *This Was Your Life.*[60] To properly sort out these matters, however, we must look to Scripture.

Do not marvel at this, for an hour is coming when all who are in the tombs will hear his voice and come out, those who have done good to the resurrection of life, and those who have done evil to the resurrection of judgment. (John 5:28–29)

And I saw the dead, great and small, standing before the throne, and books were opened. Then another book was opened, which is the book of life. And the dead were judged by what was written in the books, according to what they had done. (Revelation 20:12)

I tell you, on the day of judgment people will give account for every careless word they speak. (Matthew 12:36)

For nothing is hidden that will not be made manifest, nor is anything secret that will not be known and come to light. (Luke 8:17)

As we can see, based on these verses, God's ultimate and final judgment occurs at the resurrection of the dead after the return of Jesus Christ. What, then, happens when people die? Do they go to Heaven or Hell depending on their standing with Jesus at the time of death? Is this their place of residence until the final judgment? Is there any coming back from this temporary residence or status before the final judgment? Furthermore, what do we do with the idea that God will give some people one last chance to repent at death?

To answer these questions and more, we have to remember that an NDE is not death, and in every NDE case, the experiencers are always meant to return, meaning they do not suffer the permanent loss of physical life. Instead, they may come close to the edge of the cliff—so close they can see all the way down to the bottom, but do not fall off and undergo the crushing blow of contact with the earth below. If a person has an NDE and is given a chance to repent, does that count as a "second chance," or is it really a continuation of the first chance they had prior to the NDE? Certainly, not every person who experiences an NDE ends up receiving Christ as Savior; therefore, a rejection is still possible. What does Scripture say about second chances after physical death?

The Lord is not slow to fulfill his promises some count slowness, but is patient toward you, not wishing that any should perish, but that all should reach repentance. (2 Peter 3:9)

It would stand to reason, given this verse, that "to perish" means there is no going back. Death is when the choice is set in stone. Why else would God be patient? If there were second or even third chances, why would God be patient with the first chance? Second Peter 3:9 seems to indicate that there is one chance for repentance, that of physical life, and God is willing to be patient because He doesn't want anyone to squander his or her chance and perish with no hope of being reconciled to Him in eternity.

Come now, let us reason together, says the Lord: though your sins are like scarlet, they shall be as white as snow; though they are red like crimson, they shall become like wool. (Isaiah 1:18)

As it is my eager expectation and hope that I will not be at all ashamed, but that with full courage now as always Christ will be honored in my body, whether by life or by death. (Philippians 1:20)

These verses speak to the reality of sin in our lives and how we are reconciled to God through Christ despite sin. They wouldn't make much sense if we were allowed multiple chances through cycles of life and death to come to the saving grace of Jesus Christ. If sin is like scarlet, but then can become as white as snow, how could sin then become scarlet again? If an NDE was the same as death, when a believer dies, his or her sins become white as snow. If that Christian is allowed to return, how could he or she become red with sin again after already being washed clean?

Of course, throughout Scripture, there are cases of resurrections; certain people were literally raised from the dead—which is different from an NDE. NDEs can happen to believers and nonbelievers alike who come back with a wide variety of ways to interpret their experiences. It seems that the resurrections in the Bible (not counting the final resurrection of the dead, as that includes everybody who has ever lived) center around believers in the God of the Bible specifically. (We will delve deeper into this topic later, as it is a theologically heavy matter.)

> But, as it is written, "What no eye has seen, nor ear heard, nor the heart of man imagined, what God has prepared for those who love him." (1 Corinthians 2:9)

This is our promise as believers. This is also how we know that, from a Christian perspective, NDEs and death are different, yet related. We've never seen or heard—nor could we even imagine—what's in store for us if we love the Lord Jesus Christ. If NDEs could give us any indication of what actual death is like, this verse would be rendered useless. In that case, eyes would have seen, ears would have heard, and the hearts of men would have imagined—providing they had an NDE. As stated earlier, the best way to understand NDEs on a very basic level is to imagine looking down the face of a cliff without jumping off past the point of no return. You might be able to get a sense of what it could be like past the edge of the cliff, but you could never really know for sure unless you took the leap, in which case you absolutely would not be coming back to tell anyone about it. This brings us to supernatural revelation (what it would be like looking down the face of the cliff, whereas most others haven't) and the element of reaching a point of no return (jumping off the cliff).

Supernatural Revelation

This aspect of an NDE is probably one of the most profound. Fifty-six percent of NDEers claimed that they received some sort of supernatural revelation—an extra-earthly understanding of "special knowledge, universal order, and/or purpose."[61] Many felt they had obtained a higher level of comprehension about God, humanity, the universe, and even of the realm of time. Because of this disclosure, most NDEers return to life with a great sense of mission and purpose. Furthermore, they report that "trivial matters" diminish in importance, while weightier matters such as "loving one another" or "learning more about love" become central priorities for the rest of their lives.

Tom Horn's Experiences[62]

Excerpted from *The Boy From El Mirage* by Tom Horn

One night after going to bed next to [Horn's wife,] Nita, I drifted off to sleep, and at some point in the middle of the night, my consciousness was jerked to a place I had never seen. I couldn't comprehend its brilliance. Contemplating my surroundings, I wondered where I was, where I had come from, how long I had been here, and why I had no memories of getting here...wherever "here" was.

At that moment, I knew this was no dream; it was too vivid to be anything less than real. In fact, it felt more real than any previous reality I had known. Had I died?

Yes, I had.

I barely became aware of this supernatural backdrop when I abruptly found myself standing somewhere before a spectacular pillar of light (or was it a throne?). It was so bright, so intense and penetrating—glistening with vibrant streams of silver and blue and gold emanating the most unexplainable, yet awe-inspiring presence—that I could hardly keep my eyes open or my face toward the radiance.

And I was urgently exclaiming something I couldn't possibly understand: "Please, Lord, don't let me forget. Please don't let me forget! IT'S TOO WONDERFUL!"

How much time had I spent in this surreal place? What had I just observed that so profoundly influenced my desire to remember it? And what was it I was even talking about? Why was I so desperate to recall something I had obviously feared forgetting? And how had I known I was standing before the LORD?

Suspended there like a marionette hanging on wires, I was somehow aware that "memories" from only moments before stood just beyond my ability to summon back into my conscious mind again. (But were "moments" or "time" even factors in this place?) Whatever had been revealed to me was already gone, leaving a hungry void in the place of a great revelation.

But I had known something…of that I was sure. A disclosure of vast importance had dawned within my cognition like a great, vibrating bell, alerting the depths of my very soul to a certainty that trumped any knowledge I've ever held in my finite brain…and it had come through no invitation of my own. It hadn't been my idea. That much was clear. It had been a truth that electrified my deepest consciousness…something about the future. The data was there. I had visualized it, I had seen it, and then it had been blocked from my access again; I had been told I would not remember the details.

But why? What would be the purpose in that?

Something else had happened, too. Somehow, I knew that a scroll of some kind had unrolled before me depicting scenes of a distant tomorrow, a hereafter, a time ahead—my time ahead—playing out on what looked like silvery parchment. The image of this was as clear and as believable as if I were watching a movie, with rich depictions of a destiny or possible future where something extraordinary and miraculous was taking place. A cinematic conveyance of a personal fate. A "potential existence" that had been downloaded into my subconscious mind—or soul. Then, for some reason, it departed my intellect as quickly as it had appeared.

Had a revelation of some type been sealed within me, perhaps something intended for a later time?

My thoughts raced, and I started to repeat, "Lord, please, don't let me forget," but I stopped short as, just then, a deep, still, small voice countered, "You will not remember…and it is time for you to go back now."

I heard a thunderclap and found myself falling backward, gliding rapidly, as if I had been dropped out of an airplane window or was let loose by some heavenly hands that had been holding me above, my arms and legs gliding up and down now against a cloudless sky.

As I fell, I gazed unblinkingly upward in amazement. The brilliance, which had just been in front of me, was moving swiftly away into the distance, yet I wasn't afraid. A high-pitched whistling sound began rushing in around my ears, and I thought it must be the sound of the air carrying me aloft as I plummeted toward the earth. A moment later, I observed the oddest thing: The roof of my house literally enveloped me as I passed effortlessly through it, and then it felt as if I had landed on my bedroom mattress with a thud…

I sat straight up, took a desperate, shuddering, deep inhalation, and then slowly let the breath out as I realized that something extraordinary had occurred. Wherever I had been, whatever I had seen, now I was back to the "real" world, and this material, earthly substance all around me straightaway felt far less authentic than the other place I had been. It was like this cosmos, this dimension, this realm that everyone calls "life" was merely a temporal and trivial matrix of existence that I was now being required to return to after tasting the marvelous phenomenon of a genuine, superior domain.

It was the middle of the night, and I sat there for a few seconds, possibly in shock, trying to determine what had happened.

I could feel my chest burning…and then I heard something.

Sobbing. Right next to me. As the tears flowed, my young wife had her head bowed, resting on her hands.

Once my eyes adjusted to the darkness, I found Nita's isolated stare. She looked as if she had been crying desperately, and she had an unfamiliar expression conveying what I somehow already understood: We had both gone through an experience far more irregular than anything we ever could have prepared for.

"Nita," I said softly, "what's going on? Why are you crying?"

It took a while for her to collect herself, but once she did, she tearfully described how she had awakened to find me dead. I had no pulse, no breath, no heartbeat, and my skin was cold to the touch—and not just for a few seconds. I had remained in that condition for approximately fifteen minutes, she estimated, while she had screamed for me to wake up, pounded on my chest, and attempted something like CPR. My face was contorted in wild expression. My hands were crumpled up next to my head, fingers partly curled inward on themselves like a man creeping up on someone in a classic "boo" scare. My skin was ashen, and my muscles were stiff as a board.

I had been absolutely, beyond a doubt, dead.

I had been, for the third time in my life, "as good as gone."

We didn't have a phone in those days, and because it was somewhere around midnight, Nita had been unsure of what to do. She told me she had been about to try pulling me outside to the car to take me to the hospital when I had jerked up, taken a deep breath, and looked at her.

No matter how incredible this narrative seems, it really did happen to me a long time ago. Later, and since then, I understood why God had allowed my wife to wake up and find me in that condition. Without her eyewitness account that night, uncertainties about the supernaturalism of the experience would have undoubtedly crept into my mind over the years. That I had been dead for a significant period of time—not breathing and therefore not taking in oxygen, yet experiencing no brain damage beyond the disruption that had occurred to my long-term memory when I had been run over as a boy—also attested to the preternatural aspect of the event.

But why would God show me something and then not allow me to remember it? What would be the point in that, right? I struggled to make sense of what had obviously been an extraordinary incident in my and Nita's life. I prayed daily, seeking understanding, and during this same period (undoubtedly God had all this timing in control from the very beginning), I happened to be reading the Bible from cover to cover for the first time in my life. I had made it to the book of Job, and one day my eyes suddenly fell upon Job 33:15–17. The Word of God dramatically came to life in what some charismatics might call a *rhema* moment: a time when the Scripture went from being ink on paper to *the living Word of God.* The text that instantly conveyed the dynamic truth behind what had happened to me that fateful night I died read:

> In a dream, in a vision of the night, when deep sleep falleth upon men, in slumberings upon the bed; Then he openeth the ears of men, and sealeth their instruction [within them], That he may withdraw man from his purpose, and hide pride from man.

Though I was a young and inexperienced believer, I clearly understood what this text was saying to me. Like the apostle Paul who could not tell whether he was "in the body…or out of the body" when he had been "caught up to the third heaven" (2 Corinthians 12:2), God, on that momentous night, had taken me to a heavenly place and "sealed instructions" within me. These directions would be there when I needed them, as they were like a road map that the Holy Spirit would "quicken" when I could use guidance or information. Nevertheless, I was not to remember these details ahead of time; otherwise, I might be drawn away into my "own purpose" and lifted up in "pride," according to this oldest book in the Bible.

In other words, if, as a young believer, I had seen the ministries that God would later allow Nita and me to participate in, it's likely I would have made two huge mistakes: First, I would have immediately aimed at the later ministries and started working toward making them happen—all without the benefit of the struggles, trials, setbacks, side roads, and experiences that "seasoned" me and (hopefully) qualified me to eventually operate in them (thus God "withdrew me from *my* purpose"). Second, I would have been tempted by pride to think more of myself than I should have as a young man if I had envisioned winding up in high-profile ministries. So, God, in His benevolence, "hid pride" from me by keeping the revelations "sealed" until the appropriate times.

In the Bible, it is clear that God does "seal" knowledge, wisdom, and revelations in the hearts of those who follow Him. That these concealed truths can be "quickened" or made alive at the right moments as they are needed is depicted in such texts as Matthew 10:19–20, where Jesus says to His disciples: "But when they deliver you up, take no thought how or what ye shall speak: *for it shall be given you in that same hour* what ye shall speak. For it is not ye that speak, but the Spirit of your Father which speaketh *in you*" (emphasis added). That this reflects a deep partnership between our personal devotions and studies (2 Timothy 2:15; Psalm 119:11) and the indwelling Holy Spirit as part of the mystical union God holds with all members of the true Church—the Body of Christ—can also be seen in Proverbs 3:6, which says, "In all thy ways acknowledge him [that's us doing our part], and he shall direct thy paths [His part]." Again, the book of John (6:63) refers to the Holy Spirit as the one "that quickens" (Greek *zōopoieō*—"to cause to live, to make alive at that moment") the Word of God as well as those "sealed instructions" Job talked about.

If you are a sincere believer and haven't clearly received your call from God, keep seeking. It's there as surely as the Lord lives. Only within His Divine timing will your calling dawn upon you.

If, at some point, you thought that you received your calling, but it turned out to conflict with the direction your spirit felt led initially, embrace the lesson you learned during that time. No time is wasted when knowledge is being imparted. Perhaps, like me, the Lord has "locked" your ultimate call from you until He sees the moment has arrived for you to follow it. But it will only be after the preparation for the call—the benefit of the struggles, trials, setbacks, side roads, and experiences along the way—that the call will be revealed.

Finally, if you have experienced a supernatural event and later sought the advice of a ministry leader or fellow believer whose advice didn't ring true in your spirit, rest assured that the answer will come in due time. Meanwhile, pour yourself into the truth of the Word and soak up every story from those blessed pages as you can. Pray at every opportunity that you will grow in your ability to communicate with the Lord, no matter your age or circumstances. Prayer and Bible reading may not give you *an immediate* answer, but prayer and the Word *will* give you an answer, and the search will only drive you closer to the throne.

End of excerpt from *The Boy From El Mirage* by Tom Horn

Reaching a Border or Point of No Return

When hearing about NDEs, many people—31 percent, to be more precise—refer to a point at which, once past it, they would be unable to return to life on earth.[63] For some, this is when they were offered a choice of returning to earthly life or remaining in the afterlife. For others, this was when they claim to have been met by angels, God, Jesus, or even deceased family members who told them that this was not their time; they must return to the "regular world." Most people can see past the boundary into what they claim is a beautiful land, which remains consistent with other commonly reported elements of NDE: a landscape of brilliant light with bright cities on the horizon filled with vivid colors and magnificent music, and which overflows with all-enveloping, all-encompassing peace, joy, and love.

Bruce Van Natta's Experience[64]

Written by Allie Anderson-Henson and Donna Howell
in *Encounters: Extraordinary Accounts of Angelic Intervention
and What the Bible Actually Says about God's Messengers*

Thursday, November 16, 2006, began like any ordinary day for Bruce Van Natta, a married father of four small children who was active in his local Christian church. Despite the morning chill over the Lakes area of Wisconsin, Bruce left his house early and drove to work in the utility vehicle that housed his diesel repair tools. The job he would be finishing that day was rectifying a coolant leak on a Peterbilt logging truck, a project he had started earlier in the week. He had already disassembled the engine and done most of the work; all that remained was reassembling the parts and reinstalling the engine.

Little did Bruce know that before this day would end, he would face off with the grave, make a life-or-death decision, and experience magnificent, supernatural, angelic intervention.

Once at work, Bruce located some parts that had been delivered and spent the majority of the day working with another mechanic to wrap up the project. All went smoothly, and soon the only thing left to do was run a test to make sure the issue was resolved before he would be free to leave. His coworker would then finish some other fixes that the Peterbilt was undergoing. Checking the time just after 6 p.m., Bruce happily made a note to himself that, at this rate, he'd be home for dinner.

Bruce started the engine to make sure the problem had been fixed. While he waited for the engine to reach the proper temperature, he began to pack up his tools, until the mechanic he had been working with asked one last favor: Would Bruce try to pinpoint the source of an oil drip that had been puzzling him for some time? Bruce agreed, and his coworker pointed out a vague area near the front, bottom vicinity of the grill. To get a better look, Bruce would need to slide beneath the vehicle on a creeper—a flat, gurney-type platform on wheels. Because Bruce's own heavy-duty steel one was already packed away with his other tools, he quickly borrowed the assistant's plastic creeper and rolled himself into position on his back.

This Peterbilt was of a conventional style, sometimes known as a "long-nose" body type, with a hood and fenders and a tall, forward-facing chrome bumper. From beneath, the front axle was the part of the vehicle that was lowest to the ground, carrying between five and six tons of weight without a load, as it was now. To make that side of the engine more accessible and to get the hoist underneath, the front, passenger-side wheel had been removed and a round bottle jack had been placed to support the weight of the vehicle on this side. No further safety equipment had been put into place.

As Bruce began to assess the underside of the motor, he asked the assistant mechanic to climb inside the rig and read the temperature gauge on the dashboard. At this time, the front axle was stationed over Bruce's abdomen. As his coworker proceeded to enter the cab in order to read the needle on the dash, the weight of the truck shifted, momentarily releasing the downward pressure that had been holding the bottle jack in place. The lift device's angle budged, but the vehicle returned to its original position. At this, the change in weight placement caused the tool to fly from its location, which allowed the Peterbilt to drop to the concrete floor, crushing Bruce's torso beneath more than five tons of blunt metal.

"Lord, help me!" Bruce called out. His diaphragm had been shoved up into his chest, instantly restricting his breath to short intakes, and he began coughing up blood.

He pressed against the truck in an attempt to lift it off his body, but to no avail. Again, he pleaded, "Lord, help me!"

Looking down, Bruce could see that the gap between the lowest point of the steel and the ground was about an inch on the left side and about two on the right, so he quickly realized that his midsection had been crushed to those dimensions. Likewise, he was aware that the metal was approximately six inches thick, thus his injury filled a similar span across his body, comprising the entire area between his ribs and the top of his pelvic bone.

(In a later interview, Bruce reflected that, despite the severity of the injury, the shape of the damage was so defined that it reminded him of cartoons he had seen as a child, wherein the shape of the indention in an injury was exaggerated for the sake of comedy. For example, when Wiley Coyote, the misfortunate villain in the vintage *Road Runner* cartoons, was hit by a train, his body literally folded into the shape of the track. On a more serious note, Bruce also recalled that he surely would have been cut in half had he used his own steel-reinforced creeper instead of borrowing his coworker's plastic one, which had crumbled beneath Bruce on impact.)

Immediately in a panic, the assistant mechanic called 911. He didn't know how to get the vehicle up and off of Bruce because the area beneath it was far too narrow for any hoist to be inserted. In desperation, the man collected the jack that had flown from its previous position and placed it below the leaf spring of the front passenger side. Bruce tried to ask the assistant not to do that, for fear that the flexibility of the suspension system would cause the device to fly from its position a second time, this time, with fatal consequences. The subordinate, however, was determined to get the load off of Bruce and proceeded, despite argument. Soon, the Peterbilt was up and off of Bruce's body, hovering just above the wounded man. (Bruce later learned that the initial impact had severed major arteries in five places, and while the metal was still on top of him, it had blocked those injuries, minimizing the bleeding.) Once the pressure was lifted off Bruce's body, the blood was allowed to flow freely onto the garage floor.

Still worried that the rig would fall on him a second time, Bruce begged the assistant mechanic to get him out from beneath the truck, but by now, the flatness of his body was apparent to the comrade, and the man refused to move him. By now, both were convinced that Bruce's spine, as well as his internal organs, must have been damaged. The coworker refused to take any action for fear of causing further injury. In desperation, Bruce reached above his head, gripping the bumper of the Peterbilt (much as a gymnast performing a chin-up would reach for the bar with an upward motion), and pulled himself toward it. This shifted his body enough that his head was now protruding from beneath the front grill. Although Bruce wanted to move himself farther, the effort took all of his strength; he simply couldn't do it. At this point, the effect of the blood loss began to kick in, causing his lucidity to fade. Succumbing to the sleepiness closing in, Bruce's eyelids grew increasingly heavy and finally shut.

At that moment, Bruce felt himself somehow eject from his body and hover above it, near the ceiling of the garage. He looked down on the scene, strangely distant from the happenings, even unaware that *he* was that the one who lay there, dying. It was as though he were watching strangers.

All the man felt was perfect peace: no sorrow, no regret, and none of the physical pain that his broken body below had been subjected to. The colors in the scene below were more richly intense and vibrant than human eyes ever see in the physical realm. He observed as one man (himself) lay broken, bleeding on the ground, while the other knelt nearby, repeating apologetic phrases to the lifeless body as he cried and cradled the man's head. The wounded one didn't respond, but remained silently still, eyes shut.

Suddenly, a panoramic observation widened for Bruce, as if a camera lens had zoomed out. As his view broadened, Bruce noticed two more beings in the picture. But these weren't human, as the first ones Bruce had seen. Each was stationed on either side of the incapacitated man. It was immediately apparent that they were separate but identical. Light emanated from them; golden, ringlet-curled hair flowed from their heads, cascading down their backs to about their waistline. Thick, woven fabric—armor-like, seemingly made of intertwined rope—covered their masculine bodies in what could only be described as shining, white robes. Each wore a golden belt cinched tightly, exposing the bulging shape of his muscular build. Although identifiable as angels, they didn't have wings, as many images depict. The assistant mechanic maintained his position at the victim's head, apologizing for the accident. The beings' height, even from their kneeling position, reached at least two feet beyond that of Bruce's coworker. (Bruce later estimated that, were the heavenly creatures standing rather than kneeling, they would be about eight feet tall.) The figures were distinctive to look at, and piercing illumination was perceptible throughout their bodies, although they weren't transparent.

Their hands were placed beneath the truck on the injured man's abdomen, upon either side of his injury. From his position above, Bruce could see only the angels' backs as they looked down, intent on the man on the floor. They remained very still, with somber, statuesque focus. They did not speak to one another, nor did they look up to interact with Bruce as he lingered overhead, watching.

From his viewpoint, Bruce could see emergency personnel beginning to arrive. Paramedics entered through the front door and to bustle about the garage, talking busily with each other and gesturing toward the incapacitated man. The angels were undistracted by the activity around them. Despite the panicked bustle, not one person stepped through or over either of the angels at any point. It was as though the responders worked around the heavenly creatures without even realizing it.

The last two of the ten or so medics to arrive came in through a different door (Bruce's knowledge of this fact later became one of many elements that confirmed his out-of-body experience to skeptics). He could see that one of them, a young woman, had long, flowing, vibrant-red hair. By this time, the first responders had stopped life-saving attempts, because CPR would only have pushed more blood from his body. The redheaded woman walked up to the man on the floor and kneeled beside him, oblivious to the fact that she had positioned herself directly between two massive angels. Hesitating only briefly, she began to pat the cheek of the man, commanding him to open his eyes. Despite his lack of a pulse, his ashen skin, and his blue lips, she ordered him to wake up. The spiritual visitors remained undistracted. The injured man lay unresponsive. The persistent woman began to ask the other people in the room for the victim's name. When a fellow responder answered her question, she tapped the man's face again.

"Bruce Van Natta, open your eyes!" the woman instructed more than once. Each time he didn't react, she repeated the words, her voice escalating.

From his vantage point, Bruce couldn't understand why, but the command within the woman's voice gripped his attention. Suddenly, he felt a momentum sweep him from his position, forcefully pulling him downward and back into his body. Despite the fact that no CPR or other life-saving measures were being administered, the woman's words had carried the authority to usher him back. Instantly, Bruce found himself stretched out below the redhead, looking up at her. She continued slapping his cheek and telling him to open his eyes.

The physical pain that suddenly enveloped Bruce was indescribable. Only now was he aware that *he himself* was the man beneath the truck. With this realization, Bruce remembered what he had seen moments before from above. Quickly, he glanced around to see if the angels were still at their posts on either side of him. He couldn't see them.

He closed his eyes, and when he did, the peaceful painlessness returned. As this bliss surrounded him, he felt himself leave his body again, this time floating past the ceiling of the garage and into a sort of vacuum-forced tunnel filled with light. He felt himself moving farther away from his body more rapidly with each passing instant, and he somehow knew that heaven was at the other end of this indescribable pathway. But each time he began to succumb to the momentum's draw, he heard the words: "Bruce Van Natta, open your eyes!"

Each time the woman gave that order, he obeyed. And each time he did, the horrible, searing pain of his dying, crushed body returned.

A battle began to rage inside Bruce's mind. It was as though he could hear two voices arguing for his fate. One was gruff and negative, encouraging him to give up and die—after all, he would go to Heaven, so what reason was there to remain here on earth, anyway? Yet something in Bruce's discernment told him that this advice came from someone with a malevolent agenda. The second expression was quiet and firm, offering Bruce a choice. Bruce knew that in order to live, he would have to return to his body and endure unspeakable physical pain. He was aware that if he chose to remain in this life, the road ahead of him would be a rough one.

The voice that gave Bruce the decision told him, "If you want to live, you're going to have to fight, and it will be a hard fight."

Why fight? The pain was excruciating. It would be so much easier to drift off into this vortex filled with light, into eternal bliss and peace…

As the argument continued in Bruce's mind, he kept drifting in and out of his body. He would open his eyes briefly, only to close them again, unable to withstand the agony. Then he would withdraw, floating upward toward the light again.

Suddenly, something occurred that pulled Bruce out of the volley that he had been engaged in. The redhead's words shifted and echoed the quieter voice he had heard in his thoughts. She ordered him to switch into a full-on combat mode. Bruce recognized the authority of these words and knew that God was speaking through her.

"Do you have a wife?" the woman demanded of the injured man. "Do you have kids? What do you have in this world to fight for?" This was the first time that elements of Bruce's earthly life had crossed his mind since the accident. The suggestion of his responsibilities turned Bruce's mind to his obligations.

The answer was yes. He *did* have something to fight for!

Bruce had a wife and four young children who needed him. Up to this point, he hadn't recalled a factor compelling enough to motivate him to return to his body and undergo the unbearable hurt. Thinking about his family changed everything.

Bruce returned to his body and chose to stay there, regardless of the agony.

By the time he was taken by a life-flight helicopter to one of the most prominent trauma centers in the area, more than two hours had passed since the accident. During this time, Bruce found it essential to keep his eyes open. He didn't know how many more times he would be able to reopen them, should he allow them to close. For Bruce, the key to staying here on earth was his stubborn refusal to shut them again.

His strategy became finding something to focus his vision on in each new setting he was moved to. In the helicopter, he stared at the vent on the back of a responder's helmet. Medics continued to ask for his name and birthdate; he knew the answers, but since he was unable to speak, he remained silent, his sight fixated on that vent.

Later, at the hospital, one of the doctors became the focus of Bruce's vision. Too weak by now to move his head around, he followed the man with his eyes as he moved about, bustling among the nurses and other medical personnel. At one point, Bruce noticed the doctor was in a heated discussion with another physician. (When Bruce later asked what it was about, he was informed that a CT scan had provided no technical explanation for how Bruce was even alive. The anomalous results appeared like that of a "dead person," while his "heart was pounding as if…running a marathon."[65] The men had been exchanging opposing opinions about how Bruce survived.)

By any medical explanation, his severed arteries and veins *should have* caused him to bleed out within three to five minutes. Bruce had been given eighteen units of blood, but his wrecked body was unable to retain it. Finally, as he lay on the CT scanning equipment watching this exchange between the doctors, darkness closed in, and his ability to will his eyes open faded.

Summoning the last of his strength, Bruce finally spoke: "If you don't do something to help me, I'm going to die!"

Bruce's blood pressure, which had miraculously maintained life-sustaining levels up to this point, quickly plummeted to 0. Immediately, medical personnel moved him in preparation for emergency surgery. The doctors abandoned their discussion and engaged in arranging the operation.

Bruce later identified this moment as a turning point. Everything grew darker, but he somehow knew that the medical intervention that was about to take place would be effective. As the pre-anesthetic mask descended toward his face, he finally allowed his exhausted eyes to close. He believes this is the moment when the angels departed and God dispatched them elsewhere.

While Bruce was in the operating room that night, the doctor informed Bruce's wife that it was doubtful that he would live through the night because the injuries were just too extensive. Family, along with friends from church, gathered in the waiting room, and this group of prayer warriors decided that they would praise God for every thirty minutes Bruce remained alive. Over the following hours, these individuals, twice per hour, would join hands and form a circle, exalting and praising God for another half-hour of life.

Bruce surprised the doctors by surviving the night. The next morning, he was placed in an induced coma to allow his body time to heal from his extended injuries, particularly the major arteries that had been severed. (A later study by the University of Southern California on the mortality rate versus number of arteries severed indicates that Bruce not only should have bled to death within minutes of impact, but that he is also the only known survivor of injuries of this magnitude.) He is convinced that the prayers of his wife and fellow believers are what carried him through those first, difficult months following his accident. But, little did he know, there were more miracles to be seen in the upcoming future...

Four months after his accident, a segment of Bruce's small intestine that doctors had attempted to save began to die. Most adults have somewhere near twenty feet of this organ, while Bruce's remaining one hundred centimeters or so had been salvaged from several pieces patched together by surgeons. Because his small intestine still wasn't functioning properly, he was fed intravenously. Unfortunately, the human body isn't designed to take in nutrients this way for the long term. Bruce's pre-accident weight of 180 pounds dropped by more than one-third, and he was approaching danger of starvation. The doctor estimated that at this rate, the interceptive feeding would likely only keep Bruce alive for a year to eighteen months.

Upon receiving this news, Bruce lay in his hospital bed, prayerfully pondering this development. His solitude was interrupted by a visitor who, having met Bruce Van Natta in person only one time before, reintroduced himself as Bruce Carlson.

But Bruce Van Natta remembered Carlson immediately from another encounter...

About a year earlier, long before the life-changing incident with the Peterbilt logging truck, Van Natta had awakened during the night with a strange dream—one he immediately recognized as some sort of message from God. In this vision, he and a man he had never seen before were sitting together, eating sweetbread. When he awoke, Van Natta prayed for wisdom regarding the meaning of the dream. The only answer he received was that he needed to discuss it with the former pastor of his church, Ryan Clark. He had done so, but Clark was equally baffled. Two weeks after the reverie, Van Natta had traveled to visit his former pastor in person, and had also attended church with him, where he had been introduced to Bruce Carlson, the man who had shared the sweetbread in Van Natta's dream! At that time, Van Natta had talked Carlson about these strange events, but neither could make sense of its significance.

Yet, one year after the prophetic revelation and four months after Van Natta's terrible accident, Carlson stood in the dying man's hospital room. Carlson revealed that earlier in the same week, God had awakened him abruptly at 5 a.m., instructing him to fly to Wisconsin to pray for Bruce, who had been on the prayer chain at Carlson's church. The man had initially looked up the price of a plane ticket, which proved to be more than nine hundred dollars—more money than he believed he needed to spend at this time. So, shrugging off the incident as simply strange, he went about his business. The next morning, the same thing happened: God prompted him early in the morning with the same compulsion. This time, God added to the instruction: If Carlson would obey, God would perform a creative miracle.

Obediently, Bruce Carlson purchased the expensive airfare, expecting God to do great things.

Carlson began to pray for healing for the patient, specifying that his own plea was merely added to the countless others already being raised by many other saints. Carlson placed his right hand on Van Natta's forehead and petitioned with authority unlike any Van Natta had ever heard spoken in supplication.

"Small intestine, I command you to supernaturally grow in length right now, in the name of Jesus!" Carlson ordered.

At once, Van Natta's forehead began to burn as though electricity were coming from the man's hand, and a surging feeling spread throughout his entire body until it found its destination: the lower abdomen. Immediately, Van Natta felt a sensation in the afflicted region that he would later describe as feeling like "something cylindrical moving around inside of my stomach."[66]

Although doctors couldn't understand it (a response Van Natta was becoming accustomed to by now), Bruce was miraculously bestowed with what doctors estimate to be nine to eleven feet of small intestine. The medically salvaged, dying piece of this organ had grown nearly four times its previous, postsurgical length.

Bruce was able to eat again and soon began regaining weight. In an effort to obtain more insight, doctors conducted additional CT scans,

X-rays, and an upper gastrointestinal series. The only knowledge these tests yielded was that Bruce Van Natta had experienced a miraculous healing that could not be explained by science.

Over the course of the year following his accident, Bruce spent much of his time in the hospital. He underwent myriad surgeries, transfusions, and other procedures. Experts have said that he *should* have bled out and died three to five minutes after the truck was lifted from his body, and early speculation was that he would never again walk without assistance. Other injuries that Bruce sustained included broken ribs, fractured vertebrae, and damage to his pancreas, stomach, and spleen. He was told that he would be on prescription pain patches and monthly medication shots for the rest of his life, and that he would have intestinal troubles forever. But what a mighty God we serve: Bruce is thankful to report that, other than the occasional stomach upset, he has made a full recovery!

Bruce later learned that in some Middle Eastern cultures, sweetbread is made of the cooked intestines and pancreas of a lamb. He felt that his dream of eating sweetbread with Bruce Carlson was prophetic, because after sharing the delicacy in his dream, the two later shared the miracle of healing.

Bruce Van Natta resides in Wisconsin with his wife, Lori, and their four children. He is a published author and speaker and the founder and president of Sweet Bread Ministries.

Bruce believes that angelic intervention happens around us much more often than we realize. Because we don't see these beings, we often take their protection and involvement for granted.

A final thought that Bruce leaves us with is this: God gives us all both the prerogative and the power to choose what we will do with our existence. "The Holy Spirit said *if I wanted to live, then I was going to have to fight....* In the same way He still gives people freewill choices today. We get to choose if we are going to believe in Him or not as our

Lord and Savior…[and] if we are going to be warriors and fight the fight of faith or not."[67]

End of excerpt from *Encounters: Extraordinary Accounts of Angelic Intervention and What the Bible Actually Says about God's Messengers* by Allie Anderson-Henson and Donna Howell

The Return to the Body

Nearly 60 percent of individuals who claim to have had NDEs later recalled knowledge of the decision regarding the return to their body.[68] For some, the choice had been made by a higher power who informed them that it wasn't their time, while others were given the opportunity to decide for themselves. Likewise varying were the physical ramifications of the return, as those experiencing an NDE were typically doing so due to terminal illness or traumatic injury. Some felt as though the higher power guaranteed them an easier recovery from physical trauma upon their decision to choose life. Others felt they were given the choice to live and were encouraged to do so because they still had important experiences ahead or responsibilities to fulfill, such as loved ones who counted on them (often their own children), but were warned that deciding to return would result in a tough physical battle, but one that would be worth it. Many, despite the physical pain expected in earthly life and the alluring beauty promised in the afterworld, determined to return and fight for mortal life because they knew that people they would leave behind needed them.

Can NDEs Be Counterfeited?

As previously stated, the concept that an NDE could be an altered state of mind, dream, or hallucination due to traumatic injury, blood loss, etc., seems refuted by several facts. The unknowable and accurate details given by patients who were unconscious or clinically dead gives credibility to this phenomenon. And, on the rare occasion that another individual shares the NDE, that serves as further confirmation that the experience is more than a dream or hallucination.

Dr. Sam Parnia, assistant professor of critical care medicine and director of resuscitation research at the University of New York at Stony Brooke, conducted a four-year study called AWARE (AWAreness during Resuscitation; more on this later). The endeavor began 2008, wherein Parnia and "at least 20 experts, from neurology, psychiatry, various fields in neuroscience, and emergency medicine"[69] scrutinized more than two thousand cases of cardiac arrest and their relationship to an NDE.[70] As a guest in a 2014 interview that focused on near-death experiences, he stated that when the body is in cardiac arrest, the brain's cortex is not functioning, which eliminates the possibility of hallucinations being the explanation for an NDE occurring during cardiac arrest.[71] Furthermore, while some assert that NDEs take place during the brief moment when consciousness is returning to the body (such as at the instant of resuscitation), that still does not account for the unknowable details observed and later described firsthand by the experiencer, facts that would have spanned the duration of an out-of-body experience as opposed to knowledge of only the seconds before the return of consciousness. Dr. Parnia elaborates on one particular case reviewed during his study: "This is the first documented case of somebody—we can verify—who had consciousness at least during a 3- to 5-minute period when the brain would not have been functioning—we timed it—rather than when the brain was coming back online."[72]

Beyond this, a strong consistency through NDE reports crosses age, religious, ethnic, and cultural barriers. If this were a phenomenon designed within the mind of an individual, surely cultural, social, economic, or other factors would impact the visions or subsequent interpretation. Even those who are barely old enough to communicate verbally report similar factors as the elderly.

Another element that adds credibility to the reality of NDEs is the fact that those who have experienced them usually return changed. As mentioned throughout this book, most people emphasize the all-encompassing love they feel from a higher power upon crossing over. Often, after experiencing this joyous and peaceful, indescribable love, their perspective on their remaining earthly years is different. Love becomes a forerunning theme throughout the rest of their lives, and problems they may have previously spent resources on solving become trivial matters. On the other hand, the NDEers seem to transition toward spending more resources on interpersonal connection, quality of life, and their newfound sense of purpose and mission.

One uncanny wonder occurs when blind people have an NDE: They often regain their sight during the experience. In such cases, they are often able to describe in great detail what they see, despite their blindness both before and after the occurrence. What makes this particularly notable is that people who have had blindness medically corrected usually have an adjustment period wherein their brain learns to adapt to the intake of sight while they develop the cognitive process of translating visual stimuli into outgoing, verbal communication. Thus, the ability to see and then describe to others what has been seen typically involves a learning curve.

However, for those who see for the first time during the near-death experience, there is no such learning curve. Dr. Jeffrey Long explains:

> Occasionally, blind people with certain correctable conditions are able to regain their vision through surgical procedures. When blind people acquire sight, there is often a prolonged period of time in which they have trouble making sense of visual perception. This contrasts with Vicki [a woman who experienced sight for the first time during her NDE], who was immediately aware of her visual perceptions during her NDE. This further suggests that Vicki's vision was not of physical origin.[73]

This gives new perspective to other accounts of NDEs, wherein such elements as light and color are essentially deemed indescribable. The landscape visible to those who experience an NDE clearly isn't anything like what we're accustomed to here on earth, and this instant ability for a blind person to see, along with the immediate capability of understanding and describing what they are seeing further confirms that a person experiencing an NDE is doing so in the spirit realm, not the physical. Many sighted individuals who experience NDEs have reported a strange ability to see in all directions at once, a sort of "360-degree vision,"[74] which further reinforces the concept that vision, upon entering an NDE, is conducted through the spirit realm.

Other times, even physical evidence is discovered that corroborates the NDEers' claims. For example, there are cases in some have had an OBE/NDE and were able to see something they would not have been able to see otherwise, such as something in another room. When the NDEers have come back and explained what they saw, further investigation has confirmed the NDE claims, and lending incredible evidence to support the legitimacy of the experience.

Story of Lady Who Reported Shoe on HIVAC Unit[75]

Written by Cris Putnam in *The Supernatural Worldview*

Maria had never been to Seattle. America was everything she had imagined and more. Although the rain never stopped, that crazy, flying-saucer-looking building epitomized American excess. *En la parte superior!* However, this visit was only a brief respite from the arduous picking season. Like most other migrant workers, she sent her hard-earned wages home. She came to this country for the work. *Flash!* ...shooting pain, shortness of breath, darkness, sirens, traffic, and blinding overhead lights. A too-skinny nurse said she had a heart attack. She had been admitted to the Harborview Hospital coronary care unit.

While lying in the metal-railed bed, everything seemed white, clean; a bleachy aroma prevailed. Surely she would be up again soon. It came again—like a cannon shot. The pain in her chest exploded her up and out of her body. Really out—she was out of her body. Looking down, she saw the panicked staff rush to her bedside amidst the clamor of squawking alarms. Everything was realer than real…hyper-real, high-definition, holographic, multidimensional immersion. She was floating. As the staff was screaming and equipment was buzzing and beeping, she felt a blissful peace. She rose through the ceiling, through the roof, and looked down on the hospital. Floating, she thought, "Now that is odd." On a window ledge, she saw a single, tattered, blue tennis shoe sitting on its frayed lace. She wondered, "How did it get way up here on the third floor?" It had a hole in the pinky toe. All of sudden, she shot back into her body and felt an icy hot pain as she looked up and saw the doctor holding the defibrillator paddles.

Kimberly Clark was working as a social worker in Harborview Hospital when an unconscious cardiac arrest patient, Maria, was admitted. She had arrested again in the hospital, flatlining for a minute or two, but was resuscitated within the three-minute window. As part of her customary follow-up, Clark visited her the same day, whereupon Maria related her out-of-body experience (OBE) floating above the hospital. In addition to describing Maria's perspective looking down on her body and then rising through the building, Clark recorded, "Maria proceeded to describe being further distracted by an object on the third-floor ledge on the North end of the building. She 'thought her way' up there and found herself 'eyeball to shoelace' with a tennis shoe, which she asked me to find for her."[76] Anxious to prove that she wasn't crazy, Maria desperately wanted her social worker to find the shoe.

Incredulous but sympathetic, Clark investigated, and with some effort found a shoe that perfectly matched Maria's description. They were precise details that exclude coincidence, like the fact that the shoe had a hole in the pinky toe facing out from the ledge, and that it was sitting on top of its lace. This marked a paradigm shift for Kim Clark. She would never again doubt the existence of the immaterial soul. She explained, "The only way she could have had such a perspective was if she had been floating right outside and at very close range to the tennis shoe. I retrieved the shoe and brought it back to Maria; it was very concrete evidence for me."[77] This is called a *veridical* near-death experience (NDE), meaning that the experience has objective external evidence confirming it. It really happened, and has stood up well under the scrutiny of peer review.

Philosopher Dr. Gary Habermas not only verified those details; he discovered that Maria had just arrived in Seattle, was unfamiliar with area, and had never before been in that hospital. Also, the shoe could not be seen from the ground, and there were no buildings nearby that provided a vantage point from which it could be seen. Even more astonishing, neither the hole in the toe nor the position of the lace could be seen from the window where Sharp had retrieved it.[78] In other words, the perspective that Maria described from her bed could only be realized by floating in the air looking toward the building! As astonishing as this seems, this is one of many such cases with confirming external evidence.

End of excerpt from *The Supernatural Worldview* by Cris Putnam

Are All NDEs Positive in Nature?

While 34 percent of NDEers reported that certain elements within their experience incited fear or made them uncomfortable, these were often cases wherein the common NDE elements made them uncomfortable, such as encountering an angel or entering a tunnel.[79] However, among these people, after first reporting frightening elements, most were able to acknowledge pleasant aspects of the NDE as well. But not all NDEs are necessarily good experiences.

Slightly fewer than 4 percent of near-death experiences reportedly included only frightening components.[80] Fear-provoking NDEs usually fall into three categories: (1) those that follow the typical NDE pattern, but that are interpreted as terrifying; (2) those that feature "nothingness," or a sense of entering a vast void; or (3) those wherein the experiencer is subjected to hellish or demonic activity.[81] Of these categories, hellish experiences are reported the least often.[82] The late Dr. Barbara Rommer, an internal medicine physician and founder of the South Florida chapter of the International Association for Near-Death Studies, conducted research specifically on "less than positive" (LTP) near-death experiences.[83] She believed that frightening NDEs occurred as a sort of "spiritual wakeup call, causing the person to stop, look back, and review past choices."[84] In her book, *Blessing in Disguise: Another Side of the Near-Death Experience*, she explains that despite the initial, terrifying elements of the LTP near-death experience, they should still be considered gifts, because in the years following, individuals make positive life changes that they may not otherwise have made. Further, she stated:

> It appears that disavowing the reality or possibility of the existence of a Higher Power may contribute to the "why" of a Less-Than-Positive Experience: 19.4 percent of my LTP study group labeled themselves as atheist or agnostic prior to their experience. If one also disrespects life, then that just compounds the problem.[85]

She likewise correlated these events with individuals who claimed that they wanted to die. Ironically, a common theme reported by those who have faced a less-than-positive NDE is that, once they've made the changes prompted by the experience (such as the need to change their life's direction, to believe in a higher power, etc.), they usually no longer fear death at all, despite the terror incited by the NDE.

Bryan Melvin Exclusive Interview[86]

Bryan Melvin took the Christian world by storm in 2005 when he released his book, *A Land Unknown: Hell's Dominion*, which chronicles his near-death experience in which he saw Jesus and Hell, and was permitted to return to earth to inform others of what awaits in the after-life. On May 3, 2017, Bryan's testimony was uploaded to the popular YouTube Channel "2028 END," and it has since attracted 2.9 million views. To this day, Bryan is still invited for interviews and speaking engagements across the country. I (Josh Peck) have heard many NDE accounts, especially in research for this book. Some have been outlandishly fantastic and even difficult to believe; others have been reasonably believable, yet fall outside the scope of what is being detailed here. Yet others were not only plausible, but revolutionary—but still not exactly what I was looking for in this particular area of study. However, one account really hit home for me. Something unique about Bryan's experience fell in line with my areas of interest and the direction we envisioned for this specific book. So I reached out to him to ask for an interview, and I am honored to say that he accepted the invitation.

Josh: What kind of person were you before your near-death experience?

Bryan: I grew up in a great Southern Baptist home, but fell away [from the church] due to circumstances I describe in my book in the chapter titled "Bully Bully." It was not the typical story of bullying most might be familiar with, but for me, it was how culture, schools, movies, *Mad* magazine, teachers, and the climate I grew up in the 1960s [ten miles south of Washington DC during height of the civil rights movement, the Vietnam War, and a highly political environment] caused me to mirror the same bullying I was witnessing.

Around 1968, at ten years old, I fell away from the church. At that age, I fought to stay home rather than attend church. I was able to a few times until around age eleven, when I finally stopped attending altogether. Instead, I watched *Bullwinkle* on TV and read books on history and philosophy. The reading level for my generation was higher than it is now.

Everything I was reading caused me to question God's existence due to prevalence of evil, war, and the insanity I experienced [race riots, protests, leftist ideas]. These all caused me to search out answers. In junior high school, I was bused [the practice of taking students to different schools to redress prior racial segregation] to a predominantly black school [or what could be called reverse busing, which did happen at that time]. It was here I was severely bullied and beaten up.

This led me into agnosticism, followed by full-blown, militant atheism. I began stealing drugs out of family medicine cabinets and selling them. I became a big dealer overnight, all without doing drugs myself. As I became more popular, I corrupted more of the youth group from my former church. I even got into many fights. I earned protection from other kids who were as frightened as myself. We stuck together. I skipped school, my grades dropped, high school came and went, and I graduated.

As soon as I could, I moved out of the house. I was a rebellious, know-it-all, stupid mess who finally drifted into doing drugs and drinking heavily. I thought of joining a dominant East-Coast biker club. A friend of mine was in this biker club. I lived at his place for a while, thinking I'd earned my colors, but it became too crazy, so I got out.

I got a job as an electrician's apprentice and moved to Tucson, Arizona. Christians would come up and try to witness to me, but I was a hardcore, militant atheist, so I would argue with them. Thankfully, my parents, their church, some neighbors, relatives [many were ministers and deacons], and some other campus crusader types were all praying for me.

Josh: What happened to initiate the near-death experience?

Bryan: I moved to Tucson at the end of March, 1980, after accepting a job with an electrical company. There, I accidentally drank bad water that my supervisor—a Christian who had "700 Club" and "Turn or Burn" bumper stickers stuck on his truck—had left in the back in a big, orange-top Igloo cooler. I didn't know his cooler didn't have clean water in it; earlier, he had used it to collect creek water from Mexico in order to cool his overheated truck.

The cooler was in back of the truck instead of sitting on the tailgate, as was the norm for construction-worker etiquette back then. [The temperature] had been 121 degrees for several days. I and my coworker were both thirsty. I saw the cooler, grabbed it, and drank heavy and fast. I handed the cooler to my coworker. He began to drink, but spit the water out immediately.

We opened the container and [saw that] it held nothing but slimy pond water with hot, putrid algae and flat, wormy things swimming in it. After work, I went home and tried the "John Wayne" cure: shots of Jose Cuervo, Old Grand-Dad, and Jack Daniels. But, of course, these guys never practiced medicine.

Later, after my afterlife experience and recovery, I was diagnosed with cholera. I even checked the symptoms of cholera, and mine matched them all to a *T*. After I drank the putrid water, the cholera hit fast; It only took about twelve hours for the initial stages to kick in. This was also during a time when the Fourth of July weekend was fast approaching.

I rented the duplex I lived in with two other guys from Virginia. We were all planning to go to Phoenix to visit a friend who owned a small plane. We were going to fly to the Grand Canyon and party. The cholera hit me, however, so I could not go. Once my friends saw my condition, they wanted me to go to the hospital—even offering to forgo the trip to stay with me.

With cholera, before the body goes into shock and shuts down, there is a feeling of physical relief, as if you are past the illness. That's what happened to me. All the razor-blade pain in the guts [had gone] away, [so] there was no more vomiting, diarrhea, high fever, or chills. So, I told the guys they should go on the trip. I told them I was okay; I could walk and drink water. They reluctantly left, but asked our neighbor to check in on me after he got home from work.

[The next thing I remember], I was in the kitchen. I watched the guys leave, drank a little water, and then it all hit at once. I immediately collapsed onto the floor. My dog stayed at my side, whimpering. I managed to crawl to the bathroom and exploded with another round of vomit and diarrhea. I cleaned up most of the mess, but then passed out into semiconsciousness due to the intense gut pain. I crawled into the bedroom and somehow got into bed. This entire process [stretched out for] several hours. I knew something was really wrong, and I had no one to help me.

Josh: What was the exact point of death like for you; how would you best describe the experience of passing from life into death?

Bryan: I wear glasses because I'm nearsighted. My glasses and alarm clock were on table close by. My dog came over and started to lick my hand, which I extended to her. A rattling sound was coming out of my lungs. It was hard to breathe. I reached up and saw my hand go through my dog's chin. I could see clearly across the room even though I did not have my glasses on. I heard another set of neighbors fighting, and kids kicking a can down the street; all [these sights and sounds were] very pristine and sharp.

I felt no pain, no fever, no chills, and no worries at all. At first, I intuitively realized something happened. It was like waking up into a new reality more real than this mortal one. Before I could think, I floated up and out of my physical body. I lost all thoughts of atheism at that moment.

I had no idea what to expect. I [had] never heard of NDEs, and wouldn't have believed in them even if I did. I looked around the room and watched my dog circle to bed down by my bed while [she was] whimpering and looking up at my body, which was pale with bluish blotches. At that moment, I was at total peace and very glad. I had no more pain and no symptoms of illness.

I turned in the air and faced the ceiling, with my face toward a fold of ceiling texture. I noticed something there I had never seen before. Inside the fold, there was a fingerprint that cannot be seen from where I would normally be in the room. It was inside a fold of texture. In fact, after this whole experience, I climbed a ladder and a lot of awkward contortion; I found the same print in the fold, confirming what I [had seen] was real.

While out of the body, I was facing this fingerprint, then, *Bam!* I went through the ceiling, past the swamp cooler [a roof-mount type of air-conditioning unit], seeing the kids kicking the can down the street, and into a cool and pleasant darkness. I was heading toward a beautiful light.

Josh: You said earlier that you "suddenly" knew you had died. Can you tell us more about that? What caused you to realize you were dead?

Bryan: I intuitively knew that I had died the second my breath left me. However, I remained perplexed, because I believed that when someone dies, they become just a dead hunk of meat. When eternity kicks in, it is like waking up in a more alive state, more real than what we live in now. I could see and hear clearer than ever before. The peace I felt was simply indescribable.

Josh: In your testimony, you talk about being face to face with Jesus. What were the events, dialogue, and descriptions of that entire experience?

Bryan: I floated in the darkness toward the light. The closer I got to the light, the more I heard heavenly music. I heard a choir singing in a beautiful language I never heard before, yet I could understand the words. The choir was proclaiming the glories of God, revealing details of His character and nature, and answering all the whys of life.

While this was going on, I felt great love and peace. I was so very happy not to feel the illness with its pain. I had no cares in the world. I knew all who I [had] left behind would be well, including my dog.

While floating and moving to the light, I heard someone speak—not in words, but by thought. Each word contained encyclopedias of knowledge. I also saw glimpses of my life every now and then.

When I say this, folks simply do not understand. I was unaware that I was heading to a judgment: a reckoning. I didn't know that the love I felt was soon to judge me for abusing it, putting it on trial, using it for my own ends, stealing from it, placing heavy loads on it, and mocking it. I took advantage of it. I would find out the love of God does judge. It "rejoices not in iniquity."[87]

I saw that the light came from a huge rock suspended in the void of darkness. A human-shaped figure was upon the rock. The light came from Him. The light was bright and made of colors our mortal eyes cannot see. I landed before Him and fell down like a dead sack of wheat. I felt someone pick me up and place me before this figure who was wearing a hooded robe, whom I immediately realized was Jesus. People ask how did I know it was Jesus. Trust me, you know!

I could see His beard; parts were plucked out. His hands had holes gnashed in the wrists. The ankle area of His feet looked as though they had been nailed into a plank at some time. This sounds strange to some folks, so in my book I was vague about it. I found out later that is how they nailed someone to a cross in ancient times. At the time of my NDE, I knew none of these things.

Jesus spoke as *Logos*, which I learned later in Greek. He spoke in expressions of thought with tons of information within each word that exploded and downloaded immediately into my mind. Standing before the Lord was more terrifying than Hell would turn out to be. I was undone by the experience.

I saw how I [had] exploited aspects of His free gift of life, such as my great parents. I [had] abused the chances He used to wake me up. I learned how He [had] spared me from several auto accidents. I saw how I justified making my own rules and how I adapted them when I broke them. I hurt people by putting them on trial in my mind. I had fights, bitterness, and a chip on my shoulder. I understood everything about myself: who I really was at that time. I stole hearts. I was not a good old boy who never meant no harm like I thought I was.

In fact, just to interject here, I suggest reading Matthew chapters 26 and 27 and ask yourself whom have you plotted against, betrayed, abandoned, bore false witness against, put on trial, placed heavy burden on that one could not carry, mocked, beaten, and hurt? That is what is revealed [in judgment]: iniquity in the heart, which produces the fruits of sin.

While traveling through the void, I learned that God places eternity in the heart,[88] and he reneges on no gift. He gave us all life. He does everything to wake us up, but we refuse. Like C. S. Lewis once commented (and I paraphrase): In this life we learn what goodness really is by knowing what evil really is, so one can choose in accord to God's character trait of justice. God is that just to allow free moral will. If not, He would not be just.

At death, [people are] sealed forever in the state in which they died. In this eternal state, one learns more about God's good character and nature that can be used and exploited by evil people forever; however, this, God will not allow. You completely understand this, and never want God to act contrary to His own nature and traits.

Josh: What were you feeling at the exact moment you were told you would not be permitted into Heaven?

Bryan: I knew I was guilty by all that had been revealed. I didn't know what to expect. I was on trial. I absolutely knew I deserved my fate, which was totally in His just hands, but the full implications had not yet set in my mind.

As I describe in my book, Jesus spoke to me, saying that I "would see a Land unknown, best forgotten, but not to be left unseen." He also said that "returning is an option to be decided…at that particular point of overwhelming…say my name and my title."

In my book, pages 67–68, I expanded these word phrases to capture some of the encyclopedia's worth of information each of His words contained. About two years later, I came across Isaiah 26:10, which actually captures what it felt like at the time:

> If favor is shown to the wicked, he does not learn righteousness;
> in the land of uprightness he deals corruptly and does not see
> (behold) the majesty of the LORD. (Isaiah 26:10, ESV)

I had an understanding that the only land of uprightness/righteousness is the current Haven. An unredeemed person cannot enter [it] because he or she would deal corruptly with the knowledge gained concerning the majesty of the Lord that is revealed. With such knowledge, one would continue abusing and exploiting God's character traits, pitting these against each other for his or her own gain.

It wasn't shocking. It was absolutely just and fair. Jesus left no stone unturned. You know you do not deserve Heaven at all and you accept the sentence. It is proven who and what you love the most, which was not God's love at all.

After He told me to say His name and title, I began to grasp that I was heading to a place that may not be good. All this was overwhelming. It was more real than real. To see what you are really like on the inside, all Jesus offered you, and how you rejected His sparing and changing you, human words cannot convey. Tears, yes, but words, no. I unequivocally deserved wrath, not mercy, which stills haunts me to this day, as I know I did not deserve to come back.

I say this in humbleness: my concept and understanding of God's grace is profound without condemning anyone for not understanding, because humanity lives outside of eternity while looking in to see what it is. The only way to begin to grasp it is by Him revealing it.

Here's a prayer I pray; you can try it sometime: *Lord help me see through your eyes of grace and help me endure what I see.*

Josh: What was your entry into Hell like?

Bryan: I was lifted up and brought through something that looked like a tunnel or vortex, similar to the inside of a tornado. The noises were incredible. There was a heat that grew hotter the nearer I approached the end of the tunnel. I fell through a yellowish sky and landed with a thud on a hill. There was a valley and an ugly house on another hill in the near distance.

It was anticlimactic at first. I didn't know where I was. At this time, I saw no fire or devils with pitchforks. Instead, I saw people running out of the ugly house, down the valley, and up to me. They were greeting me as if they were long-lost friends. They were welcoming me to what they called "Paradise." This place was not right; I had a bad feeling about it. There was a dank light amid the gloomy darkness.

Some looked like people I knew who had died, but they kept changing their appearance and circling me like vultures. The atmosphere changed as they changed into what they really were: demonic beings of various sizes. I felt overwhelmed and said "Jesus Christ" repeatedly from that point until I left that terrible place. As I would discover, there is true power in His name. [It should be noted that "Christ" means "Messiah," so to repeat "Jesus Christ" was equivalent to saying His name and title: "Jesus the Messiah."]

Josh: What all were you shown in Hell?

Bryan: One of the beings came to me, and together we walked to the horizon. He somehow ripped the horizon open. We stepped out onto a wide, broad, circular road with a big opening in the middle. I looked around and saw many cells shaped like cubes (the Ezekiel 32:18–32 shape fits this). I turned and saw I stepped out of a cube-like cell as well. The cells next to mine were stacked six cells high.

I now understood that this was the pit of Hell. It was a bottomless pit, yet it was also enlarging itself. It was similar to how a spiral staircase looks; however, instead of stairs, there was the road. Instead of bricks supporting the staircase, there were cells. There was an opening in the middle just as with a staircase. You could not see the top or bottom of this pit. Tornados came through the opening and deposited people into cells. Demonic beings escorted other people to their own cells along the road. There were gaggles of demonic beings running all around.

These demonic beings looked like ancient pagan Mesopotamian deities and idols. Some were gargoyle-like. Others were insect-like: moths and worms with teeth. The taller ones had more authority over the smaller ones. It reminded me of a military. They also bantered with each other, called each other names, jostled each other, and so on. They were incredibly quick. It was obvious they hated me and all other people.

Some of the other demonic beings looked like lizards. This was the appearance of the entity on the road with me, serving as my guide. This entity had an extremely offensive odor. Afterwards, when I would describe my journey, my nickname for him became "Lizard Breath." What a stench! You absolutely can smell, touch, feel, see, hear, and speak in Hell. The Bible describes the chambers of death in Isaiah 24:22.

People received just degrees of recompense. The cells appeared small on the outside, but inside appeared large. This is very difficult to explain. Inside the cells, people lived in never-ending nightmares. They relived what they had done to others. It was a place designed to expose one's true sin nature fully manifest. It brought to the surface what a person is truly like on the inside, the part no one else sees in physical life.

In these cells, the people were all alone with demonic entities. What the people feared most happened. They were banished away from God. Demons hated the people with a hate I cannot describe. This, of course, is the current Hell. This is not the Lake of Fire.

I was taken along the cubes and was allowed to know the life histories of those inside in a flash. I said "Jesus Christ" nonstop during this whole experience. The entities always tried to get me to curse them, God, or myself. They challenged me. They would poke, hit, and touch, but they never could actually grab hold of me due to me repeating the name of Jesus.

I saw people enter their cells, thinking they entered paradise, only to find out a bit later it wasn't so. Others entered cells of flames or small holes. Most relived events in their lives as the victims of their bitterness, hate, revenge, perversions, immortality, foolishness, pride, lust, greed, loneliness, abuse, abandonment, neglect, and all other manners of evil that they projected on others during physical life.

This will sound strange, but I…[know that I cannot help] those already in Hell because they…[are receiving punishment for their deeds during their lives on earth, and it is too late to save them]. Instead, I truly worry about those living now who are heading there. Those in Hell, I understand what they know…[the nature of punishment that exists in Hell], which is so foreign to people alive on earth. I saw human sin nature ripped open in its rawest form. I am now so thankful that Jesus came to set us free from our sin nature by the work of the cross and fruit of His resurrection. People need that thankfulness!

Josh: How were you rescued from Hell, and why were you permitted to return to physical life?

Bryan: I came to a cube-cell with an opening in the wall and I began to feel very weak. I knew this was it. This was my final place in this current Hell. Demonic beings wanted me to enter the cell so they could have their way torturing me. I had utterly no hope. My feet were dragging through a dusty, muddy mire. I was slowly dragged to be placed inside the cell.

I felt utterly alone with no help. This was the end, and I knew I deserved this place. I stammered out "Jesus Christ" as best I could. Suddenly, I felt a strong presence coming from behind me. I felt footsteps rocking the land in a drumbeat fashion. I had no idea who it was at first. I even thought this individual was there to toss me in the cell.

The demonic entities became afraid and scattered at the close approach of whoever was coming. I was then picked up and carried out, cradled under this individual's strong arms. I saw the holes in His wrists, even to the point of seeing how His bones pulled apart carrying me. I understood that I did that to Him, as Scripture describes His bones being pulled out of joint for you and me (Psalms 22).

I suddenly knew this was Jesus Christ. I wept like I never had before onto His shoulder. He took me back through the vortex tunnel I entered from and back to the rock where I started. He stood me upright upon that rock, still suspended in the void. Then Jesus spoke to me some parting words.

He told me at an appointed time to tell of this place. He blew His breath on me, and I floated back through the void. I could still hear the choir. I floated back into my body. At first, I could not breathe at all. This part is a bit cloudy, but from what I understand, my neighbor found me and rushed me to hospital where I received treatment. Later, I arrived home, sat in a beanbag chair, and prayed, "Jesus I never want to go back to that awful place, take me, I'm yours."

That is how I became a born-again Christian. There is no afterlife salvation possible. It's only in this mortal life that [it] is possible, because after death one ['s eternal fate] is sealed.

It is by God's grace alone [that] I returned; there is no reason other than that. My concept of God's grace is different than what's commonly taught. You see, I didn't deserve to come back. It's all about grace. God's true grace changes a person. God's love is not afraid to break a person by grace so that person will wake up to the spiritual reality so many want to ignore.

I actually don't know why I was allowed to come back, other than to tell people about Jesus, see as many as I can enter into the kingdom, and train them for what is coming. The truth is, there is a spiritual war right now against a spiritual foe who wants us all dead.

Josh: What is the most important thing you want people to learn from your experience?

Bryan: I want people to wake up and return to the Lord before it's too late. I want people to know of His goodness and undeserved mercy that changes and heals people from being enslaved to the world system. People need Jesus. It is all about Jesus, not me. That is what I would like folks to learn from the experience.

I don't sensationalize Hell or those currently there. I spent years looking for answers concerning the things that happened, and only one book has the answers. That book is the Bible. Other people need to know this, too. There are other things God has shared with me over the years to pass on to others so they, too, can run the race the way the apostle Paul describes in Scripture. Again, it is all about Jesus, not me. I decrease so He can increase;[89] it's not about me at all. Grace provides that perspective to a person.

Is the NDE Phenomenon Too Limited?

In 2014, Dr. Sam Parnia, who, as mentioned earlier, is a researcher at the University of New York at Stony Brooke, reported findings rendered from a four-year study scrutinizing 2,060 cases of cardiac arrest across fifteen different hospitals.[90] The results revealed that humans experience a unique transition at death, which not only lends credibility to NDE stories, but also suggests that there is possibly even more than survivors are able to report.[91] Previously finding it difficult to find objective, nonbiased studies on what the human consciousness experiences at the moment of death, this research team set out to acquire more details about the science in the shift between life and death. Thus, in 2008, AWARE—the study mentioned earlier that took an in-depth look at

AWAreness during REsuscitation[92]—was launched at the University of New York at Stony Brook Medicine. Approaching the question from a unique perspective, Dr. Parnia explained that death is brought on differently than traditional medicine has previously asserted. For example, it has been described as a "specific moment," but this is not the case. Death is a byproduct of (sometimes) reversible developments that cause the vital organs to shut down, and thus can potentially be stopped or delayed. For example, a heart-attack survivor experiences what we call "cardiac arrest," while the less fortunate experience "death." Parnia explains that the aim of this study was to "go beyond the emotionally charged yet poorly defined term of NDEs to explore objectively what happens when we die."[93]

Parnia's report stated that 39 percent of cardiac-arrest survivors "described a perception of awareness," but were unable to outline memory of specific events, while 46 percent "experienced a broad range of mental recollections that were not compatible with the commonly used term of NDEs."[94] The physician says such statistics indicate that a larger number of people demonstrate cognitive mental activity at the time of death beyond those whose experiences fall into the category of NDEs.[95]

Neurologist Dr. Kevin Nelson explained why, for some people, the concept of an NDE is hard to study objectively. In order to qualify as having a near-death experience, an individual must be precisely that: near death. Some researchers state that necessary criteria involve proof that the person was "clinically dead." However, in an interview, Dr. Nelson clarified a common point of confusion: "In the medical literature, there has been a lot of sloppiness with the term *clinical death*. Clinical death to a neurologist means that your brain is dead, and that's not what's happening here [during NDEs]."[96] Later, in the same interview, Dr. Nelson elaborated on the changes in the brain at the time of death:

There's no coming back from clinical death…. When a brain dies, the cells, the nerves that constitute that brain, burst like water balloons because [of] an in rushing of calcium, and that causes cells to lyse [meaning break down].... Once that neuron bursts, it's gone. When a critical number of these neurons die within the brain, then the whole organ may reach a point where it's irretrievably dead.[97]

Dr. Parnia explains that, historically, death has been defined at the moment the heart stops, which happens simultaneously with the breathing ceasing, followed quickly by a halt in brain functioning.[98] However, recent decades have procured life-saving measures—including life-support technology, "modern intensive care medicine,"[99] and even the discovery of cardiopulmonary resuscitation (CPR)—that add considerable time to the process that occurs to the brain at the time of death, allowing people to linger at the edge of death and then return to the living with stories of their experiences.[100]

Parnia stated:

What then occurred over the ensuing couple decades [after the aforementioned medical innovations] was that many more thousands were now being brought back to life either because they had been very close to death or had temporarily gone beyond the traditional threshold of death.[101]

This is important, because it adds validity to the seeming upsurge in claims of NDE phenomena. Likewise, it validates the assertions beginning to surface within the medical and scientific field that the brain remains active after someone is considered medically dead. The distinction between *clinically dead* (the dying process in the brain has completed) and *medically dead* (the heart has stopped, breathing has stopped, etc.) can mean that a period between the two leaves a person standing between the two worlds of life and death until the brain has completed its dying process.

It is also apparent in NDE research that not every episode contains all, or even any, of the typical elements. Not everyone sees a tunnel or a life review. A number of NDE accounts, considered "mundane" by some, prove that near-death experiences are not "one size fits all." In fact, some NDEs that lack the expected elements still manifest amazingly miraculous events in the physical world.

Christina Peck's Experiences[102]

Christina Peck was only fourteen years old when her life nearly came to an end. It was December 28, 2000, and she and her friend, Nichole, had just exchanged gifts at a belated Christmas celebration. Since both received money, they decided a trip to the mall was in order. Following the shopping excursion, they swung by the grocery store to pick up snacks before heading toward Christina's house for a night of junk food and fun.

Nichole's brother, James, was in the car with them, along with her sister, Christy, and Christy's boyfriend, Andy, who was driving. Andy was going to drop off Christina and Nichole, and were only a couple miles from the house when an inebriated man driving a Mazda truck forced a Dodge Durango full of kids on their way home from a Bible study into the opposite lane. The Dodge Neon driven by Andy was being pelted with freezing rain, so road conditions were treacherous. Before Andy could swerve out of the way, the Durango smashed head-on into the tiny car, sending it into a dangerous spin. The drunk driver's small pick-up truck then broadsided them, but the madness was not yet over. The impact was so intense that the Durango then rolled over the Dodge Neon, completely crushing it and trapping Andy and Christina inside.

Christina, who was sitting behind Andy, was nearly sent flying through the windshield, because her seatbelt broke—which she found out later actually saved her life. Had the seatbelt not malfunctioned, the top part of the windshield would've decapitated her for sure. As it was, she had broken the lower part of the window with her head. The top part of the window came down, and the twisting metal and broken glass guillotined the left side of her face. Her head was gashed so deeply, she still carries a large scar on the left side, from the top of her head to the corner of her eye.

A stark reminder of God's grace.

Police officers, paramedics, and fire fighters soon arrived, and they had to use the Jaws of Life to cut both Christina and Andy out of the car. While several involved in the accident were bruised and banged up, thankfully, nobody else was seriously injured. Christina recalls that the whole experience seemed to happen in slow-motion flashes and shadows.

Today, Christina recalls seeing a light, but she didn't leave the car. She felt a calming presence, but heard no voices. Seeing herself and her friends in the car, she suddenly heard a massive vacuum sound, then she regained consciousness.

She gasped and opened her eyes, giving the paramedic a glazed look. He shockingly responded, "Oh, you're alive!"

A whirlwind of questions ran through her head:

"Who am I? Where am I? What's going on?"

The paramedic was asking questions, and in her mind, she heard herself giving him clear and logical answers, but he couldn't understand anything she was saying. The paramedic then started asking Nichole the same questions Christina thought she'd already answered. This confused her, since she believed she had responded normally to him.

By the time Christina arrived at the hospital, she had fallen into a coma. During this difficult period, her family rarely left her bedside. Her sister, Deborah, was there one day, sharing how Christina's cat, Precious—a short-haired, domesticated Siamese—had holed up in Christina's room. The cat was angry, lashing out at everyone who tried to enter, allowing nobody to pass through the bedroom door.

Christina recalls the entire conversation and says she told Deborah about the beautiful jewelry box Nichole had given her for Christmas. When her older sister returned to the hospital two days later, miraculously, Christina had awakened from her coma. She asked Deborah if Precious was still angry with her for not being there.

Dumbfounded, Deborah asked, "How do you know that?"

"Because you told me!" Christina replied. "Remember? We talked about it last time you were here, and I was telling you about the jewelry box from Nichole. I said you should tell Precious it's okay, I'll be home soon."

Still in shock, Deborah responded, "No, Christina you were in a coma, you never said any of that."

"That's not true," her little sister reiterated. I was staring right at you! I remember you sitting on my right side, and we were talking, we were having a conversation!"

"No," Deborah insisted, "*I* was talking; *you* were in a coma."

During the two days when Christina was in a coma, she recalls hearing conversations between medical personnel regarding her health. Doctors had been in her room, trying to predict her future. She would never walk again, they deduced, and her brain function would be severely affected. Additionally, according to these doctors, she would never be able to bear children.

Two decades and four children later, Christina is a testament to the truth of Luke 18:27: "What is impossible with man is possible with God."

Her journey, though, has not been an easy one. After the accident, half of her body was nearly paralyzed, and she stumbled out of the hospital five days later, dragging the right side of her body behind her, similar to a stroke victim. She had to relearn basic skills such as walking, talking, and doing simple math. She spent eighteen months in physical therapy, retraining her brain how to remember and how to put together comprehensive thoughts.

"I couldn't talk in complete sentences for the first six months," she recalls.

Another hurdle she had to overcome was the fact that, for the first three months after the accident, she refused to eat. The smell, look, and taste of food literally made her sick, and the former lover of steak and potatoes suddenly couldn't stomach the thought of even one bite. At five feet, nine inches tall, her weight plummeted to an emaciated eighty pounds, and her family was understandably terrified. Her mother, Louise, tried to get her to eat, but to no avail.

"You're fourteen years old," Louise would lovingly prompt her daughter, "So we're going to take fourteen bites of food." But try as she might, Louise was unsuccessful at getting her daughter to consume food during this difficult time.

Christina's story is chock-full of miracles, however, and this problem simply vanished one April afternoon when a friend of her sister came to visit. The family decided a steak dinner was in order, and as they always did, invited Christina along. They figured it was a futile request, but couldn't allow themselves to abandon hope.

They were startled, though, when she responded, "Oh, thank goodness. I'm starving!"

Her mom, her sister, and indeed the entire family began to weep. Christina asked what all the fuss was about, as she had just experienced a fully unconscious transition back to having a healthy appetite and eating normally. Three months prior, her hunger had vanished, only to return instantaneously. The prayers of her worried parents, siblings, and friends were answered, just as simply and beautifully as that.

"You haven't eaten in three months!" her mom stated in tears.

"Oh, wow," Christina said. "Well, I'm hungry, let's eat. I want a steak!"

She tried to return to school, but teachers didn't know what to do with her. She was too advanced for the special-needs class, but wasn't able to concentrate in a regular classroom situation. She would get overwhelmed and frustrated with the hectic pace and the noise, and her mind would just shut down. This once bright, cheerful, and outgoing girl was now subdued and withdrawn, completely isolating herself from all but her closest friends and family.

"It took me a long time to get my personality back," Christina explains. "I used to be the most outgoing person you'd ever meet, always wanting to go out with my friends and have fun, but after the accident I turned into a closet introvert. I didn't want to be around anyone, and I didn't want to talk to anybody. I went from being sociable and friendly to a person who was easily agitated and stressed out."

Since she felt incapable of attending high school, her big sister Deborah, a licensed teacher, discovered a home-schooling program she could personalize to fit Christina's unique learning challenges. Thus, nearly half a year later, Christina set about catching up with her former classmates, eventually surpassing them to graduate high school early.

One interesting result of the accident was that she discovered her brain worked differently than before. For example, she began to use words she had never heard. Once, from the corner of her eye, she saw her cat jump up on the chair next to her.

Startled, she blurted out, "Oh my word!"

When her sister asked what was wrong, she tried to say the cat was "sneaky" or "stealthy," but instead found herself blurting out, "Precious is being so inconspicuous!"

"How do you know that word?" Deborah asked her, knowing her little sister hadn't used that word before.

"I don't know," Christina responded. "It just made sense."

Something else that suddenly "made sense" was complex math problems. She began solving them without knowing exactly how she'd done it. Deborah would ask her to show her work, but she couldn't. Christina knew her answers were right, and they made perfect sense, but she hadn't the slightest clue how she'd gotten the correct responses. She would try to describe how she'd arrived at her answer, but her explanations made sense to no one but her. It took her several months to learn how to show her work when solving arithmetic problems.

Slowly, Christina got to the point at which she desired to be around people again. The learning process was gradual and painful, and it took her eighteen months to complete her freshman year of high school, but her rate of learning sped up so dramatically that during her senior year, she was taking college courses.

Today, Christina still experiences minimal effects from the accident, such as arthritis in her hands and short-term memory loss. Christina says there are times when she's talking with her husband, for example, and mid-conversation she trails off into a whisper or completely stops talking. Her husband will ask her what she was talking about, and she'll reply that she wasn't aware she was talking, or she won't remember the topic. There's simply no recollection of what she was even saying.

Most of her memory came back over a four-year period, in pieces, a little bit at a time. It was emotionally grueling for her to look at family photos and be unable to remember the events pictured. She would get extremely frustrated and begin to cry as she tried, in vain, to remember. Though, over time, she has been able to recollect most of it, there are still some pictures that don't jog her memory. She explains that some of this is normal for someone who survived a near-fatal accident.

A few years after Christina's traumatic event, her father, Daniel, was diagnosed with cancer. While the disease was labeled as a "cancer of unknown origins," many believed it stemmed from his exposure to the lethal chemical Agent Orange while he was serving his country in the Vietnam War. Christina's mom, a nurse, became Daniel's caregiver, although toward the end of his life he required in-home hospice care. Sadly, he had declined to the point that he required assistance with the routine activities of daily living, such as maintaining personal hygiene and eating.

A bed was set up for Daniel in the first-floor dining room; Louise slept upstairs in the couple's bedroom. So she could continue to avail herself to him when she was upstairs, she set up a baby monitor beside both their beds. One day, through the cheap, crackly speakers, she and Deborah heard what sounded like a large group of people in the room. Knowing only she, Deborah, and Daniel were in the house, mother and daughter were nonetheless hearing voices and commotion wafting through the monitor.

Then they heard a calm, patient, and loving female voice. "It's okay," the voice said. "They've had a really long day. They're tired, so we're going to take care of this for them." They also listened as Daniel spoke to the woman as if she were a close friend or family member.

A few minutes later, when Louise and Deborah checked on Daniel, the dressings from the incisions that remained following surgery and bed linens had all been changed, and were fresh and clean. Louise and Deborah had been together upstairs, and the only outside access to the dining room was through the windows.

In his last days, Daniel would carry on conversations with people only he could see. Just a few days before he passed away, Daniel had stopped all his chemotherapy treatments, and it had quickly become apparent that he was not long for this earth. Christina, pregnant with her now five-year-old son, Nathan, her husband, Josh (yes, one of the authors of this book), and their two-year-old daughter, Jaklynn, went to say their final goodbyes.

When they approached Daniel, he said, "I'm sorry there are so many people in this room right now; I can't hear you."

"Daddy, we're the only ones in here," Christina replied.

"No," he said, scanning the breadth of the room. "Everybody's walking around here."

It was obvious that he was seeing into a different realm, and angels were not only there, but were assisting Daniel and his family during his arduous last days. Christina believes heavenly messengers were both comforting her dad and preparing him for his trip to see Jesus.

Soon after that, Christina and her mom, knowing that the man's time was short, sat near him, privately saying their goodbyes, when the dining room lights abruptly went off. At this moment, the family dog walked over and put her head in Christina's lap—and both mother and daughter knew Daniel was gone. Louise walked across the room and flipped the light switch a time or two, and the room lit up once more. No problems with electricity had been experienced by the family either before or since.

In two very different fashions, father and daughter had been propelled to the threshold of life's abyss. Both looked over the edge, but only one survived to tell the tale. Christina knows her father is dancing with the angels, though, and longs for the day she can see him once more.

> For we know that if the tent that is our earthly home is destroyed, we have a building from God, a house not made with hands, eternal in the heavens. For while we are still in this tent, we groan, being burdened—not that we would be unclothed, but that we would be further clothed, so that what is mortal may be swallowed up by life. (2 Corinthians 5:1, 4 ESV)

Extradimensional Perception

One of the strangest types of reports in some NDEs is the shift in perception addressed briefly earlier. Without a background in quantum physics, it seems impossible to imagine what extra dimensions (above our own three of space and one of time) would be like. However, some NDEs seem to describe just that. It also seems implausible that the brain would make up an extradimensional reality and perception, seeing as, in my (Josh Peck's) humble opinion, Hollywood and the modern entertainment culture have described these things woefully inaccurately. Could it be that the most sensible explanation is that there really does exist an extradimensional reality that we enter at the point of physical death?

Imagine drawing a square on a piece of paper. Put that paper down on a table and look down at it. The square exists in two dimensions of space. You exist in three. For the square, up and down doesn't exist. You can look down at the square and see all four sides, and even the inside, all at once. To the square, you are an extradimensional being. You have access to one dimension that the square does not.

Let's say you now draw another square next to the first one. Imagine, if the squares were able to see, what Square 1 would look like from the perspective of Square 2. Square 2 could see one—or, at most, two—sides (depending how Square 1 was oriented in its two-dimensional space). If Square 2 wanted to see all sides of Square 1, it would have to physically travel around Square 1, observing the sides one at a time. Even then, Square 2 would not be able to see the inside of Square 1 unless it found a way to slice it open. Square 2 might be able to imagine how a three-dimensional being could see all sides at once, but it would never really be able to form that image in its mind with its limited, two-dimensional perception. Yet you, as a three-dimensional being, can look down at both squares, see all four sides—including the inside and out-side—at the same time, and your brain can process that image without any trouble.

If we take this example and add another dimension, we can begin to understand how something consisting of an extraphysical dimension would see us. An extradimensional being would be able to see all sides of us, including the inside and outside, at the same time. Such a thing is impossible for us to form a clear picture of in our minds due to our limited, three-dimensional understanding and perspective; yet, we can at least grasp the concept.

Now, to stretch this thought exercise to the limit: Imagine that the squares were actually cubes, yet they still had a limited, two-dimensional perspective and understanding. In essence, they would be cubes that "think" they are squares. They believe there is more to them than the physical, two-dimensional form they can see, but they have no physical, two-dimensional proof. They call this extra "stuff" the soul. Their three-dimensional soul is the "real" version of them, but they are limited by their two-dimensional environment. Their extradimensional selves must operate in a two-dimensional body, which in turn is used to operate within their two-dimensional environment.

Now imagine that Square 2 has a near-death experience. For a brief time, Square 2 can see and experience three-dimensional reality in the cube version of itself that it always has been, only couldn't really know it until now. It is able to look down and see Square 1, only this time it can see all sides, inside and out, at the same time. And, even more, it finds it makes perfect sense. This is now the real reality, and the square's former, two-dimensional reality was only a shadow. Square 2 then comes back to two-dimensional life and tries to explain to Square 1 what it saw and experienced. Only now, to its dismay, Square 2 is back to using a two-dimensional brain, and thus cannot really explain or put together in its mind what it saw or how it saw it. Square 2 is no quantum physicist, so it uses the best language it can. Square 1 is amazed, yet understandably confused as it struggles to understand.

Believe it or not, this type of thing is found in certain NDEs. A person has an incredible NDE, experiences extradimensional perception, comes back to his or her limited physical form, and has difficulty explaining exactly what he or she saw. Yet, astoundingly, what the person is able to explain lines up perfectly with modern scientific research and thought into extra dimensions commonly found in the field of quantum physics.

In 2011, Jean-Pierre Jourdan, MD, the French president and director of medical research of IANDS (International Association for Near-Death Studies), published a paper in the *Journal of Cosmology* in which are documented NDEs involving strange extradimensional experiences.[103] In it, Dr. Jourdan tells of an account wherein the person who experienced the NDE could apparently see all sides of objects:

> I was able to see the sofa and my body simultaneously from all directions. I saw my body through the sofa, I could see the top of my head and in the same time I saw my left and right sides and the sofa from below and from above, and all the room like that, I was everywhere at the same time! Dashing off several sketches, front and side-on views as well as views from above, below, etc., he repeated "I saw all that."[104]

Also documented is a study that looked at seventy cases of NDEs, forty-eight of which included an OBE in which the experiencer could see his or her surroundings. Of the forty-eight, there were some surprising descriptions of perceptions:

- Seventeen described "global perception."
- Fifteen described "360 degree or spherical perception."
- Twelve described perception from "everywhere."
- Eighteen described "perception by transparency."
- Fifteen described "zoom/instantaneous displacement."

Along with this, current, non-NDE-related scientific research suggests that the brain actually operates in four dimensions rather than three. Putting this together with the amazing descriptions provided in NDE accounts involving extradimensional perspective, is it more plausible to say that these accounts are all made up, that they are a trick of the brain (which is incapable of imagining even a simple object composed of more than three spatial dimensions), or that we ourselves are in fact akin to cubes who believe we are squares?

Conclusion

As we've seen, there is a clear distinction between NDEs and actual, physical death. There is also a difference between NDEs and physical resurrection as described in the Bible. Now that we've built a foundation for this research by first discussing some personal experiences and current research in the field of NDEs, we can get into the far stranger topic of bodily resurrection after the point of physical death. The most famous resurrection, of course, is that of Jesus Christ. It is described in full in the biblical Gospels, but what if there was left behind an actual artifact attesting to the reality of the resurrection of Jesus Christ?

Immediately what comes to the minds of most people who are even remotely interested in this type of research is the Shroud of Turin. Is it real? Is it a hoax? Is it even possible for us to know for sure? What are some details about the Shroud of Turin not commonly known? Should the Christian response to the burial cloth be the same as or different from the secular response? We'll discuss these questions and more in the next chapter.

PART TWO

HISTORICAL IMPLICATIONS
REGARDING THE AFTERLIFE

chapter two

Science of the Shroud of Turin

A seemingly unremarkable piece of linen fabric endlessly sits at the center of controversy. It measures a little over fourteen feet in length and almost four feet in width; it was woven with fine flax fibers into a herringbone pattern; and it almost imperceptibly bears the likeness of an average-height, lean, muscular male of about 165–175 pounds who had shoulder-length hair and a beard. This cloth is the most iconic historical artifact in the world of Christendom, and has been the root of some of the lengthiest and most heated debates in academia for the last several centuries. The man whose likeness appears in the fabric could easily be missed if the viewer didn't pause to concentrate on the story the tragic figure tells once the image comes into focus. At first glance, the natural sepia impression shows blurred and undefined edges that just barely formulate a human shape, somewhat resembling an early canvas painting of an ancient pharaoh at rest in a sarcophagus. Upon closer inspection, however, the dramatic bloodstains on the wrists, arms, feet, head, and the side of the chest draw a startlingly accurate visual journey of Jesus Christ's final hours.

It is the Shroud of Turin.

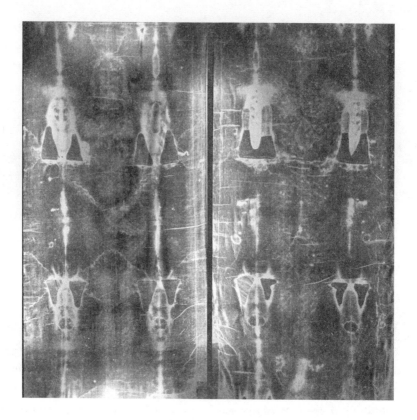

To some, this artifact inspires a sobering reverence for our Lord and Savior—a tangible and earthly connection to the Lamb who was sacrificed for our own redemption, as well as evidence of Scripture's authenticity. For others, it's an elaborate hoax that persistent religious folk simply refuse to acknowledge for what it is in their zeal, trading "scientific proof" and logical reasoning for fairy tales. (These authors find it extremely annoying that so few people even consider the idea that, rather than a forgery, the Shroud might have been a reverent work of art created by someone with good intentions. In the ceaseless debates surrounding the origin of this beautiful cloth, it's almost always referred to as *either* "authentic" or "forgery," never allowing for a third possibility: that a Christ-follower might have created it to honor God by putting on display another reminder of His suffering.) But no matter how we perceive the cloth today, the fabric still contains a host of mysteries that the most advanced contemporary science cannot completely crack—a reality that is certainly exacerbated by the fact that we can't easily gain access to the artifact. Therefore, until proven otherwise, the opposing worlds of religion and science have hit an impasse…each blaming the other for narrow-minded and ill-informed assumptions. Believers are "irrationally hopeful" for wanting to have faith in the Shroud of Turin as the burial cloth of Christ, since such a thing can't currently be proven true (though many claim it can); skeptics are "narrow-minded" for dismissing that possibility outright so long as it can't currently be proven false (though again, many claim it can). Radiocarbon dating tests on the fabric in 1988 assert that it was created circa AD 1260–1390; countless disputes have challenged the reliability of these tests from many reasonable angles. Notable intelligent personalities on both sides present their own evidence for or against the Shroud's authenticity as Christ's burial cloth, and the debate rages on. (It's also relevant to note that there is some disdain between Protestants and Catholics as well: Protestants are at times uneasy to follow the issue of the Shroud too closely, lest the *article* itself become an item of worship, the caution against which comes from many Scriptures addressing idolatry; Catholics largely venerate the Shroud and some even claim it has power of its own, with support for this practice usually stemming from the healing garments the apostle Paul referenced in Acts 19:12.)

But until we're given boundless time and access to the Shroud of Turin; until we can study it to the fullest, most microscopic degree without altering or damaging it; until we reach a day and age when all sindonology (research related to the Shroud of Turin) can be conducted and reported *honestly and objectively*; and until we get to a point that the researchers, scientists, scholars, historians, religious personalities, news reporters, bloggers, YouTubers, and other influential voices can revisit the Shroud without bias or preconceived and unfair assumptions that line up with past (and therefore out of date) discussions (fake news anyone?), it will be an error (if not entirely negligent and dishonest) to claim that we have all the answers and therefore a rock-solid conclusion about the Shroud and the man (Man?) it depicts. We don't know for sure right now what the cloth represents; we *can't* know for sure right now.

Therefore, Christians and/or believers in the Shroud—*as well as scientists/skeptics*—should be willing to hold a certain level of diplomacy and decorum when debating with those whom they perceive to be opposition. The Shroud will always have the potential to pit intellectual snobbery against religious snobbery, as long as we're all fallen humans capable of exchanging decency for self-aggrandizement and boasting. Because of that tendency, we need to remain vigilant at all times that *both science and religion* are matters of faith; that has never been truer than it is concerning the Shroud of Turin. (For religion, this "faith" statement is obvious, but for those who may be wondering how science relies on faith, just ask a scientist where the first living cell came from.) Even human DNA and DNA replication machineries present the unanswerable question: "Since they all rely on each other to function, which came first between DNA, RNA, and proteins, and how could one exist without the other in the beginning of all life?" Questions like this and many others form the basis of what scientists and scholars refer to as "the cosmological argument"—theories relating to the "first cause" of the cosmos (universe). The systematic arrangement of the universe and all life as we know it (including the interdependency between the earth's weather patterns, seasons, plants and animals, and human biology) is complicated enough that, to believers, assuming it was all a random accident makes as much sense as throwing rocket parts in the air and having them "accidentally" or "coincidentally" fall together into the first fully functional and operational NASA space shuttle. When the rubber meets the road: a) Science is never able to completely explain the conclusions of religious faith; and, perhaps more importantly, b) Science is constantly updating its own database of facts with new technologies, amending and sometimes altogether negating the discoveries of previous generations…which were developments that experts at the time claimed were tested, proven truths. (Hey, does anyone remember that time when ancient Hippocratic medicine "proved" that hair was a mass of congealed intimate bodily fluids? Interesting fact: This is why women were told in the New Testament to keep their heads covered. More info in Donna Howell's *The Handmaidens Conspiracy*, [Defender Publishing, 2018.])

That is why this brief overview of the Shroud of Turin will not make a definitive statement one way or the other about whether it is, in fact, the burial cloth of Christ. Though these authors have their own opinions, this book will *not* try to tell readers what to believe.

That said, here is one fact: Whether the Shroud is the burial cloth of Christ, an artistic (and apparently unreproducible) hoax, or a relic unrelated to either of these two possibilities, it does tell a tragic tale of someone's journey into the afterlife from the first flogging to the grave—*and quite possibly the flash back to life.*

Without further ado, let's take a quick, crash-course visit through the background of this controversial fabric for those who may be less familiar with it than others. The authenticity of the Shroud as being the burial cloth of Christ relies on, literally, *hundreds* of factors, and this book would be far too long if it dealt with the matter in exhaustive detail (as other works have already done). The chief issues related to the Shroud being eventually deemed genuine have been the following:

- What Scripture describes about Christ's death, and whether the cloth matches that description
- Whether the linen could have been a forgery or work of art
- How the image on the cloth was created in the first place, and whether it could ever be reproduced
- Where the cloth has traveled from Christ's death to its current location in Turin, Italy
- Whether the dating of the cloth is reliable
- What science has to say about all of these issues

133

We will visit these subjects in this order, but note that the scientific issues will be addressed as we go along, because it is as intrinsically woven into every topic related to the Shroud of Turin, as the man's image is within the Shroud's fibers.

The Body on the Linen

It's fascinating to think that the Shroud of Turin could possibly be the very *sindon* (the Greek word for linen cloth) that Joseph of Arimathea bought and handled just prior to lowering Christ's body from the cross.

The image embedded in the cloth shows the following wounds:

- Significant, numerous lacerations all over the body, front and back, consistent with the flagellation of Christ as described in the Gospel accounts (John 19:1; Mark 15:15; Matthew 27:26; a discussion of the "thirty-nine stripes" is forthcoming).
- Thick, red drops of blood all around the forehead from multiple deep punctures, in proportion to wounds that might have been caused by Christ's crown of thorns (John 19:2, 5; Mark 15:17; Matthew 27:29).
- Dark, prominent impalement marks on the wrists and feet, in line with the location where nails would have pierced the body during a Roman crucifixion. To the lay observer, the thumbs on the hands appear to be missing. On the front of the arms, the blood stains travel upward to the elbow, demonstrating that the victim's arms were in a raised position when the wounds to the wrists were inflicted.
- A pronounced stab wound in the man's side gives the most dramatic of all blood stains. Once again, this is consistent with the Gospel account of Jesus being pierced with a spear in His side to ensure His death (John 19:34).

Forgery Theory Proved Wrong by Blood and Anatomy?

On May 28, 1898, Secondo Pia had the privilege of capturing the very first photograph of the Shroud. Photography at the time was still fairly new technology, so there would have been little to no expectations that anything extra luminous would show up on the negatives in the darkroom when he attempted to develop the photos. When his eyes finally did land on the negatives, which caused the image of the suffering man in the linen to "pop" from the flat picture, Pia almost dropped and broke the photographic darkroom plates in shock. His were the first truly clear portrayals of the face and body of the messianic artifact.

These images, and those made by other photographers after him, show anatomical details and facts about the blood that point to the idea that a forgery (or reverent work of art) is an impossible conclusion.

Anatomical Shapes and Cloth-Wrapping

Most immediately noteworthy to sindonologists, physicians, medical and forensic experts, and scientists who have studied the Shroud is the anatomical accuracy of the body's impression on the cloth. An artist or forger would have needed a high level of knowledge regarding the muscular/bone shape of every human body part shown on the fabric in order to produce this realistic depiction, front and back. (Remember, there weren't any "how-to-draw-anatomy" sections at a local Barnes & Noble store back in the 1200–1300s; a forger might be able to make a perfect human hand imprint somehow, but not easily an entire body. If the dating of the cloth is accurate, the artist/forger would have had to make a conscious effort not to be influenced by the art in the culture at the time, which gave little concern for accuracy in the human form.)

Additionally, comparative anthropometric analysis (scientific measurement of human body proportions) of the ventral (front) and dorsal (back) sides of the cloth show the forger would have had to make it a) align perfectly enough that both sides are anatomically superimposable (showing it is the same person and in the same position on the ventral side as the dorsal), and b) align irregularly enough in some places to allow for naturally occurring outline deviations in what one study calls "the cloth-body wrapping effect."[105]

For years, many claimed the Shroud had to be a fake because the legs on the dorsal side are shorter than the ventral side (in other words, the legs appears "taller" on the front side), but this actually substantiated the cloth further once the anthropometric analysis was completed showing that the man's knees are slightly fixed in a bent position in the front, the contour of which creates a slight elongation of the ventral side of the cloth as it "spends" more space traveling over the knees.

Rigor mortis would have set in before Jesus was taken down from the cross, which would have fixed His knees in a bent position. For Christ's body to lay flat, the rigor mortis would have had to have been broken at major joints, but the irregularity of shape and forward bend of the knee would have likely been maintained, though at a smaller degree, which lines up perfectly with this study. Had a forger made the legs on the ventral and dorsal images identical in height—a move that anyone likely would have done if they were attempting to make the front and back sides of the image manifest as the same person—the rookie mistake would have backfired, proving the Shroud to be a great deal more likely a fraud since the bend of the knees is visible. (Bent knees also challenge claims that the body of the forger's model was "standing" while the cloth's image was created, though that line of thinking doesn't garner much attention anymore. The initial theory was created because the Shroud man's hair doesn't "fall back" the way it would if He had been on his back; that indicates He must have been standing. However, many sindonology experts agree that this detail is, once again, more evidence of authenticity, because the hair would have been caked with blood and filth [despite the minor body-washing burial methods of the Jews], and therefore stuck in an awkward shape from when Christ hung His head forward on the cross.)

This isn't the only time this occurs in the image. For instance, the shoulders of the man are raised awkwardly, and the arms are bent stiffly at the elbow; neither of these areas is resting naturally. This, too, shows that the shoulders and arms were fixed firmly upon the horizontal support beam of the cross when rigor mortis took hold of the muscles. The rigor mortis would have had to be broken in order to lay the body in position upon the Shroud, but the arrangement of the arms and shoulders would reflect a remaining stiffness that makes His "rest" markedly awkward. Further, the body's right shoulder bears evidence of a scratch, which ties to another scratch on the left scapula (shoulder blade), consistent with wounds that would have been made while carrying a cross. This is a perfect explanation for why the Shroud man's right shoulder is tensely positioned a little lower than the left in the image.

The bend of the legs creating the "taller" illusion on the ventral side is the most prominent measurement deviation from a natural human body in a prone position, but it's not the only place where posthumous anatomical expertise (including extensive understanding of rigor mortis) would have to be in play for a forger.

Other paintings in antiquity were also mentioned in this study and compared against the Shroud. Not surprisingly, the Shroud "showed the incompatibility of the images painted by artists who at that time did not have enough anatomic knowledge."[106] Indeed, an artist or forger would have had to be nothing less than an expert in both posthumous anatomy and body wrapping to have fabricated the burial cloth of Christ.

Other elements and features of the image are equally difficult to imitate, considering the relationship between anatomy and biblical prophecy. As only one example of many: Exodus 12:46 and Numbers 9:12 prophesied that not a single bone of the Messiah's body would be broken. The Shroud displays much swelling, but according to sindonologists, there are no visible signs of broken bones. The injuries of the man in the image have been studied and documented (the long list having been buttressed by computerized VP-8 image enhancement, a system that analyzes depth of brightness) showing an in-depth analysis of each injury, all the way from the crown of thorns and spear wound to what appears to be a tiny rip in the man's right eyelid.[107] Yet, one "oops" move from a forger/artist might have suggested a concave in the artwork suggesting bone breakage, even in the tiniest (and therefore most inconspicuous) places, such as a finger or brow bone. It looks to be far more than just an interesting coincidence that the body's swelling is abundant, but not a single bone appears to have been broken.

But all this only scratches the surface; a forger also would have needed to be aware of another relationship between blood and fabric that the world wouldn't have known about at the time...

Forgery Ruled Out by Blood Alone?

When the Shroud of Turin was examined under ultraviolet lights, something called serum albumin retraction was discovered. In short, this represents blood protein "rings" around the wounds where the blood and the serum separated just after the cessation of the heartbeat. When this appears on all the wounds imprinted on the Shroud (of course under examination with modern instruments), a "halo" effect appears, with the outermost edge of the stain traveling farther than the bloodstain itself.

Once again, there would have been no way a forger could have known about this posthumous blood-protein relationship, since this information was unknown at the time. Even if the forger had known about it, this assumes he would have found a way to reproduce this feature invisibly, until technology later produced the ultraviolet means necessary for viewing it.

Microchemical and spectroscopic tests carried out by Dr. Alan Adler and Dr. John Heller in 1980 showed that human blood composed of hemoglobin was most certainly present on the cloth, and that it was type AB. (This is according to many tests, not just one or two. The scientific method was responsibly applied in this issue.) Further microscopic and proteolytic enzymatic hydrolysis (blood removal) tests by Dr. Adler show that the blood and the image imprint don't occupy the same fibers. Put more simply: Wherever blood is present on the cloth, the image is no longer present.

This discovery was an enormous factor in the ongoing debate regarding whether the Shroud of Turin is a forgery or work of art!

Forensic pathologist and chief medical examiner in Rockland County, New York, Dr. Frederick Zugibe, has long been considered an expert on the Shroud. His background in crime-scene analysis and his personal quest since 1948 to find answers about the cloth have come together to produce numerous fresh perspectives. In his book, *The Crucifixion of Jesus: A Forensic Inquiry*, Zugibe makes an intelligent assessment of Dr. Adler's findings as they relate to whether the Shroud is a hoax:

If this [the Shroud] were done by human hands, the artist [or forger] would have had to paint all of the bloodstains with the albumin halos in all of the wounds and blood flows, including the blood of the scourge marks, using human blood and then paint the body image around them in their precise locations and eliminate images wherever there was blood.[108]

Zugibe is not alone in thinking that a fourteenth-century forger could not be responsible for producing the Shroud. Nevertheless, assuming such a counterfeiter technically might have existed, let's continue our investigation.

Putting the Shroud to the Cross Test

Zugibe shows his dedication to putting the image to the test. He writes about the life-size, experimental cross he had built by the blacksmith and sculptor Father Weyland, from which Zugibe hung willing male volunteers (obviously nobody was nailed or killed), all of whom were around the same size and weight (165–175 pounds) as the man in the Shroud in order to test the "statements" the Shroud man makes with his visual testimony. The gravitational pull of the arms and legs is a matter of experimental evidence and mathematics during full-bodied suspension with repeat documentation of the variables, not solely of anthropometric (survey of the proportions of the body in relation to the size and weight of a person's frame) analyses on paper (though he writes about that report with respect and refers to it several times in his work).

To begin, leather "hand gauntlets" were constructed for each volunteer, so when they were hung on the cross, the two "Omega Digital Programmable Strain Gauge Panel Meter" cables provided an accurate measurement of the pull on each hand without the volunteer having to hang on with his own strength. The volunteer was then subjected to three different positions: 1) the full body hanging from the hand gauntlets; 2) the feet separately secured to the cross; and 3) the feet secured with one foot atop the other. (Many other details abound regarding Zugibe's work of suspending volunteers, including the use of the oximeter [which challenges the asphyxiation-death theory of Christ] and many other pieces of monitoring equipment. Volunteers were instructed to report any complaints that they had about such things as pain, cramping, and difficulty breathing. This information was used to identify commonalities from one "victim" to another.)

These experiments were conducted in such a way that they certainly provided scientific methodology from which others could learn about the execution of Christ, but the primary purpose was to compare the findings with the Shroud's image and its relation to the position the body was in when it came into contact with the cloth after death. (Another central purpose was to refute Barbet's "missing thumbs" theory, which we address in the following pages.)

After considering the compiled notes on the cross experiments, it's not a leap to say that a forger would have had extreme difficulty mimicking such postmortem anatomy even today, let alone in the fourteenth century.

"Thirty-Nine Stripes" and the Evidence of the Spear

The Bible doesn't say how many lashes Christ received during flagellation, but a popular tradition/assumption is thirty-nine. Because of a stipulation in the Mosaic Law stating that a criminal should not be given more than "forty stripes" (Deuteronomy 25:3), Jews didn't normally punish a criminal beyond thirty-nine lashes during flagellation. Paul wrote in 2 Corinthians 11:24 that on five different occasions, he had received "forty lashes minus one" as a result of the Jews' interpretation of maximum flagellation punishment around the time of Christ. It has therefore become a traditional belief that Christ's punishers would have struck Jesus thirty-nine times as the accepted maximum.

However, this idea is quickly discredited. It is necessary to remember that Christ's execution was carried out by the Romans—who weren't under any obligation to follow Jewish laws or convictions—not the Jews, so there is no reason to assume the number thirty-nine has anything to do with Christ's severe beating. (This is relevant to the number of lacerations on the body imprinted on the Shroud, certainly, but it's also relevant in pop-culture Christianity as well. A number of ministers in recent years have connected the "by His stripes we are healed" prophecy of Isaiah 53:5 to thirty-nine particular diseases, afflictions, conditions, et cetera, that we are allowed to claim healing for today. These presentations are intriguing, but from what we've seen, they conveniently avoid addressing how they've managed to cut the Romans out of this equation, and they further limit Christ's healing abilities today to a number, which is suspect.)

Additionally, much medical research has been dedicated to how the hasta (the Roman spear used at the time of Christ) in the side of our Lord would have resulted in the "blood and water" phenomenon (mentioned in John 19:34). These discussions have been carried on for two thousand years apart from, and unrelated to, the Shroud's image involving far more than the thirty-nine lashes. There are currently eleven leading hypotheses, some assuming that Christ might have still been alive when the spear was thrust in, while most adhere to what the Word said regarding the soldiers confirming His death before illustrating what they already knew with a spear (John 19:32–34). However, the theory most popularly considered credible among doctors, surgeons, forensic analysts, and scientists describes how the spear pierced through the right atrium of Jesus' heart, releasing a small amount of a "massive pleural effusion (fluid around the lungs),"[109] that was present as a result of the insanely cruel beatings and lashings that Christ received in the hours prior to the cross. If this hypothesis is as spot-on as the experts think it is, then the odd "blood and water" note from the Gospel of John points to a much greater physical torture than thirty-nine lashes on the back and a few hard punches. Therefore, the Shroud, once again, defies traditional beliefs from early Jewish and Christian cultures as well as amateur assumptions potentially made by fourteenth-century forgers, and this conclusion has been reached without the help of the picture on the cloth.

The authenticity of the Shroud appears to be holding firm through many of these reflections. Many objections assert that believers are grasping at anything they can to prove that it is the real burial cloth of Christ. We need to rewire our thinking about this: Sindonologists are not "proving the Shroud to be real." Much the opposite, science and medicine have sought to explain what must have physically occurred in Christ's last hours, regardless of the Turin cloth. We are merely at a point of observing the Shroud's many former "puzzling oddities" showing a more advanced level of credibility amongst contemporary medical understanding. And, not unexpectedly, the cloth has more to say about the "stripes."

Studies on the reported number of lashes given to the man whose image is on the Shroud contrast widely, and for good reason. The bloodstains alone cannot prove how new or possibly frayed the flagrum (the scourging whip, aka "cat-o'-nine tails") was, how long the thongs (leather cords fixed to the flagrum) were that extended from the handle to the metal-tipped end of each, and therefore how many of the marks across the flesh each thong individually accounts for, how many pieces of small bone (or other debris) might have been threaded along the thongs for deeper penetration into the flesh, and whether the whip involved nine thongs—or more, or less, and so on. Many interesting hypotheses exist addressing just how many lashes the man whose image is depicted on the Shroud would have had to receive to appear the way he does on the fabric, but the jury is still out on an exact count for now—and possibly for forever on this side of eternity.

However, due to the historically accurate shapes and angles of the stripes upon the image, if the Shroud is a work of religious art or a forgery from the fourteenth century, the artist/forger would have had to know precisely how a Roman flogging was conducted around a thousand years after the practice had ceased—in an age when he or she couldn't find this information on the Internet, at a local library, or from a neighbor. It definitely was not shown correctly in the art of that time. Today, there are charts all over the place for inquiring minds regarding how much distance there would be between the Roman soldier/executioner and the victim, and at what diagonal directions the lacerations would have torn through the skin, but this is a convenience that a fourteenth-century forger wouldn't have had. We also know that many of the scourge marks on the Shroud's image are dumbbell-shaped (two or three metal pieces affixed in succession at the end of the thong, leaving their mark in the skin like tiny dumbbell weights), which is quite an obscure, antique detail for a forger to include. Our guess is that the forger/artist would have: a) had to have researched Roman flagellation to the point that every created stripe was a realistic strike, or b) had to have gotten really, really lucky in guessing. Either way, the stripes on the body show a positive match to what we know of the punishment methods of that time, and the evidence of the spear likewise points to the idea that the beating Christ endured was far more dramatic than a traditional "thirty-nine stripes."

By no means does this prove or disprove a thing about the Shroud's authenticity. At this point in our quick analysis, we're simply stating the first of many puzzling factors about a potential forgery/work of art.

Missing Thumbs: Barbet vs. Zugibe

The "missing thumbs" of the image on the cloth is a key element on the believer's list of arguments in favor of authenticity.

It is well known that *koine* Greek (the Greek language as it had developed at the time of Christ and in which the New Testament was written) used the word *cheir* to refer to both the hand and the wrist. It is equally possible, then, that Jesus was nailed to the cross by His wrists, not through the palms. (Our insistence that the word "hand" be used in many modern translations can probably be traced to the Latin Vulgate, a fourth-century work that therefore occurred well after the *koine* Greek Gospel accounts were written.) The Romans technically could have used either entry point, as historical documents and artifacts have shown they enjoyed a variety of torture methods. Remains of crucifixion victims—dating to the time of Christ and discovered during excavations (especially the one at *Giv'at ha Mivtar*)—have shown that some endured being nailed through the forearms. Upside-down crucifixions were not uncommon, adding to the proof that we shouldn't get stuck on one hand or wrist theory over another for any ancient victim, including Christ. There is also little backing to the claim that a nail would hold a victim to the cross more efficiently through the wrist than the palm (Zugibe's cross experiments effectively refuted this theory, proving that a man's palms would hold him up without a hitch all the way up to 225 pounds total body weight), so in regard to Jesus Christ, we can't know for sure.

The location of the Shroud man's nail wounds appears to be on what's known as the Destot's Space (at the center of the lunate, triquetral, capitate, and hamate bones, named after the French anatomist and pioneer radiologist Étienne Destot). The late Dr. Pierre Barbet (1884–

1961) was known for his career as chief surgeon at St. Joseph's Hospital in Paris and his book, *Doctor at Calvary: The Passion of Our Lord Jesus Christ as Described by a Surgeon*, although his truest claim to fame is linked to his postulations about the Shroud of Turin. Barbet, because of his line of work, frequently had access to amputated limbs. Observing the Shroud, he concluded that the Destot's Space on the wrist must have been the origin of the wound, and he decided to conduct the experiment personally. Using a freshly removed human arm, he drove a nail through the Destot's Space and observed as the carpal bones cooperated to let the nail pass through. At the moment the nail was hammered through the wrist, the thumbs "snapped" inward toward the palm—a result of the trauma to the median nerve. Barbet explains:

Is it possible that trained executioners would not have known by experience of this ideal spot for crucifying the hands, combining every advantage and so easy to find? The answer is obvious. And this spot is precisely where the shroud shows us the mark of the nail, a spot of which no forger would have had any idea or the boldness to represent it.

The contraction of these thenar muscles, which were still living like their motor nerve, could be easily explained by the mechanical stimulation of the median nerve. *Christ must then have agonised and died and have become fixed in the cadaverous rigidity, with the thumbs bent inwards into His palms.* And that is why, on the shroud, the two hands when seen from behind only show four fingers, and why the two thumbs are hidden in the palms. *Could a forger have imagined this?* Would he have dared to portray it? Indeed, so true is this that many ancient copyists of the shroud have added the thumbs; in the same way they have separated the feet and shown their forward faces with two nail holes; but none of this is to be seen on the shroud.[110] (emphasis original)

Barbet felt from this (and several other) experiments that he had proven: a) why the Shroud man's thumbs appear to be missing, and that b) if the Shroud man is Jesus Christ, then the Messiah was absolutely nailed to the cross through the wrists. Further, his question herein poised "Could a forger have imagined this?" has been quoted uncountable times in books, magazines, articles, blogs, and documentaries. The question, itself, offers an obvious answer: No. It's a *huge* stretch to assume that a fourteenth-century forger would think to create the image with anatomical information not yet discovered about a nail-to-cross method that wasn't in practice at the time to which the cloth is dated. Nor is it likely the forger would have done it even if he or she *had* known, because an oddity like the missing thumbs of Christ wouldn't make sense to contemporary aesthetes (people who study and appreciate art). And there doesn't appear to be any sensible explanation for why a *fourteenth-century* forger would relocate those wounds to the wrists a thousand years after the Latin Vulgate translation (which was, again, a fourth-century work) had already widely introduced the concept that the nails were driven through the *palm*. This would have made the forgery suspect at that time.

Thus, Barbet concludes that the only person capable of creating a forgery would have had to be present on the day of the execution and standing close enough to see the "snapping inward" of Christ's thumbs when the nails pierced His Destot's Space. But…if the fourteenth-century dating of the cloth is accurate, then the "forger" couldn't have possibly been alive at the time as an eyewitness to Christ's death.

However, not everyone agrees that the missing thumbs are relevant.

Dr. Zugibe states in his book that in his thirty-four years of experience in the medical examiner's office, he has many times observed the same "missing thumbs" appearance on various fabrics that bodies have been wrapped in. When the hands are crossed in front of a body and at rest, the only parts of the flesh that comes into contact with the fabric in that area are the wrists and the fingers; the thumbs are naturally tucked underneath, producing an image similar to that of the Shroud man's hands.[111]

If Zugibe's explanation is correct in regard to the Shroud as well, then we need not assume anything spectacular about the missing thumbs. He goes on to point out that other hand surgeons and medical professionals have convincingly challenged whether the "snapping" would have occurred as a result of injury to the median nerve, *or* that the median nerve would even be struck by a nail driven through the Destot's Space.[112] Therefore, as amazing as the "missing thumb" theory of Barbet was for many years, an honest believer would remember that this major argument for the Shroud's authenticity is heavily contested.

This theory hasn't been rendered entirely inconsequential, though. It still means that the forger would have had the artistic wherewithal to depict the hands without thumbs, which, once again, goes back to him or her conveniently being an anatomical expert well-informed of "the cloth-body wrapping effect." Whether the thumbs are missing as a result of injury or not is a matter the experts of science and medicine may continue to debate, but this fact remains: Whenever someone first studies the image on the Shroud, the missing thumbs stand out as an oddity, an awkward element that seems anatomically *incorrect* (at least to an untrained eye). Why would that detail be one the forger wished to include? The idea that a forger would know about or choose to include such an element is at the very least far-fetched when it would have been easier to just put complete hands on the image to avoid confusion and appeal to believers everywhere who would be more drawn to an image of a complete Messiah, instead of one of a Deliverer with missing thumbs.

Of course, at the end of the day, the question that lingers regarding the hand section of the image is not about whether the victim's skin could have come into contact with fabric anyway. It's interesting that Zugibe and Barbet both spent so much time on that specific conundrum when it has been proven countless times that our best sciences *cannot* reproduce the Shroud (which they easily could if it were a matter of skin/fabric contact).

Tridimensional Findings: Forgery Theory Takes a Blow

The Shroud is what experts call "tridimensional." This means that, when subjected to three-dimensional, computer-imaging studies, the image on the Shroud "pops" with accurate contours. This three-dimensional data is mysteriously stored within the cloth itself. Viewing this information download into the corresponding programs appears much like a model has laid down under the cloth and all of the body parts are raised where they should be. When regular photographs are examined with this same experiment, the contours are confused, at times falling flat or even under another dimensional layer, impossibly disproportionate to the original object photographed. In other words, a photo of a man's face might show all features flat, just like a picture we hold in our hand, instead of contoured like the tridimensional Shroud, but even when the program is adjusted to pick up and "pop" features involved in the photo, the nose might suddenly become inverted and concaved, traveling backwards into the head. (These 3D studies also showed no trace of discernable directional brushstrokes, ruling out the idea that a painting was present on the cloth anywhere.)

New Insights on the Injuries

Under these new observations, the Shroud showed every injury (along with swelling) in a way that bolstered the forensic and scientific analyses that we've just reflected upon. Believers don't find it surprising that, even when transformed into a 3D image, the image on the cloth had no broken bones (in line with Scripture). The imaging even showed details that the linen could not, such as pronounced blood clots under the skin in correspondence to their nearby injuries. (This "forger" is getting more and more impossibly advanced, creating otherwise invisible blood clots in his "art.")

New Insights on the Face

Additionally, the now-multidimensional face of the image on the cloth revealed Semitic facial features relating to the Hebrew blood-lines (yet another "expertise" the "forger" would have had to master so that the "Jesus" of the hoax didn't appear Asian or Mexican, etc.). The face did not show any wrinkles, which the image experts said would appear under such a delicate 3D analysis, showing that the person depicted in the Shroud was young at the time of death (right about Christ's age).

Coins Over the Eyes?

One peculiar and unexpected detail that appeared on the 3D image (but is undiscernible on the cloth) was a button-like object on the outside of each of the Shroud man's eyes. A closer look at the right eye revealed what appeared to be the letters "UCAI" in one corner and a swirling astrologer's staff in the center. The men behind the tridimensional experiments—who didn't know at first what they were even looking at—dug deeper into the existing literature on Hebrew burial methods during the Intertestamental Period (the era between the end of the time covered in the Old and the beginning of the New Testaments) to see what may have been placed there. They discovered that the Jews at the time of Christ held to an odd custom: Coins were placed over the eyes of a recently deceased loved one so they could not view their journey to the afterlife.

(Quick note: Whether those who cared for Christ's body believed in such a thing is to some degree irrelevant, because, as every reliable study on Jewish culture at this time shows, they were creatures of habit, often clinging to customs out of tradition [often even favoring oral tradition over Scripture, like the Pharisees have accurately been accused of doing]. We put flowers on the chests of casketed loved ones today according to tradition, even though our modern embalming methods have far surpassed the need to cover the odor of a decaying body, which is where that custom originated. Therefore, arguments about whether Joseph of Arimathea or the disciples (male or female) would have "tried to prevent Christ from seeing His afterlife" by adding coins to the eyelids are fascinating, but not necessarily significant.)

Researching the "UCAI" letters and the staff on what they now assumed was a coin, the researchers made a stunning connection: The common Roman lepton (small currency) coin of Pontius Pilate issued between AD 29 and AD 32 had an astrologer's staff (a lituus) in the center, and the letters surrounding it spelled "TIBERIOUKAICAROC," which translates "of Tiberius Caesar"—the Roman Emperor during Jesus' ministry years. The lituus staff was a symbol of Pilate's rule, but after him, no ruler of Rome was ever associated with it. This would place the coins in common use precisely at the time of Christ's death, as well as rendering them nearly impossible to get hold of not long afterward. But the rabbit hole goes deeper…

There was an unexplainable "C" where the "K" should have been on the coin (TIBERIOUKAICAROC). This oddity raised curiosity (and skeptics' balking) for a while, until it was discovered to be an even more unbelievable phenomenon relating to a minting error: At one point, the coin's design had been misspelled, and only a limited number of them were released into circulation before the problem was evidently corrected. (We still have these coins today.)

Over the Shroud man's left eye, however, was an image that looked like a bundle of barley. Not surprisingly, the "Julia lepton" coin was minted for Tiberius Caesar's wife, only produced one time in AD 29 (very limited printing), and it reflected her rule with barley.

Once this "coins" theory gained ground, more experts were brought into the project and confirmed that the remaining letters of "TIBERIOU-KAICAROC" were almost certainly discernable when studying which portions of the coin's surface hadn't been scuffed or destroyed.

Furthermore, the coins-over-the-eyes burial custom ceased early in the second century. So, the "forger" who somehow created an imprint of Pilate's coins—invisible to the naked eye until the cloth was subjected to modern 3D imaging—would have also known to include this burial custom feature to keep his hoax perfectly accurate to Christ's day... Oh, and he also would have needed to get his hands on two of the rarest coins in the world, including one with a minting error. But as a final thought on this subject: If the coin findings can be considered reliable, then suddenly the radiocarbon dating (discussed later) would not be.

(Note that countertheories relate this entire coin phenomenon as a flaw in the linen. These arguments are strong, but the mathematical likeliness of the letters and staff images showing up in exactly the same era as when the coins were released—and appearing on both eyelids [instead of an atypical place like a shoulder or kneecap]—makes the coin theory stronger, in these authors' opinions.)

The Unreproducible Image

Other books on the Shroud of Turin have covered the following experiments at great scientific length, and have made a case so solid for the "unreproducible image" that, for the sake of space, we won't go into the same level of detail. For those just joining the discussion, however, we'll briefly outline what has already been done in the unsuccessful attempt to explain its origins.

To begin, however, it's necessary to mention what the scientific groups—including STURP (Shroud of Turin Research Project)—have already learned about the linen's makeup. Methods used were *in part*:

...microscopy (light, polarizing, phase, fluorescent, stereo, petrographic, scanning, electron), immunochemical analysis, enzymatic chemical analysis, serological analysis, textile analysis, microchemical tests, laser microprobe Raman spectroscopy, mass spectroscopy, spectroscopy (optical, infrared), energy dispersive X-ray analysis, X-ray diffraction, micro FTIR (Fourier Transform Infrared) spectroscopy, electron microprobe analysis, Fourier analysis, VP-8 computer imaging, computer studies, pyrolysis mass spectrometry, and others.[113]

No paints, dyes, or stains are present on the linen; pigments present on the cloth are trace amounts and have been ruled out as the primary origin (more information on this in the next subsection); microchemical evaluation proved that the body did not leave behind any oil or biochemical imprints; the body-image area tested free of any added materials; and the colors within the fibers of the linen cannot be dissolved or diluted. (Also, organic dyes change to a deeper color when subjected to extreme heat; if the Shroud's image was a result of dyes, the fire in 1532 that left gaping holes in the linen would show an increase of color near the locations of fire damage, and it does not.) Bloodstains show that the present human blood type AB on the cloth was absorbed into the fibers, not painted on or applied artificially. Had any archaic type of paint or glue been used that is unfamiliar to our modern scientists, the numerous pollens present on the cloth (and linking the linen to the ancient world) would be stuck *under* that substance, which is not the case.

The discoloration of the fibers belonging to the body-image areas was determined to be the result of decomposition by aging (meaning that somehow the fibers holding the image of the man are more *aged* than the rest of the non-body-image areas of the linen). However, since the body-image and non-body-image areas of the cloth are connected by the original herringbone linen weave, one portion of the cloth cannot be "aged" more than another portion, *unless*, experts say, the body-image fibers were exposed to a sudden source of heat, accelerating the deterioration of the fibers *only* in the body-image area.

Reproduction Attempts

Despite what has been ruled out regarding the Shroud (such as the presence of paint), true scientific method requires even unlikely origins to be tested on the chance that the process may reveal additional details pertinent to the overall data.

Not a Work of Art

No attempted artistic reproduction (regardless of the method, which varies from paint and dye to pigments, and so on) has been able to hold up to the same intense "photo negative" effects when submitted under photography testing as was the Shroud. Likewise, they have lacked the ability to satisfy the demands of any tridimensional (3D) imaging tests, falling hopelessly flat in comparison. No reproducers had a reliable answer for how, on the Shroud, the body-image areas cease to exist wherever there is blood (proving that the bloodstains would have had to be painted on first before the body image). Each artistic-reproduction test resulted in altering the state of the fibers and present pollens in an unnatural way (like "gluing them down" with paint, etc.), and was therefore eliminated as a possibility.

Noteworthy about this particular origin theory is the sticky-tape analysis done by Walter McCrone, who later reported the body image was created with glair (egg white), and that rod ochre (a red pigment) and mercuric sulfide (a vermillion pigment) were found on the linen. His findings, however stimulating to skeptics though they may be, have been repeatedly debunked as an origin explanation. To begin, the glair would have produced proteins on the body-image area, and those are not present; microchemical tests disprove the body-image color could be from glair. Whereas there are trace amounts of pigment, and the "red ochre" association is a leading go-to for skeptics who cling to the idea that the Shroud is a work of art, these particles are extremely rare and hard to locate—and, unlike the irons pulled from the Shroud (which tested chemically pure), these pigments were tainted with manganese, cobalt, nickel, and other contaminants.

Additionally, the bloodstains and the body image are not a color match to these pigments. If pigment was the source of the image, we would have found plenty of existing particles in the fibers, and at least microscopically, the color would be a match. As for why a trace amount is present, that, again, has been repeatedly explained: Artists throughout the years have been allowed to paint a reproduction of the Turin original while viewing it on display in person so that they can take the reproduction back to their own home churches and display it as a reference to the true "holy sindon" for veneration. But a reproduction cannot be venerated unless it has been physically laid upon the Shroud of Turin (as a kind of "absorbed blessing," so to speak). Thus, not only have the artists of the reproductions ground and mixed their pigments only a few feet away from the original (with trace pigments wafting and landing on whatever they're next to), when the secondary work dried, the reproduction was laid upon the original, face to face. To name a few reproduction shrouds that have certainly been involved in this "laying-together" process: "the Spanish churches of Guadalupe and Navarette in 1568, Torres de la Alameda in 1620, La Cuesta in 1654, and Aglie in 1822, and in the United States in 1624 at Our Lady of the Rosary (Summit, New Jersey)."[114] Actually, though there's not even close to enough pigments to account for the origin of the Shroud of Turin, it's surprising that we haven't found more than we have, considering how vulnerable it's been to that exposure throughout the centuries.

(Other popular artist-design theories have gained a lot of attention, like Craig-Bresee and Joe Nickell's "rubbing" hypotheses, but they have the same problems discussed previously: They rely on certain chemicals or particles to be heavily present on the Shroud, which they are not, and they can't explain why the Shroud image is chemically pure, while their own compounds would produce contamination; they can't ever recreate the same sharp, clear, intense negative effect as the Shroud; and they fail the 3D test every time.)

Not Substance, Diffusion, Oils, Sweat, Bacteria, or Bodily Secretions

All attempts involving diffusion or oxidation of substances (like aloes or spices; cf. John 19:39–40) result in a blurred image—nowhere near as clear as the Shroud man. So, too, did experiments involving the covering of human skin (either corpses or volunteers) in oil, sweat, salts, etc., and introducing catacomb-like, damp air conditions. The body-image area of the shroud has also shown by tape-extraction tests to be surface level (only applying to the outermost, superficial layers of the fibers), which rules out any image-creating method that would "breathe through" the cloth on both sides.

Yet, if the body image had originated from a spice, oil, or related substance diffusing through the linen, washing it out would have resulted in altering the bloodstains, so the substance would have to remain today… and no one substance is present over the whole body-image consistently.

One theory (the Volckringer hypothesis) nominates lactic acid through sweating as an origin idea, but it conflicts with the enormously stacked forensic evidence that the Shroud man's body was washed (ceremoniously) before it was laid to rest (which, by the way, is the reason for the intense bloodstains on the cloth; the washing process reopened the wounds that would have otherwise been clotted and filthy), so the sweat would not have accumulated to the degree of the Shroud's image. Also, there likely would have excess lactic acid in the fibers, but there is not. Even if these two factors weren't an issue in the Volckringer hypothesis, the body-contact distortion factor (addressed next) would have meant that the Shroud man's sweating body was flat.

Numerous other similar theories assume that the body came into contact with a foreign substance or that it created its own substance— whether as a result of physical trauma or bacteria (like Stephen Mattingly's bacteriological explanation)—and each fails for many reasons, not the least of which is the fact that they rely on something being chemically present on the cloth that is entirely absent or only present in trace amounts (that could not accumulate to image formation).

Not a Matter of Body Contact

Without getting into all the numerous attempts to prove the Shroud image is a result of the linen's contact with a body, suffice it to say they have all shown the same result. For a quick explanation, imagine rolling around in the mud or jumping in a pool of paint—something to that effect—and then lying flat on your back while a person drapes a length of linen over you. If the cloth is peeled away immediately, it leaves an impression nowhere close to as defined or detailed as that of the Shroud man. If you have an assistant press the cloth into you to make a more pronounced impression, then, when you get out from under the cloth, the image distorts and elongates your features when it's laid flat. The Shroud man is a perfect, anatomically believable specimen while the cloth is flat. The only body-contact explanation that makes sense is one in which the body moves completely through the cloth from a lying-down position, leaving the imprint of the most external layer as the body emerges to the other side, which we all know is impossible…unless the man (Man) under the cloth is known for passing through things (John 20:19).

Not a Medieval Photo

Some origin theories have surfaced recently that suggest the Shroud is an early form of an actual photo negative that simply wasn't developed (which is why, when photographed, the lights and darks produce the positive image). Sometimes these ideas involve body chemicals' exposure to heated silver from the container during the 1532 fire, though that trail cuts off as quickly as all the artist-origin ideas, because no silver is anywhere on the cloth other than near the scorched areas. Other times, like with Professor Nicholas Allen's interesting photographic hypothesis, the Shroud man would have been a model fixed outside, while the sun slowly worked its magic onto a linen inside a darkroom-style building through a quartz lens in a window or aperture. This idea—although extremely clever!—has even bigger holes to fill. The direction of light (as in the shine from the sun above, the shadows under the arms, etc.) that results in these images is very strong, whereas the Shroud has no light direction at all; the body on the linen has crisp edges, and the Shroud does not; and there is still the issue of how the blood "got there first" (since the body image is not present where blood is).[115] (Zugibe adds to this that a human body—which would have been necessary to produce the Shroud of Turin's man—would have been decomposing [not to mention facing the outside elements like birds, etc.] while the medieval photo would have taken weeks to complete the picture impression.)[116]

Another theory you may have heard of is the "da Vinci hypothesis," which goes as far as to involve Leonardo da Vinci, himself, in a massive anti-Catholic conspiracy, using his early camera obscura invention to create a photograph of a cadaver. This is immediately debunked by simply looking at the year da Vinci was born (1452) and knowing that we have solid historical documentation of the existence of the Shroud of Turin from as early as 1349 (more on this shortly).

But in any case, for the same reason, an actual photograph lacks the tridimensional contours on the Shroud; due to sharper imaging on a photo than this mysterious sindon, the Shroud proves itself not to be an actual photograph negative.

Not a Stamp
Some believe that a statue-like object—flat enough to avoid the feature distortion described in the previous "Not a Matter of Body Contact" section, but contoured to the point that it still allows a fade-away at the edges—was heated and pressed into the linen, scorching the body's form into the fibers. Of all the origin theories, this one makes the most

sense alongside the scientific information we currently possess about the Shroud, because: a) that process can accelerate the aging of the fibers rapidly, resulting in the kind of body-image discoloration we see everywhere but the blood; b) we don't have to find any bodily secretions, substances, paints, dyes, etc. on the cloth for it to be feasible; c) such scorch-stamping experiments have shown to produce more of a "photo negative" effect than many other recreation attempts (although still nothing as intense as the Shroud).

However, when a scorch-stamped image is viewed under ultraviolet lighting, it reveals a unique fluorescence of the affected material, wherein that entire area turns bright orange, and this is not a reaction that we can see on the Shroud. Scorching on flax linen also shows an alteration of the crystal structure of the fiber's cellulose—the body-image area does not have any scorching to the fibers at all, save for those in the fire-damage areas. Therefore, the stamp theory can't be viable, as the alterations of the fibers brought about by thermal decomposition (pyrolysis) don't add up to what we see on the Shroud, and we still have the blood to answer for (which, again, does not occupy the same fibers as the image).

Probably Not Radiation

No matter the experiment or explanation, all radiation theories (and there are many) rely on the single factor that the linen would have been subjected to heat. In addition, this heat would have had to be applied gently enough not to damage the fibers beyond that of the Shroud, and in such a way as to dodge the feature distortion. (Most radiation theories involve the use of such intense heat that both the blood and the cloth fibers would have been incinerated.)

One idea is that the earthquake that occurred during the death-and-resurrection narrative—or an electrical storm—charged the stone in the tomb with electricity, and therefore used Christ's body as a conductor for high-voltage energy that released into the linen, scorching the image we see today. Yet this "corona discharge" theory has problems: The energy required to produce a lasting image on linen would have to be extremely high—much higher than energy accumulated by an electric storm or earthquake; the present plasma involved would likely destroy the entire Shroud in the process; areas where the body made contact with the cloth would be entirely free of color due to the relationship of electron acceleration with points of conductivity; and when experiments were conducted to test how an antique flax linen would hold up under these plasma-treated circumstances, the subjects that survived showed a change in the organic materials that is not present in the Shroud.

The theory that the Shroud is a series of early X-rays—created by a repetitious reaction between electromagnetic radiation rays and the dirt and salt on the body's skin, producing a single image—was fascinating. Like only few other hypotheses, this explanation has the potential of creating the intense "negative" feature of the Shroud, as well as the body-image discoloration by accelerated aging of the linen. Likewise, because the image would have been created by emissions into the air, the Shroud man's outline would fade into nothing and never create a definitive edge. However, the amount of radiation that a body would have to contain in order to make this theory feasible is outrageously high. The cause of death would have been documented as radiation poisoning, and no person could have lived long enough to go through any ordeal even close to the crucifixion narrative (or sustain the beating that the Shroud man obviously did). Also, the X-ray emissions would have created an image even where there is blood, the image of the Shroud man would be on both sides of the cloth, and this dirt-and-salt-on-skin reaction could not have happened if the body was washed before burial.

These certainly are not the only theories relating to radiation, though the rest have similar issues and appear unlikely with the sciences we do have to test them. Additionally, the chemical tests carried out on the Shroud have proven that the cloth was never heated enough to remove the hydrogen sulfides from the blood areas, completely ruling out intense radiation.[117] Many faithful Shroud believers want to think that in a sudden resurrection event, a burst of radiation created the image on the linen, but scientific findings have rendered this theory as a "probably not."

Not Anything Else We Have Ever Known

The bottom line is: Although we can prove many origin theories wrong, we don't currently have any scientific method that can prove an origin theory. We simply cannot remake the Shroud. How in the world would a fourteenth-century forger achieve such a work that our greatest minds today cannot?

Or perhaps a better question is this: How in the otherworld might a recently deceased entity create a photo-negative style image of itself? And if it is Christ: Would an event such as a resurrection by a Man who can instantly pass through linen bow to our finite explanations, anyway?

History, Travels, and Chronology of the Shroud

Assuming the Shroud of Turin might be the actual burial cloth of Christ, then the first place to start regarding its history is in Scripture, itself. However, before we address the solid references to the burial cloth of Christ, we must visit one obscure passage commonly (but probably erroneously) linked to the tomb.

Did Paul Tell Timothy to Bring Him the Shroud?

Believers in the Shroud's authenticity have consistently treated 2 Timothy 4:13 (when Paul instructs Timothy to bring "the cloak" [Greek *phainoles*] that he left "at Troas") as a direct reference to Christ's burial cloth. Although this can't be ruled out—since the meaning of the Greek word for "cloak" in this instance is still being debated—it's not as likely as Shroud-believers wish it to be. In fact, following the proper principles of exegesis, it's rather unlikely.

First, the Greek words are not the same. If Joseph of Arimathea bought a *sindon*, Paul probably would have asked for the *sindon* had his intent been to obtain what we now know to be the Shroud. At this time, certain fabrics with importance to the Jews (like those used in ceremony, burial, etc.) were referred to by the kind of cloth they were (like "linen"), not commonly by their use, unlike garments that were worn during daily life, which were referred to by their function (like "robe" or "veil"). Paul was writing a letter, and it would have been strange for him to risk confusion by using an ambiguous word.

Second, most of the historical evidence relating to a *phainoles* points to the conclusion that it was a traveling cloak with a hood used as a protective layer from rain or cold. Some evidence suggests that it was a kind of book bag, as Greek grammarian Hesychius of Alexandria (who specialized in obscure words) understood it to be. The word is only used one time in the Bible, so we can't consult Scripture elsewhere on the context in which it was used. However, both a book bag and a journeyman's hooded cloak fits with the lifestyle of Paul, as he went about on foot all over the ancient world church-planting at that time (when he wasn't imprisoned), and he would have needed proper clothing and a carrying case for his study materials. Furthermore, if most scholars' dating of the epistle is correct, at the time Paul's second letter to Timothy was written, winter was also approaching, so an extra covering from the cold fits the circumstantial needs of Paul.

Third, the casual manner with which Paul refers to the cloak—in contrast to the importance he places on his parchments at the end of this same verse—argues for the idea that the *phainoles* was nothing more than a coat or a bag. After only briefly mentioning the cloak, the apostle entreats Timothy to "especially" (Greek *malista*, which translates "most of all") bring his parchments. It seems odd that Paul would speak about the Shroud of Turin like it's a "by the way" memo and then treat the parchments with chief importance.

As a conclusion to this popular theory, there's more evidence against it than for it, so believers in the authenticity of the Shroud may find their positions more credible if they discontinue their insistence that it is a "fact" that Paul told Timothy to bring him Christ's burial cloth as many of them claim (or at least heavily insinuate) in their writing.

Moving right along…

Biblical References to the Burial Cloth of Christ

To begin with what we know the Bible *certainly* says about the *sindon* of Christ, Mark 15:42–46 describes the event following immediately after Jesus' mortal body expired:

> And when evening had come, since it was the day of Prepara-
> tion, that is, the day before the Sabbath, Joseph of Arimathea, a
> respected member of the council, who was also himself looking
> for the kingdom of God, took courage and went to Pilate and
> asked for the body of Jesus. Pilate was surprised to hear that he
> should have already died. And summoning the centurion, he
> asked him whether he was already dead. And when he learned
> from the centurion that he was dead, he granted the corpse to
> Joseph. And Joseph bought a linen [*sindon*] shroud, and taking
> him down, wrapped him in the linen shroud and laid him in a
> tomb that had been cut out of the rock. And he rolled a stone
> against the entrance of the tomb. (ESV)

This allusion to the *sindon* cloth was referenced in the other two synoptic Gospels (Matthew 27:59 and Luke 23:53). John 19:40 further states: "So they [Joseph of Arimathea and Nicodemus] took the body of Jesus and bound it in linen cloths [*othonion*] with the spices, as is the burial custom of the Jews." The Greek word *othonion* here describes thinner strips that were wrapped around the Lord's wrists and feet, pre-sumably to keep His limbs from flailing about as He was carried from the cross to the tomb. (These are the same kind of linen strips that were affixed to Lazarus' hands and feet after Christ raised him from his tomb of death in John 11:44.) In the Gospel of John (20:5–9), the *othonion* strips and the "face cloth" (or "sweat cloth"; Greek *soudarion*, from where we now gain the word "sudarium," which is another important artifact we will visit later on) are both seen, but the *sindon* cloth (possibly the Shroud of Turin) is no longer present in the scene:

> And stooping to look in, he [John] saw the linen cloths [*otho-nion*] lying there, but he did not go in. Then Simon Peter came, following him, and went into the tomb. He saw the linen cloths [*othonion*] lying there, and the face cloth [*soudarion*], which had been on Jesus' head, not lying with the linen cloths [*otho-nion*] but folded up in a place by itself. Then the other disciple, who had reached the tomb first, also went in, and he saw and believed; for as yet they did not understand the Scripture, that he must rise from the dead. (ESV)

John's reaction to seeing the *othonion* and *soudarion* cloths ("he saw and believed") is noteworthy to many scholars. Just happening upon cloths wouldn't automatically prove anything to John about the resurrection of which he was now convinced. If anything, it might have first inspired the fear that someone had stolen the body (which we can assume certain personalities had an interest in doing in that day, for both nefarious and honorable reasons). It likewise would have been odd for the face and binding cloths to be present, but for the *sindon* shroud to be gone (as it is now missing from the scene). Perhaps it wasn't the cloths, themselves, that wowed John; rather, maybe it was the shape he found them in. What if, as many sindonologists and scholars have postulated, John found the *othonion* strips still coiled and tied in the exact arrangement they were in when they had first been fixed to Christ's wrists and feet, as if Christ had passed straight through them? (The *soudarion* cloth might have been set aside for a while by this time, as readers will soon see.)

But then...where would the burial shroud be?

Allusions to the Shroud's Travels Prior to 1349

Only from the year 1349 and forward are the travels of the Shroud of Turin known for sure. Important note: Though this part of our study will address the chronology of the linen cloth that believers trust to be historical references to the Shroud of Turin, it should be understood that: a) these authors are not endorsing these views, and b) any pre-1349 allusions to a burial shroud of Christ have not (and cannot yet) be proven to be one and the same Shroud of Turin, Italy. We will, however, list the leading pre-1349 references because, due to their resemblance to the Shroud, they have been continuously relevant to the subject of the Shroud, and any study on this ancient cloth is incomplete without them.

The Gospel of the Hebrews

Of course, as mentioned, all three synoptic Gospels and the Gospel of John refer to the sindon cloth Christ was wrapped with. Other apocryphal (and therefore noncanonical) works acknowledge Jesus' burial cloth (and its travels) as early as the following century (Acts of Nicodemus, Gospel of Gamaliel, Acts of Pilate, Gospel of Peter, etc.).

One famous example is the Gospel of the Hebrews. The original text is lost, but some of the core doctrines and narratives remain by proxy (now called the "Fragments"), as many early authors (including Church Fathers) and theologians (Clement, Jerome, Origen, Didymus the Blind, etc.) quoted from it, and it is through the works of others that we gain insight to the first manuscript. At the close of the fourth century, when the New Testament canon was formed, the Gospel of the Hebrews became an obscurity.

The Sixth Fragment relays, in part, the following: "And when the Lord [Jesus] had given his linen cloth to the servant of the priest he went to James and appeared unto him."[118] If this reference is accurate, then the first movement of Christ's burial cloth from the tomb took place just prior to Jesus' appearance to His half-brother ("James the Just," as the apocryphal text identifies in the immediate context), when Christ, Himself, placed His burial cloth in the hands of "the servant of the priest." This particular "servant," Edward Byron Nicholson (translator and classical commentator of the Gospel of the Hebrews) goes on to say, is the one and only Malchus (servant to High Priest Caiaphas), whose ear was severed by Simon Peter during the scene of Christ's betrayal (Matthew 26:51; Mark 14:47; Luke 22:50; John 18:10), and whom Jesus wasted no time in healing (Luke 22:51). Nicholson's commentary explains:

> He [Malchus] had helped in the seizure of Jesus, and had had his right ear cut off with a sword by Simon Peter. But touched and healed by Jesus.... One must guess in the absence of context that he had been entrusted with the setting of the watch (mentioned by Matt. only) over the tomb, had been witness to some of the phaenomena of the resurrection, and had thrown himself at the feet of Jesus.[119]

According to this source, then, Jesus' burial cloth was hand delivered by our Lord and Savior to a believer whose political and social influence at that time was significant.

Not all sindonologists agree on Malchus as the referred-to servant. Some also interpret the Gospel of the Hebrews as indicating the apostle John is the recipient here. Nevertheless, by far, the crux of this small historical testimonial is the idea that Christ would have personally entrusted His shroud to someone He knew would care for it in the way He wished, and less about whether the receiver was John or Malchus. (It is noteworthy to point out that although the second-century manuscripts don't have perfect parallels regarding the recipient either, they concur that the sindon was taken from the tomb and moved to safety.)

Early Art Depicts Shroud?

Turmoil by religious leaders, by this time, had begun what became known as the Byzantine Iconoclasms. These were periods when claims of idol worship brought down an attack against art (icons), and many paintings, sculptures, and varying forms of Christ's likeness were destroyed. Therefore, although this would explain why the Shroud of Turin may have disappeared for hundreds of years, a vast number of images were lost, and we are today somewhat limited in how we can honestly approach what artistic styles dominated the ancient world during this era. Directing our focus on what we can analyze does, however, introduce an odd phenomenon.

Centuries prior to the Shroud's assigned fourteenth-century dating, classic works of art (including Byzantine icons) began to appear with striking—sometimes startling—resemblance to the man in the Shroud. Prior to about the year 450, almost all the artistic depictions of Christ had Him looking baby-faced, unweathered, and clean-shaven; many show His hair cut short in a Greco-Roman fashion. If He was deceased in a painting or sculpture, He was often pictured as being wrapped in many linen cloths, like a mummy. Then, suddenly, a trend began that showed Christ appearing like the man in the Shroud.

In the early years of the twelfth century, professor of biology at the Catholic Institute of Paris, France, Paul Vignon, made it his *magnum opus* to compile a list of all known works of art that resembled the Shroud of Turin. These works—the most well-known of which originate between the year 544 and 850 (thus predating the "fourteenth-century forgery" theory by many centuries)—included features "such as [a] forked beard, absence of a neck, straight nose, one raised eyebrow, a divided mustache, staring, owlish eyes, [and] wide nostrils."[120] Many of these "guesses" put onto canvas by devout artists are so similar to the Shroud of Turin that the paintings can, even today, be superimposed over the cloth and, once made somewhat transparent, the painted image tends to trace right over the image in the sindon cloth. And when Jesus appears in a painting with other men (apostles, rulers, etc.), He is the only one painted similar to the image of the man featured in the shroud. (These similarities between art and the Shroud are now called "Vignon Marks.")

One celebrated painting that has captured more attention than any other is the "Christ Pantocrator" of the Saint Catherine's Monastery at Mount. Sinai. The artist is unknown, and the work has been dated to the middle of the sixth century. At first glance, Christ's eyes appear to be gazing in two slightly different directions, which to a lay observer suggests that the artist—having shown immaculate precision and skill everywhere else in the painting—either flubbed that part of the picture and never fixed it, or was attempting to give Christ a flaw (such as a "lazy eye"), perhaps to further identify with His humanity. After considering other "Pantocrator" (Greek for "Lord of Hosts" or "God

Christ Pantocrator

Almighty") paintings of this era, it becomes clear that "Christ in two natures" was the flavor of these icons: On one hand, Christ always gives the benediction (the sign of the gift of blessing), and in the other, He holds a book (representing either the New Testament or one of the Gospels, depending on the artist). (This icon is still central to the Eastern Orthodox Church.) Particular to the Mount Sinai painting, however, is the "two natures" interpretation that manifests in two separate, but joined, natures. In other words, if you trace an invisible line down the center of the canvas from top to bottom and hold a mirror against the *left* side, you have Christ in gentle features: mouth relaxed, eyes slightly heavenward, both hands giving a blessing, beard and hair neatly combed against the flesh, slightly pale skin tones, solemn eyebrows...and on His neck, buried in the shadings, you have the hill and cross on which Christ was crucified as a human. If you mirror the *right* side, Christ becomes an immediate, divine force to be reckoned with: firm mouth, intense eye contact with the viewer, both hands commandingly clutching the authoritative Gospels, beard and hair flowing out a bit like a lion's mane, dramatic lines and shading in the skin, eyebrows like those of a respectable judge...and on His neck, once again buried in the shadings, Christ's spiritual form is ascending into the clouds.

Christ Pantocrator with both halves split and mirrored

What's even more unbelievable, however, is that, whether the artist intended to or not, when he chose to "split" the image and make half of Christ's face different than the other, he also happened to show how each side of the face of the man in the Shroud differentiates as a result of swelling: the right cheek is hollowed out farther than the left; the right eyebrow is arched; the neckline stops sharply at the "garment" line; the left nostril is a bit wider; a patch of hair is missing between the lower lip and the chin; there is a swollen point in the middle of the nose bridge; the hair is "stiff" (as opposed to loose or flowing); and these are only the most obvious similarities. Depending on which report we might read, there are up to seventeen nearly exact facial measurements and features between the "Christ Pantocrator" painting and the Shroud of Turin, and that's not including other parallels, which number at nearly two hundred, according to researcher and analyst Dr. Alan Whanger. In his report for Applied Optics, entitled "Polarized Image Overlay Technique: A New Image Comparison Method and Its Applications,"

Whanger made other connections, including painted creases or folds the artist featured in the same areas they show on the Shroud.[121] Could the anonymous craftsman who originated the "Pantocrator" painting have been standing near the Shroud of Turin when this classic work was created?

Yet, not all of the "proof paintings" are about comparing facial features. At times, even the anomalous details of the Shroud were brought into art, and for no evident explanation other than the artist copying what he had seen on the linen.

Christ Pantocrator with an overlay of the Shroud of Turin

Countless other works of art around the sixth century show where the artist involved an otherwise anomalous crease or line in the work that corresponds to a known flaw on the Shroud of Turin. At times, these defects are interpreted to be something related to Christ—such as when an artist turns the small "box" between the Shroud man's eyes (a flaw in the threads) into a phylactery or extra-pronounced eyebrows (like the oft-referenced Bust of Christ from the catacomb of St. Pontianus, Rome). (According to Vignon's research, this "box" between Christ's eyes shows up in some form of artistic interpretation in close to 80 percent of Byzantine icons.) And although an enormous number of paintings created at this time could only be depicting Jesus with a single lock of curly hair at the forehead, so many match the curvature of the Shroud image's "reverse-3" bloodstain identically (and in the exact same place) that it's relevant to mention the oddity here.

Two coins from 692 and 695, even from far away, inspire a viewer to do a double-take. Not only do these solid gold tresmissis and solidus coins of Byzantine Emperor Justinian II look like every stroke was fashioned after the head of the man on the Shroud (including the apparent line across the middle of the image's nose bridge and the "reverse-3" mark on the forehead), they were also the first coins in antiquity to feature the Messiah, proving not to be influenced by any other "Christ coin" up to that date. These coins, too, feature "creases" and "wrinkles" in the background design in the same places they appear on the Shroud, as well as an awkwardly interpreted point where the Messiah's neck bulges into a very high collarbone in the same shape as the Shroud man's "garment line," which was only certainly a "wrinkle" or "flaw in the weave" of the linen after more recent and higher definition negatives were created on the cloth. (At the time the coin was created, prior to the sharper images we have now, the Shroud man's "garment line" likely would have looked like a high collar bone.) Aside from these artists' interpretations of flaws in the shroud, most of these messianic features don't make artistic sense!

If the Shroud originated in the fourteenth century, then why are all these sixth-century-forward painters and coin designers including random visual "crease" and "flaw" references in precisely the same spots?

Other questions pop up as well, the longer we dig into the anomalies of this epoch: During the tumultuously fragile Byzantine Iconoclasm eras, why would any artist dare to paint Christ nude like the "Flogging of Christ" included in the ninth-century Stuttgart Psalter, folio 43v? That bold move alone allows for the possibility that the artist was getting his ideas from somewhere, and it certainly wouldn't have been from the general public at this time, since such an indecent and graphic concept would have been shocking and was nonexistent in art at that time.

As another example, consider the Hungarian Prayer Codex, consistently dated to 1192–1195 (a little more than a hundred years before the fourteenth century, from which our "forger" was dated to have created the Shroud). The "burial of Jesus" illustration is only one of five images the codex contains. It depicts Christ, just after the crucifixion, being laid down on the sindon on the upper half: He is unclothed, with "missing-thumb" hands crossing over His nakedness, and a bloodstain is painted on His forehead.

Just to point out a few odd observations so far: First, it wasn't at all common to see a "naked" Christ pictured in classic artwork. Out of respect, and not in the interest of historical accuracy, Christ was almost always shown in art wearing a loincloth, so His arms wouldn't need to be crossed to ensure His modesty. However, if the artist had set out to create a work that paralleled the image on the Shroud, a loincloth would not be featured, and Christ's arms would be crossed. Second, like on the Shroud, Christ's thumbs cannot be seen. Third, the location of the forehead bloodstain is a precise match to the deep, squiggly bloodstain on the Shroud man's face (referred to in studies as the "reverse-3" bloodstain, as it looks like a backward "3"). If much of the ancient world at that time was paying more attention to the "face" of Christ (Image of Edessa, Sudarium, etc.), could a conservative artist (who didn't want to overstress Christ's blood) choose to feature only one bloodstain, and do so in the most iconic and recognizable place?

The bottom half of the image goes even farther, showing that the outside layer of the sindon (if that's what it is) is made up of a herringbone-type weave, while the artistic interpretation shows the inside layer (where Christ would have been) covered in crosses. Though the shroud in this codex image doesn't picture Christ's likeness on the linen, one detail that continues to create questions for skeptics is a peculiar set of small holes drawn through the fibers, making the shape of the capital letter *L*. These holes are in the same location and proportion as the Shroud's famous, *L*-shaped "poker holes." (The Shroud of Turin's "poker holes" are little burn perforations in the cloth. Their cause is unknown, but one theory is that someone swung a censor (a metal sphere that dangles on a chain, often used to simmer incense for religious rituals) with hot coals over it and spilled a tiny amount, singing the fibers through several layers. Also note that many analysts believe this item in the lower half of the artwork is not a cloth at all, but a sarcophagus, though they still acknowledge the herringbone pattern and poker holes to be at least a symbolic reference to the Shroud.)

Sudarium of Oviedo: AD 570–700?

The Sudarium of Oviedo is a bloodstained cloth measuring 33 by 21 inches, currently safely housed in an ark in the Cathedral of San Salvador in Oviedo, Spain. John 20:6–7 says: "Then Simon Peter came, following [John], and went into the tomb. He saw the linen cloths [*othonion*] lying there, and the face cloth [*soudarion*], which had been on Jesus' head, not lying with the linen cloths but folded up in a place by itself." The Sudarium of Oviedo is believed to be the one and the same "face cloth" that covered Christ's head, as mentioned here in the Gospel of John, in part because the blood the fabric absorbed is consistent with crucifixion and a crown of thorns.

It's no secret that "the history of the Sudarium is very well established and there are definite references to its presence in Jerusalem in AD 570 and at the beginning of the fifth century."[122] Therefore, about the same time that artwork was changing Jesus' appearance from a baby-faced, Apollo-looking image to one that eerily matches the image depicted on the Shroud of Turin, the location and travels of the Sudarium of Oviedo was established in the ancient world. In 614, the face cloth was carted away from Jerusalem (to avoid Byzantine invasions ordered by Persian King Khosrau II) to Seville, Spain, where it remained for several years before its transition to Toledo in 657, then to the cave of Montesacro circa 718, and finally to the Oviedo chapel specifically built to house it in 812, where it remains today.

If Jesus was laid to rest with two cloths over His head (the face *soudarion* and the full-bodied *sindon*), then we could assume reasonably that the blood types and bloodstains on both cloths should match, and that the cloth would be dated to the same time in history. Straight out of the gate on this one, the first two items are old news: The blood type on both the Shroud of Turin and the Sudarium of Oviedo are human, group AB, and the complicated bilirubin and blood-protein patterns, as well as the patterns of bloodstains, on both cloths match so closely that, according to blood and chemistry expert Dr. Alan Adler, it suggests that "these two cloths were in contact with the same wounded body, presumably within the same short time period."[123] Historical dating, on the other hand, is the fascinating part.

In 2007, it was announced that radiocarbon dating has concluded the Sudarium's origin to be near AD 700.[124]

Did you catch that? The Sudarium of Oviedo, Spain, was radiocarbon dated to "AD 700," but we have a solid, definite, reliable historical record that it was in Jerusalem in AD 570, then in Seville, Spain in 614, and so on. The dating must be off by at least 130 years. There simply is no other explanation.

Additionally, if the blood type, bilirubin, proteins, and bloodstain evidence is enough to show these cloths as originating from the same victim (or Victim)—and so far, the evidence points to that conclusion—then, as Adler states in his report, "the accuracy of the 14th century date of the Shroud will be clearly doubtful."[125] In fact, the Sudarium would prove the Shroud to be at least as old as AD 570.

These facts, compiled, make the Sudarium a suitable "allusion to the Shroud prior to 1349" (which is why it is mentioned at this point in our reflections).

But wait, one might think: Why wouldn't the Sudarium also carry the image of Christ's face if He was buried with both cloths?

That is a valid question. Yet at least one source—in this case, the Bible, itself—acknowledges that the soudarion of Christ was "not lying with the linen cloths but folded up in a place by itself." Then the question becomes: Was the "face cloth" of John removed prior to the resurrection event that likely created the image on the Shroud of Turin?

Actually, not only is that possible, it's probable. Hebrew law required a bloodied face to be covered with a soudarion as soon as possible after death. However, once the body of the deceased was moved to a more proper burial cloth (such as the sindon), the soudarion was frequently removed. If we adopt this theory for these two fabrics, then the man in the Shroud of Turin was no longer covered by the Sudarium of Oviedo by the time he was laid to rest in the tomb; the face cloth would have been removed and set aside, just as the Gospel of John describes.

The Image of Edessa

The following has been called both beautiful truth and polemic myth, depending on the speaker, and we're only scratching the surface of this narrative, but this is the story that eventually leads to the next assumed travel of the Shroud of Turin. It's almost certainly a legend, but it needs to be briefly recounted to separate it from the more reliable account:

1. Close to the time of Christ's crucifixion, King Agbar V of Osroene (modern Turkey) was struck with an incurable dis-

ease. From his capital in Edessa, he sent a messenger to locate Christ and hand him a letter telling Him that the king of Edessa believed He truly was the Messiah. The message involved mention of the king's afflictions and a request for healing, but it also extended an invitation for Christ to flee from the Romans to a place of safety to avoid the then-rumored crucifixion.

2. Christ wrote a brief response to King Agbar, telling the king that He must remain where He was so that He could fulfill the purposes for which He had been sent. He went on to reassure the king that, after His death and resurrection, He would send one of His disciples to heal the king and bring life to the people of Edessa.

3. After the crucifixion, Thaddeus—one of the seventy (or seventytwo) disciples mentioned in Luke 10 and a native to Edessa—responded to the plea in earnest and brought healing to the king, as well as Christianity to the region.

4. King Agbar, now miraculously healed, endorsed the spread of Christianity. After years of successful reign, the world became alerted to the Image of Edessa, a holy relic, which was brought to the king at the time of Thaddeus' arrival.

The Image of Edessa, also known as the Mandylion, is, by tradition, only a rectangle cloth with Christ's face in the center. However, this is about the only detail the historians, scholars, and sindonologists all agree upon.

One legend has it that Thaddeus brought the burial cloth of Christ (the Shroud of Turin, believers say), after he had it folded numerous times and placed in a frame so that the only portion of the image of Christ showing outward would be His face, while the rest of the double-sided *sindon* cloth was neatly tucked underneath. (It this scene that the famous painting, "King Agbar Received the Image of Edessa," on display in Egypt at the St. Catherine's Monastary, depicts.) In this version,

King Agbar was healed by the *sindon,* not Christ's letter. Thereafter, the burial cloth was placed in a coffer away from the public at the St. Haggia Sophia Church in Edessa. (Many believers in the world at this time would have still felt bound to keep an "unclean" or "impure" burial cloth folded and stored in a container that would not defile the hands that carried it. As such, the Jewish customs of the day supported this "folding" theory. Likewise, to look lovingly upon the sindon of a dead man, *even Christ's,* would have been a divergent experience. That might explain why the cloth would have remained hidden away until much time had gone by. Nevertheless, apart from the "folding," this remains the most suspect version of the story.)

Another leading tale states that the king was healed by Christ's letter, the healing came immediately at the return of the messenger, and there is no mention of a cloth being brought to him when Thaddeus later came to Edessa. The Image of Edessa, this tale says, was hand-painted by the messenger, himself, a man who had been given the privilege of seeing Christ's face in person before he transferred his memory to a painting.

A third variation that gets enough attention to be mentioned here is that Christ, while He was alive, miraculously created an image of His face on a piece of cloth and sent that back to King Agbar with the messenger. *That,* this narrative says, became the Image of Edessa.

The letters between King Agbar and Christ were presumably copied and displayed all over many churches. It has been documented in several places that early Christians made pilgrimages to Edessa to see Christ's letter in person, and that the Edessa document differed from the one at each person's home church. (One popularly referenced pilgrimage is that of Spanish nun Egeria in AD 384, who reportedly claimed that when she was shown the letter, it was then affixed to the city gate.)

Worthy of note, however, is the relationship between these varying tales and the city's official archives.

Compelling evidence indicates that, circa AD 180–200, King Agbar VIII (three generations after King Agbar, who allegedly wrote to Jesus) felt that the story of his great-grandfather's dealings with Jesus—*and the involvement of one of His direct disciples*—needed to be embellished for the sake of Edessa's glittery reputation and to fight back a resurgence of paganism. Thus, the "Legend of Agbar," as we know it today, involving Thaddeus and the healing by cloth as told in the *Acts of Thaddeus*, is a far less reliable account than the predecessor *Doctrine of Addai* written two centuries prior. Therefore, despite all conflicting stories, if we apply the common exegetic principle that the older writings are truer than the younger, we arrive at this:

1. King Agbar send a request (probably *verbal*) to Jesus through a messenger.
2. The messenger returned not with the famed Image of Edessa or Mandylion, but with the response (again, probably *verbal*) from Christ that He could not respond in person at that time. (Because of the possibility that this communication was only delivered in spoken words, nearly anything could be written with "decorative" details and claimed to be a letter that either of these men sent. It also leaves Christ's response to the messenger entirely up to anyone's best guess. However, the sensationalism of an existing letter of Christ is erased in this account, making the whole story more plausible: A king got sick and asked Christ for healing. Christ responded how He felt was appropriate. *That* part of this issue can be accepted readily by anyone who has eyes to see the sheer number of people Christ healed in the Bible and the number of those who sought Him for healing.)
3. This exchange is entered in the city archives.
4. Somehow, sometime (presumably after the resurrection event that believers of the shroud say created its image), and by some carrier whom history cannot solidly identify, the folded shroud showing only the face of Christ was brought to Edessa for safekeeping. (This is likely because the king had extended

protection to Christ and it may have been assumed that he would offer the same protection of this holy cloth.) The description of the cloth as it's recorded (in *both* the fourth-century and sixth-century archival entries) reasonably matches the face of the man on the Shroud of Turin.

5. The holy cloth remained in Edessa for centuries, hidden when necessary for safe-keeping.

6. In 944, the cloth was sent to Constantinople. By this time, ceaseless variations to the Legend of Agbar influenced a number of other myths, including that of the Holy Grail.

Now, moving away from conjecture and continuing forward with the factual, historical details:

1. In 325, Eusebius the historian, in his glorious *Church History* work, personally attested to seeing the letters between King Agbar V and Christ as they were eventually entered into the city archives, but *did not allude to any cloth being involved.*

2. In 375, the *Doctrine of Addai* as written, alluding to the earlier claims of the story (not involving Thaddeus). Hannan, the keeper of the archives, was mentioned therein as painting a portrait of Christ's face, Himself; however, as sindonologists have reflected, this painting by Hannan was likely a work of art based on a holy cloth he had seen; therefore, it does not have to be confused with the Shroud of Turin or Image of Edessa.

3. In 384, Spanish nun Egeria wrote of her pilgrimage to see the letters of Agbar and Christ, but made no mention of any cloth resembling Christ.

Varying accounts of letters, miracles, and the rectangular Image of Edessa aside, however, it's too complicated to dismiss the idea that the Shroud of Turin made it to Edessa and stayed there for quite some time.

Centuries of documented pilgrimages and stories of iconic veneration from the sixth to thirteenth centuries allude to the notion that there was *some* kind of Christ-created cloth in that area that people were writing home about. And whereas there is no "solid proof" that the Shroud of Turin was that relic, one sixth-century testimony (quoted again in the tenth-century *Codex Vossianus Latinus* [Q69] in the Vatican Library) states that a church in Edessa had a *faciei figuram sed totius corporis figuram cernere poteris*: "a fabric upon which one can see not only a face but the body whole."[126]

Those who document the travels of the Image of Edessa also refer to several historical letters, testimonies, travel journals, and biographies wherein the Edessa relic was not just a framed face, but a complete, full-bodied sindon. The letter from Constantine VII to his troops in 958 referenced many sacred items in his palace, among which was "the *sindon* which God wore."[127] This reference was written a mere fourteen years after the Image of Edessa was delivered with enormous celebration to Constantinople in 944. If the Edessa cloth and the Shroud of Turin are one and the same, then this reference makes sense; if not, then what full-bodied sindon might this Macedonian emperor have had in his palace?

Two years after Constantine's letter, in 960, the historical liturgical record, *Synaxarion*, reflecting the work of Symeon the Metaphrast who personally witnessed the cloth upon its arrival to Constantine in 944, also refers to the Image of Edessa as a full sindon.[128]

But for the most convincing of all historical references: In 1201, while the Image of Edessa was housed in Constantinople, Nicholas Mesarites (a palace priest and keeper of the Bucolean Chapel's sacred artifacts) attested:

In this chapel Christ rises again, and the sindon with the burial linens is the clear proof…the burial shrouds of Christ: these are of linen. They are of cheap and easy to find materials, still smelling of myrrh and defying decay since they wrapped the outlineless, fragrant-with-myrrh, naked body after the Passion.[129]

Think about this for a moment.

The Shroud man has never had an outline; the edges of the image just fade into the cloth. Even if Mesarites was lying about the Shroud's whereabouts, he still described a burial cloth of Christ wherein the "naked body" was "outlineless." Why would a person in 1201 describe the Messiah of the world as having been buried "naked," when it would have been far more a presentable or believable lie to refer to a "clothed" or "loinclothed" Christ in a tomb, unless he had seen the legitimate (and shocking) Shroud of Turin for himself? Further, why would he think to include—*evidently entirely out of the blue*—a detail about Christ's body not having an outline? Unless a person has *seen* the Shroud of Turin, mentioning such a specific detail doesn't make sense. And finally, why would the keeper of the Image of Edessa be describing a full-length sindon here, unless they were one and the same cloth? (The plurality of Mesarites' account likely references the *othonion* [wrists and ankles] cloths.)

Three years after Mesarites' words, in 1204, Robert de Clari, soldier and chronicler of the Fourth Crusade, wrote that he had personally witnessed the shroud of Christ that Mesarites had made claims about, and he, too, described a linen imprinted with the entire image of Christ's body.[130] The Fourth Crusade obliterated Constantinople, and many religious icons were destroyed. Among those that survived, believers in the authenticity of the Shroud of Turin say, was the Image of Edessa: the full-bodied burial shroud of Christ, at times folded and framed—the same cloth as the Shroud. Following the fall of Constantinople, many correspondences from notable historic figures (including Epirus's ruler, Theodore Komnenos Doukas, in 1205 and Gervase of Tillbury in 1212) referred to the holy relics that were destroyed or seized, and many detailed the same sindon of Christ. Over and over in these letters (the full account of which has been more thoroughly covered in other works by sindonologists), the Shroud of Turin is referred to in ways that can't simply be explained away as mass confusion. There are too many personal eyewitnesses of the cloth using slightly different words to describe what we know today to be the Shroud of Turin. If even a fraction of these pre-1349 references to the Image of Edessa as a full-length burial cloth are reliable—*and* if we remove the more poetic (but adulterated) version of the Agbar story from the equation—then it not only suggests that the image and the Shroud are the same cloth, it *also* alludes to the idea that the image/Shroud was an established historical artifact, well known by Christian pilgrims all over this area of the world, possibly as far back as just after the resurrection.

The leading theory about where the image/Shroud went next (as supported by mounting evidence in sindonology circles) is that it was taken by prominent Crusader Othon IV de la Roche, direct ancestor of Jeanne de Vergy—Geoffroi (Geoffrey) de Charny's wife. As will be explained shortly, de Charny was the first *certain* owner of the Shroud of Turin in 1349 as acknowledged in history books, so it makes sense that the Shroud would be passed to his wife's family following its abduction in the Fourth Crusade in Constantinople, where the Image of Edessa was celebrated.

Forgery Claim Introduced in 1359

From the moment the first undisputed owners—de Charny and wife de Vergy—owned the Shroud of Turin to 1359, there wasn't any serious challenge to its authenticity.

Geoffroi de Charny was a French knight during the reign of King Jean II, as well as the celebrated author of *Livre de Chevalerie* (*The Book of Chivalry*) written circa 1350, at about the same time that he built the Lirey Church in which his family would soon display the Shroud of Turin. The "Pilgrimage Medal" designed to memorialize the Shroud's first public displaying includes a depiction of the Shroud on exhibition with the de Charny and Vergy family coat-of-arms crests in the corners. (One of these surviving medals is currently featured in the Cluny Museum of Paris.) These public presentations, however, caused a bit of a controversy, because the family was benefitting monetarily—including (allegedly) from the sales of the "Pilgrimage Medal" as souvenirs. This angered Henry de Portier, the bishop of nearby Troyes, who thereafter ordered that the de Charny family desist in the displays. Whether Portier truly believed the Shroud to be a hoax or claimed so for his own purposes (discussed below), it was through his vociferous resistance to the Shroud's authenticity that the theory of a forgery was presented in the beginning.

In 1390, Bishop Pierre d'Arcis wrote the infamous *d-Arcis Memorandum* (supposedly with the intent of alerting the pope to the forgery; but see the bottom bullet below) telling how Bishop Portier had located the artist responsible for "painting" the Shroud, therefore "proving" that it was a forgery. Since then, many skeptics refer to this account of how the original forger confessed everything as proof that we already know the artifact to be a hoax. However, there are several serious problems with this memorandum report:

- Considering the era we're dealing with (soon after the end of the Byzantine Iconoclasts, when churches were freely allowed to display *and venerate* their icons and relics), we have every common-sense reason to believe that *both* bishops might have been pulled into the battle surrounding the commercialization of pilgrimage displays. In fact, the *d'Arcis Memorandum* openly addresses this issue, though the approach is obviously a stance against holy-relic-profiteering games, as any other position on the matter would be reputational suicide to the peers of the day. But regardless of how offended either bishop may have sounded as their opposition blared off the pages of the memorandum document, their own personal bias against the Shroud as a forgery in order to redirect foot-traffic to their own local churches is an absolute possibility that *many* historians and sindonologists have already written a good deal about. A hefty chunk of the Christian world at this time in history was fighting over whose church could bring in the most attention (or money) based on what icons they were celebrating. As such, this "confession" report might have been its own hoax from the beginning.

- The "confession" took place when we couldn't prove whether the Shroud was a painting. Today, we know that is a *no* (more on this shortly). This alone should be reason enough that modern skeptics would drop the *d'Arcis Memorandum* confession as irrelevant, since the "forgery" lists an artistic method we've now ruled out; but tragically, it remains one of the heaviest arguments against the Shroud's authenticity.

- The "artist" who "painted" the Shroud in this confession is anonymous. Nobody now and nobody *then* could ever trace this "forgery" back to the guilty party. Even Bishop d'Arcis, who wrote the memorandum with the confession, never knew the forger that his predecessor, Bishop Portier, claimed to have interviewed.

- There is *zero* proof—no paper trail, no documents, no official records of any kind—that the inquest leading to the confession ever happened to begin with. Not only is he anonymous; he doesn't exist in any contemporaneous evidence suggesting he was a real person. For all we know, though d'Arcis believed Portier (or co-conspired alongside him), the confession might have been Portier's grandest lie.

- All existing copies of the original *d'Arcis Memorandum* report are undated rough drafts that have no seal or signature, as if they were a letter d'Arcis *intended* to send to the pope, but never polished a final copy. (In earlier copies, there are also personal notes written on the edges of the pages.) Much evidence exists to question whether the bishop penned the antique letters or if they were scribal compilations. Pope Clement's personal writings never mention this matter being brought to his attention, supporting the idea that the letter was at least never received (though it's more likely that it was never sent). As such, historians, scholars, sindonologists, and researchers question (translation: refute) whether the oft-referenced *d'Arcis Memorandum* should even be part of any official paper trail case against the Shroud's authenticity.

Nevertheless, when a few key people in history (including Reverend Herbert Thurston of the *Catholic Encyclopedia*) insisted that this "confession" be considered key evidence of artistic origins, the Shroud was officially doubted.

From 1359 to Today

Because the remaining history of the Shroud's chronology is a matter of undisputed fact (and that information can be found just about anywhere), we will conclude this section of our study briefly.

From the first forgery claim to the year 1452, the Shroud remained in the de Charny family line, stationed in the Chapel of Lirey, until it was traded to the Duchess of Savoy for real estate in France. It remained in the Chapel of the Saints in Chambéry, Eastern France, until 1471, when it was moved repeatedly throughout Northern Italy, coming back to settle in Chambéry in 1502 in the Royal Chapel of Chambéry Castle.

After being fitted in an elaborate, expensive, solid silver reliquary, in 1532, a fire broke out in the chapel and melted the casing. Molten silver fell on the Shroud and damaged its folded edges, creating the large, mirrored, triangular holes once unfolded. Two years later, nuns from the Order of Saint Clare (popularly known as "Poor Clare Nuns") patched the Shroud with fresh linen and stitching, and then affixed it to the Holland backing cloth.

The Shroud was moved around on another loop of travel until it landed in its current location in Turin, Italy, in 1578. In 1946, the rule of the House of Savoy came to a close, and the cloth became property of the Holy See in 1983, a short five years before the cloth was subjected to radiocarbon dating.

Pollens: Testimony of a Silent Witness

The famous Dr. Max Frei has a long list of accolades related to his accomplishments in criminology. Some of his cases might have remained unsolved forever had he not used his genius to reveal what the world of botany proved about a person's whereabouts. Sometimes, all it takes is a speck of pollen to link a perpetrator to a crime scene, and that fact is taken much more seriously in the justice system today because of the work of Dr. Frie. As the University of Zurich professor of criminology as well as the founder of the Zurich Police Scientific Laboratory, Frie has used his doctorate in botany and his celebrated expertise in the pollens of the Mediterranean world to make a few interesting observations about the Shroud.

Fifty-seven species of pollen were identified on the surface of the linen between Frei's extraction pursuits. Of those, only seventeen could have come from Italy or France. Almost every other of the remaining forty were from the Jerusalem area, including a group of pollens originating from the Paliurus spina-christi mill, or the "Syrian Christ Thorn" plant (probably the plant from which Christ's crown of thorns was crudely fashioned).

Some say the wind blew these pollens to Europe while the Shroud was on display there, but that is not feasible, because the Shroud was only displayed out in the open a few times. The winds would have to be so gusty and mighty—specifically on those "Shroud display" days, and specifically during those pollination seasons—that it would bring a wealth of almost forty species of Jerusalem-area pollens over 1,040 miles to land on the linen and overpower the seventeen European pollens that were "there first."

Although a few have questioned whether certain of Frei's pollens could have been subjected to a deeper level of microscopy, it appears to be clear that the Shroud spent a significant amount of time exposed to the air around Jerusalem.

From the criminology expert who can convince a jury where a suspect has been based on the pollens in the fibers of his or her clothes, the Shroud has made a journey through Constantinople, Turkey, the Negev Desert, and the Dead Sea.

The Perpetual Dating Debate

To anyone who has looked into the Shroud of Turin for longer than three and a half minutes, the raging battle surrounding the linen's radiocarbon dating will have already surfaced. It's no secret that the material was tested and found by scientists to be too recent an artifact to possibly be the authentic burial cloth of Christ. It's likewise no secret that the methods applied by the team that dated the cloth have been questioned by reputable experts in science and sindonology over and over again, since the day they released their findings to the public.

As a discredit to both sides of the argument—believers versus skeptics—vitriolic comments have been exchanged that amount to little more than immature mud-flinging, which makes each side hard to take seriously: Believers in the authenticity of the cloth make snide remarks about how the scientific community is unintelligent or silly for buying into this whole "radiocarbon dating" idea when it's clear that the whole process has been historically unreliable. Too often, these jabs originate from clergy or religious people who don't have an ounce of training in these systematic methods, attacking the principles of science and insinuating (or directly declaring) that the dating was born from a conspiracy against faith and religion. Scientists and skeptics (*especially* those personally involved with the dating of the Shroud) have encouraged believers to let go of their vice grip on faith in the authenticity of the Shroud, since fact and scientific method have irrefutably won the day over fantasy. (Teddy Hall, scientist on the carbon-dating panel and director of Oxford's Research Laboratory for Archaeology and the History of Art, famously gave the following intellectual-pomposity slap to the faithful just after the public announcement of the Shroud's dating: "We have shown the Shroud to be a fake. Anyone who disagrees with us ought to belong to the Flat Earth Society."[131] His comment only made the science team look unprofessional; it also served as backfire-fuel to believers, who thereafter resisted the carbon-dating results with more determination.)

Most important to remember when reflecting upon the battle surrounding the radiocarbon dating of the Shroud are the following:

1. The scientists who performed the dating tests were intelligent researchers, whom we cannot assume were dedicated to anything less than providing the world with answers it sought. Their methods were transparent and well-documented, and they approached the task from the most advanced available sciences at the time. If they did have a hidden, conspiratorial agenda, it's not anything that can be irrefutably proven based on their findings; until one comes forward with a confession of dubious intentions that reflect the character and integrity of *all* the scientists on that assignment collectively, we shouldn't accuse such a thing.

2. The believers who refuse to accept the dating are inclined to do so for great reasons: The sample used in this testing wasn't likely taken from the original sindon cloth that would have been laid in the tomb (more on this shortly); there is significant evidence that the Shroud existed in its current form well before the date given by scientists; we cannot explain or reproduce the Shroud—every scientific attempt to do so "using state-of-the-art instrumentation and techniques" has been what many experts refer to as a "dismal failure"[132]—so it's a challenge to accept the voice of science as a final word on the dating as well. And so the list grows…

This ongoing rivalry has, as even the smallest amount of research on the Shroud will show, become so hostile that it's nearly impossible for a book like this to be written without someone out there assuming that we, too, are setting out to make one side or the other look foolish. Please understand: These authors have *no intention* of jumping in on the doling out of insults. For too long, that war has produced animosity for no apparent reason other than to magnify the fallen nature of humanity's pettiness and expose just how much more we need God's grace.

That's why we chose to start with what the image on the cloth had to say for itself *before* we addressed the dating debate (backwards in order compared with the approach of many other works like this). On our end, the evidence stacked against a potential forgery—based solely on the unlikeliness of that scenario, as discussed—was so dense that it naturally drew the dating into question, not the other way around. To say this another way: We are open to the idea that the dating process was flawed because the forgery theory appears to be so, *not* because any of us wanted so much to believe in the artifact's authenticity that we would trade the integrity of truth for that age-old, blissful feeling that cohabitates with willful ignorance.

With this firm disclaimer aside, let's move on to the curious dating debate.

Questions of Accuracy

The carbon-14 dating of the Shroud was tested by three separate laboratories, each having been supplied with a small section of the cloth. The results of the tests were announced to the public on October 13, 1988. Scientists agreed that the Turin fabric was as young as "AD 1260–1390 with at least 95% confidence."[133]

To this point, the only evidence from science and history that had been compiled was immensely in support of the Shroud's authenticity. That's not to say that everyone was a believer; it is to say that the mysteries spoke for themselves about this unreproducible and miraculous sindon, and we never had hard evidence to say it was anything less than believers claimed it to be. (That is, of course, setting aside the contribution of a confession that probably never happened from an artist who probably never existed in the d'Arcis Memorandum.) The world was shocked. Christians and sindonologists all over the globe engaged in a lengthy, corporate pause. If the cloth was a forgery, the way almost every newspaper was claiming in an enormous and overwhelming media barrage, then it didn't make sense to keep trying to prove it was real. On the other hand, most science was still in favor of authenticity, so many sindonologists agreed that something was odd about the carbon dating.

Despite the massive onslaught of discouraging and bewildering "hoax" claims that exploded overnight from every angle, almost all of the leading experts who had been examining the cloth before the dating announcement kept right on working as if nothing had changed. It wasn't because they wanted so much to believe in a religious relic or that they hung their faith on the Shroud to begin with. To them, believing a cloth that had been validated by science as the Shroud of Turin to be a fake required more faith than simply believing it was a miracle. Therefore, they all agreed it was time to take a deep breath and reevaluate the situation.

After reviewing all the data that had been collected up to this point, as well as conducting fresh tests—just to make sure there wasn't crucial oversight by an overzealous expert somewhere in the past—sindonologists produced updated documentation showing that yesterday's findings were as relevant as they'd always been, and that the foundation of data they'd always stood on was solid. Their focus was then turned toward investigating the radiocarbon dating.

The Science Isn't Perfect...and It Isn't a Secret

At first, the hypotheses the sindonologists put forth were related to the usual truths about radiocarbon dating: As Dr. Zugibe also recognized, this science, although often reliable, has been wrong "by hundreds or even thousands of years" many times in the past.[134] Countless other experts have repeatedly acknowledged this in recent history. Major media outlets like the *New York Times* have historically noted this openly and frequently, even before the "fake news phenomenon," like this article from 1990 entitled "Errors Are Feared in Carbon Dating":

> New research shows…that some estimates based on carbon may have erred by thousands of years.…
>
> Scientists…reported today in the British journal *Nature* that some estimates of age based on carbon analyses were wrong by as much as 3,500 years.…
>
> But scientists have long recognized that carbon dating is subject to error because of a variety of factors, including contamination by outside sources of carbon.[135]

If the Shroud had ever been contaminated by coming into contact with another human's bare hands—like it repeatedly was when it was brought out and venerated in the earlier days, or again when it was continuously and meticulously handled when it was restored and attached to the Holland cloth—then contamination of outside carbon would be a concern for those who oversaw the dating. If the Shroud had ever come into contact with any other foreign fibers—like it was when other artists' reproductions were laid face-to-face with it to absorb a blessing, etc.—then younger carbon would have been introduced to the surface, possibly causing inaccurate results. Because we know the Shroud *has been frequently subjected to contamination since the beginning*, then we must, if we're honest, allow for a high probability that the final-word carbon on the Shroud has been compromised.

Most experts, when explaining the statistical reliability of radiocarbon dating, allow for the following equation when considering the age of an item: If the majority of the data compiled on a certain object disagrees with carbon dating, then the results of the carbon dating are considered faulty, *not the other way around.*

Here's an example of this concept: As of right now, archaeological sciences and the historical record have long since proved the existence of the Egyptian Queen Nefertiti. We know about her life and relationships. She was wife to Pharaoh Akhenaten (previously Amenhotep IV), who was the radical and heretical ruler just before his well-known son, King Tutankhamun, took the throne. We have discovered artwork in Nefertiti's likeness—including the iconic "Bust of Nefertiti" currently housed in a museum in Berlin—giving us a glimpse of what she looked like. Thanks to the tireless work of expert linguists who studied the vast hieroglyphs that spoke of her, we know that "Nefertiti" means "the beauty has come," and that she had more than ten other titles during her reign. We even know that she, alongside her husband, was a bold, controversial ruler for her monotheistic worship of only the Aten (sun god).

The point: There is *much* we know about Nefertiti. All the data that we have about her points to her being alive around 1370–1330 BC. However, despite all we *do* know, we've still never found her body or identified any place that may have been her designated resting crypt.[136]

With that in mind, let's say for a moment that a group of archeologists' stumble upon an Egyptian tomb a year from now. The tomb is one they've never seen before, but it's one with very clear marks identifying it as the crypt of Nefertiti. Gorgeous curtains are hanging around the queen's heavy casket in the center; otherwise, the tomb is empty. One compromised and crudely replastered wall suggests that, at some point in recent history, tomb raiders have helped themselves to every other treasure in the room, and the remaining curtains look disturbed, handled, and repositioned—as if the raiders' initial intentions were to take them as well, before an unknown change of plans left those items abandoned. With great care, the archeologists eventually pry open the casket to discover that the body inside also remains, and indicates no signs of disturbance.

Later on, through DNA testing of the mummified remains, Nefertiti's identity is further confirmed. A swatch of ornate burial linen found inside the casket is subjected to radiocarbon dating, and the result links the linen to approximately 1400–1300 BC.

Because everything known about Nefertiti corroborates this timeline, then the date supports what is already known. It serves merely as a final confirmation of a conclusion that the rest of science and history had already determined to be true.

Upon closer examination, the linen inside the casket of Nefertiti exactly matches the weave style, the materials used, the pollens embedded in the fibers, and the colors, etc., to the curtains hanging around her resting place. Through much microscopic and microchemical analyses by the best in the industry, it is determined that the curtains and the casket linen were weaved on the same loom by the same craftsman. Further, the testing indicates that the curtains and the casket linen came into contact with the same atmospheric substances and originated sometime during Nefertiti's reign. Yet, a few weeks later, radiocarbon dating results come back on the curtains. They are, according to science's most advanced dating methods, a thousand years younger than the other sample from the casket.

Because everything known about the curtains lines up with all other dating data not related to radiocarbon results, then the carbon dating of the curtains is considered flawed or suspect, and is therefore dismissed. The carbon dating does not "prove the curtains young," and it does not "prove the curtains to be a planted forgery." Much to the contrary, the accumulated facts and data about the curtains on their own "proved the dating wrong."

Finding such a contrast to be thought-provoking, indeed, archeologists and scientists go back to the drawing board in an attempt to explain. They come up with many theories and hypotheses, and eventually connect the dots: Tomb raiders had repeatedly handled the curtains that they likely deemed to be less valuable as they plundered the rest of the treasure. As they turned the curtains about, they contaminated them with younger carbon, producing invalid results. Another set of samples of the curtains—taken at the ceiling where the cloth appeared to be untouched—was tested again; this time, the tests show the curtains to be the same age as the casket linen sample.

Do you see the approach of the men described in this illustration? The radiocarbon dating was *never* the golden standard to which all other data must bow.

Applying this logic to the Shroud of Turin, we shouldn't assume that one single cut-and-test of the linen is the golden standard when we have so much evidence (scientifically and historically) that the *sindon is much older* than AD 1260–1390. Scientific method stands behind radiocarbon dating—and even believers of the authenticity of the Shroud should be willing to acknowledge the accuracy of this tool from an unbiased position!—but the very definition of scientific method also, in this case, demands that the results be considered as a *possibility*, and *not as an absolute*, until more data can be compiled. Archeologists are actually quite bewildered at how seriously this single radiocarbon dating test in 1988 has been taken by the world.

As one example, Dr. William Meacham—a celebrated archeologist known for his vast experience in carbon dating ancient artifacts—had an opinion to share concerning the Shroud of Turin. He, too, believes that the world too eagerly established a *possibility* as an "absolute," and he quotes from several reliable sources to make his point:

I doubt that anyone with significant experience in the dating of excavated samples would dismiss for one moment the potential danger of contamination and other sources of error. No responsible field archaeologist would trust a single date, or a series of dates on a single feature, to settle a major historical issue, establish a site or cultural chronology, etc. No responsible radiocarbon scientist would claim that it was certain that all contaminants had been removed and that the dating range produced for a sample was without doubt its actual calendar age. The public and many non-specialist academics do seem to share the misconception that C-14 dates are absolute.

Even the most elementary textbooks of archaeology and geology give a very different picture. "Contamination of samples may cause error in determination of reliable dates" (Heizer and Graham 1967: 165); "contamination of the sample may take place…and removal of the contaminant from the pores spaces and fissures is almost impossible" (Goude 1977:10). "Carbon from other sources may easily be trapped in porous materials…" (Stuckenrath 1965:279). Excavated samples are "liable to absorb humic matter from the solutions that pass through them (resulting in) contamination by carbon compounds of an age younger than its own…there is also the possibility of exchange of carbon isotopes under such conditions… That there are other risks of contamination and other pitfalls involved in this method is obvious enough" (Zeuner 1970:341–6).[137]

Meacham goes on to say that one of these scientists (Stuckenrath) even pretreated some samples to remove carbon contamination before dating a few specimens from an ancient home found in Alaska. Oddly, the support beams that made up the structure of the house and the charcoals in the fireplaces differed by a thousand years.[138]

Radiocarbon dating science is reliable to the extent that it supports what we already know about an artifact. Scientific integrity and transparency depend on us continuing to acknowledge that across the board… and yes, that standard prevails even when we're dealing with an artifact drawn into such provocative debate as the Shroud of Turin.

Questionable Methods

Sindonologists also understood that much of dating accuracy boils down to the method carried out in each case.

The original radiocarbon dating orders for the Shroud included the proportional gas counter method and the accelerator mass spectrometry method. The tests were to be conducted in seven laboratories; samples were to be taken from several places on the Shroud; and the carbon testing was to be done while following "blind-study" protocol. (This means that samples of other non-Shroud linens were to be included so that the carbon-dating laboratories didn't know the Shroud from the others, so the report would be honest.)

In the end, Turin authorities panicked and switched the plan to involve less handling of the sacred cloth. This ended up eliminating the more reliable, proportional gas counter method, and sticking only with the faster (but more questionable) accelerator mass spectrometry method, hailing from only three labs (instead of seven) when all was said and done. Now cornered into taking only one cut of the Shroud, the scientists agreed to take a sample from the same spot that Professor Gilbert Raes had clipped in 1973 for deeper examination (the very edge of the cloth, most vulnerable to carbon contamination). Blind-study protocol was not followed, as spokespersons from the dating labs were present when the samples were collected. So, by the time the linen cuts landed at the labs for testing, the scientists knew which labeled cuts were from what cloths.

After the tests were complete, the results were announced right away, without giving any time for peer review. Scientific integrity is compromised when data is announced as fact without allowing for peer review and when the regulations of a "blind study" are ignored.

You can understand why some passionate Shroud-believers want to claim "conspiracy" on the dating, just because of how many rules were broken in a rush.

Another incredible story surfaced in 1991 proving that the opposite bungling (newly created materials dated as antique) can occur when rushed methods are applied. A contemporary artist by the name of Joan Aherns painted Indian rocks from crushed wheat during an art class sometime in the 1970s. Her paintings were stolen, swept away to South African jungles, and were found eleven years later hidden in the bushes. Oxford University—often considered an authority in scientific affairs—submitted the paintings to their radiocarbon accelerator unit (the less reliable method discussed above), and confirmed that the paintings were 1,200 years old. For a brief stint, the museum in Natal, South Africa, celebrated these paintings as originating from an African bushman and placed them on display. Later, when the "artifacts" were credited to the original source (artist Joan Aherns in the '70s), no explanation could be found for why the wheat-based paint would have dated to such antiquity.[139]

But frankly, believers of the Shroud's authenticity don't have to rely on conspiracy. The dating on the cloth could be accurate or not, and it wouldn't make a hill-of-beans' worth of difference if the cloth they tested wasn't even a part of the Shroud.

…And it probably wasn't.

Raes' and Riggi's Compromised Edge

As mentioned earlier, Professor Gilbert Raes took a cut from the edge of the Shroud in 1973. In 2000, at the Sindone Worldwide Congress (Orvieto, Italy), new research was announced to the public: Sixteenth-century patchwork had been applied to that edge. Therefore, the sample cut for the 1988 dating and further divided for the three labs, experts acknowledged, was far more vulnerable to younger dating than just the typical carbon contaminations.

The report, compiled by sindonologists Joe Marino and Sue Benford, showed that, in addition to known maintenance patchwork (such as that done by the Poor Clare Nuns), "extraneous material was skillfully spliced into the…original Shroud" by unknown hands along Raes' edge.[140] Enzo Delorenzi of the Turin Commission acknowledged as far back as 1976 that "more pairs of hands have carried out the darning than is suggested in the historical records."[141]

As far as whether these "darning" sections could have overlapped the 1988 sample, even Giovanni Riggi—the man responsible for that year's cutting—acknowledged that the eight square centimeters he had been given permission to extract were "reduced to about 7 cm because fibres of other origins had become mixed up with the original fabric" in the same area he cut from.[142] Later, when Oxford University analyzed the linen piece, Professor Edward Hall of that lab stated that the fibers showed foreign interference; about this same time, a lab in Derbyshire concluded that the extraneous material was not flax linen like the Shroud, but a yellow cotton perhaps "used for repairs" historically.[143] Dr. Adler, whose chemistry work on the blood proteins has been paramount, also stated that the infamous Raes' edge had "obviously been repaired," the proof of which was in the sections of missing cloth, distinct discoloration on opposing sides of Riggi's cut, and in the differentiating patterns of chemical composition between Riggi's cut and the non-body-image area of the Shroud.[144]

However, there is one telltale sign that Raes' and Riggi's extraction was from a piece of cloth that had been attached to the Shroud during a more recent restoration: There is a clear and present seam where the non-body-image bulk of the Shroud linen adjoins to this other fabric. Multiple textile experts—all of whom were operating from a properly conducted "blind study" (they didn't know they were looking at pictures of the Shroud of Turin!)—weighed in on this seam. Each made educated observations about the otherwise inexplicable differences on either side, including, but not limited to: the thickness of the thread being more pronounced on one side than the other, and a thick/thin, thick/thin patterned weave on one side while the other side was consistent. Collectively, the conclusion from all textile experts was that the seam did, in fact, join two completely different pieces of cloth using a sophisticated, S-directional hand stitch on an overlap repair method commonly used when one lot of yarn ran out and another was added to continue the weave.[145] This, scientists have since said, would certainly account for why the Shroud extraction weighed twice what it should have.

The cut Raes and Riggi took went just past the seam and followed lengthwise along the other material, capturing a thin strip of the original linen as well as a thick width of younger fabric. When Riggi collected his sample in 1988, the last centimeter of the eight was discarded because he deemed it contaminated. Later, despite Riggi's reassurance that none of that pesky "other origins" cloth was involved in the samples he sent the participating labs, strange blue satin and red silk fibers were inexplicably present, entirely inconsistent from known and studied Shroud fibers.

However, though mounting evidence backed this new report by Marino and Benford, some skeptics understandably found it hard to believe that the dating crew of 1988 would have made such an oversight. Celebrated chemist, University of California Los Alamo National Laboratory Fellow, and charter member for the Coalition for Excellence in Science Education, Ray Rogers, wasn't buying it at all, so he got his hands on both the 1973 Raes sample and a portion of the 1988 Riggi sample and set to work examining it against other non-body-image areas of the Shroud to disprove what he thought was mere conjecture. Microchemical/microscopic testing and analysis showed that the fabric: 1) had cotton fibers (which the Shroud does not); 2) had been dyed with alizarin and purpurin extracted from madder plant roots (a dying process that we have zero evidence existed prior to sixteenth-century France or England); 3) had been glazed in a gum medium (to act as a repair glue); and 4) contained no proteins—all of which is in absolute contradiction to the Shroud—he recruited Anna Arnoldi of the University of Milan to conduct her own tests.

The most significant find of all from both scientists came when they discovered the presence of vanillin, a polymer of lignin, which is found in the cell walls of plants. Because vanillin fades away over time, it can only be present in more recent linen, and therefore the Raes/Riggi area can't possibly date back to the earliest verified appearance of the Shroud circa 1349.

After these findings, both skeptics, Rogers and Arnoldi, became believers and confirmed that the samples taken by Raes and Riggi could not possibly be the same linen as the Shroud.[146]

As other experts caught word of Rogers' and Arnoldi's conclusions, further ultraviolet photography and spectral analyses were conducted, revealing that the sample area would not fluoresce, demonstrating an intense contrast in chemical composition from the rest of the Shroud.

This research alone proves the radiocarbon dating sample to be invalid.

Duchess of Savoy's Cut

Back in 1531, the linen had been cut when the Duchess of Savoy stipulated in her last will and testament that a strip of the holy cloth would be left behind for her home church. Upon her death in early 1531, her wishes were carried out, leaving a section of the cloth susceptible to unraveling. Thus, before the Royal Chapel of Chambéry fire in 1532, there would likely have been a reparation of the duchess-ordered cut. But, because the Poor Clare Nuns' Holland backing cloth didn't exist yet, this stitching would have to be more "sophisticated"[147] in order to prevent fraying, so every thread would have been intricately analyzed and repaired along the herringbone weave line, befitting medieval "starching" methods of fabric repair at the time. (Oh, and by the way, the Raes' edge had tested positive for starch content in 1982, consistent with this deduction.) The post-fire reparation in 1534 would have backed the entire Shroud against the Holland cloth, further blending the nearly invisible 1531 splice into obscurity.

So, what were the "fibres of other origins [that] had become mixed up with the original fabric" that Riggi recognized when he made the 1988 cut? Most likely, experts say, Riggi had flip-flopped "other origins" from what was "original." Put simply: The remaining seven centimeters he kept (those later involved in the C-14 radiocarbon dating) were from a reparation to the duchess-ordered cut in 1531, and the foreign (or "other") fabric that he discarded were from the original Shroud…and therefore, possibly, from the authentic burial cloth of Christ!

(Those fibers that were thrown away… Where did they come from, and why would they be considered inconsequential? The fact that foreign fibers suddenly mixed with the collected sample shouldn't equal irrelevance. It's quite the opposite in a fabric-dating process! That quick changeover Riggi saw from one "other origins" cloth to "original" means everything in an experiment like this. It doesn't take a scientist to see that an unexpectedly anomalous material threaded into a retrieved sample mandates a serious pause-and-reflect, even if it meant that Turin authorities panicked again and delayed the radiocarbon dating. Although these authors aren't fans of assuming the dating team was masterminding a conspiracy, this particular "throw it away" move they pulled certainly does appear questionable…but we digress.)

Even with the naked eye, when viewing photos of the sample Riggi collected, there is a detectable change of color leading into the one centimeter that was discarded. Those responsible for the reparation of the duchess cut matched the shade precisely with the madder-root dye at the time of the initial reparation. The now-observable discoloration is likely due to heat exposure during the fire, which would have accelerated the aging of this foreign cotton at a different rate from the rest of the cloth.

Concluding Thought Regarding the Dating Debate

And now for the dagger-point to all of this data: Scientist Ronald Hatfield of the world's largest radiocarbon dating service, Beta Analytic, stated that if a thin portion of a two thousand-year-old cloth was spliced to another from around AD 1500 and tested altogether (with the newer material making up the larger mass portion of around a 60/40 ratio), the C-14 age result would be—drumroll please—approximately AD 1210! "This correlates very closely with the Oxford mean date of AD 1200 as reported in Nature,"[148] the study states. But this math also brings us far closer to the 1988 dating results, showing that these labs likely did conduct a radiocarbon dating test on two separate pieces of cloth connected by seam; the younger cloth was probably from a reparation on the 1531 duchess cut and the older cloth was quite possibly right at two thousand years old, which was, of course, the time of Christ.

Therefore, despite all the arguments on both sides for or against the reliability of radiocarbon dating, the results of the 1988 tests may well have been spot-on.

...If only someone could hire them to test the actual Shroud. Wouldn't that be cool...?

What Does It All Mean?

Over and over in this study on the Shroud of Turin, the point has been made: We simply cannot—with the greatest of archeological, anthropological, and scientific studies, equipment, instruments, and minds—account for how this mysterious artifact came to be. We can land a man on the moon across space, but we can't explain this linen. We can biologically integrate humans with machines, literally making the deaf hear, the lame walk, and the blind see...but we can't provide a solitary rationale to explain an image on fabric.

It would be one thing if the image was of a tree, house, landscape, or dog. That might still fascinate, but it wouldn't cause the level of stir that a deceased and possibly resurrected man meticulously matching the description of the Savior of the world has caused. It has become the picture that just won't go away. It is so many things to so many people—but one thing it cannot be is *insignificant*. Although many don't believe the Shroud of Turin is Christ's authentic burial cloth, they can't give any more answers for what it is than the best scientists ever have.

Some theories have suggested that the Shroud is evil—some kind of plant by the enemy in ancient times to bolster the Antichrist's claims of divinity as he rises to rule. Although we can't dismiss that idea with anything more than solid faith (science can't prove that theory incorrect, obviously), neither can we prove it true, so it remains yet another layer of speculation. Other "fringe" theories relate to the cloth being of extra-terrestrial origins; and these, too, can't be proven, so they add another layer…

These authors—though we do *not* hang our entire faith on what the Shroud may someday prove to be—find it interesting how quickly the world will find *any explanation under the sun* except the most obvious, just to avoid admitting that maybe, just maybe, we actually do have our hands on "the" holy sindon of the Son. Honestly, if science proved tomorrow that the Shroud was some sophisticated work of art or a forgery, our belief in Jesus as the Man who came to accomplish exactly what Scripture says would not falter. None of us believes in Jesus *because of* the Shroud.

But one thing needs to be said: Most often, alternative origin theories about the Shroud (alien, Antichrist, forgery, "natural" origins, etc.) take far more faith to believe than just believing the cloth is what it represents itself to be.

And if it *is* the authentic burial cloth of Christ, then it *does* tell the story of a Man who died for the sake of the world…and quite possibly the story of a Man who left behind proof of His deity and likeness in a photo-finish artifact that we couldn't ever—and maybe weren't ever supposed to—decode.

chapter three

Ancient Influences

Now that we have looked at the most famous piece of potential evidence of a true, physical resurrection from someone who made it past the point of physical death and returned to tell us about it, we might ask ourselves, what did He say about the afterlife? Surely, He would know better than anyone else? Did He give us some information about what we're all in for?

In fact, He did. But before we can delve into the teachings of Christ regarding the afterlife, we need to understand the stark contrast between His teachings and the backdrop of the ancient world, and the cultural influences affecting the setting into which He was born. After that, we'll be able to more deeply understand the truly wonderful and terribly horrifying things Jesus taught us about Heaven and Hell.

Of course, it's impossible to launch into an exhaustive study of all the religions of the ancient world, even if we only focus on afterlife beliefs. Therefore, for this chapter, we've selected a few of the most influential ones to give you an understanding of the ancient world. After you have a look at what the rest of the world's population believed, you'll gain deeper insight on and appreciation of how unique Christianity (and Judaism before that) truly is.

For some people, there is confusion regarding terms like "Hades," "Sheol," and even "Gehenna" as they appear in the Bible. Do these locations represent the same place, or do they refer to different places? If they are the same, why so many different terms—why not just use the same word? Furthermore, some of the terms can be perplexing, referring to more than one person, place, or thing. Beyond the confusion regarding the interchangeability of these terms is the context in which each appears within its own cultural usage.

For example, in Greek mythology, the term "Hades" represents multiple ideas: First, it denotes an actual being—"the son of Titans Cronus and Rhea…[and] god of the underworld."[149] Second, the term refers not to a person, but to a *location*—the afterworld, which, according to Greek mythology, is where all deceased souls go and which is divided into three regions: one of reward, one of neutrality, and one of punishment. Third, there is the modern, superficial concept of Hades, which can vary, depending on a person's religious views, but for which the word "Hell" could easily be interchanged.

In order, then, to adequately grasp the meaning of each of these terms, the pages that follow include a chronology of the cultures that influenced the usage of each one, introducing the phrases as context presents opportunity. However, before proceeding, we must consider yet another element: how—and why, for that matter—each of the biblical writers would have referred to these terms in the first place, understanding that many (such as "Hades") stem from non-Christian religions. The issue isn't that the word held only Christian association; rather, in each case, the term would have been the one that local culture of that day would have recognized and related to. In other words, the essence of the truth being conveyed to the culture at that time is more important than the origin of the terminology. Just as our example of the term "Hades" shows, those who wrote to the surrounding culture regarding this place did so understanding that the audience would know the meaning of the location.

The fact that some ancient (and modern) religions parallel Christianity in several ways shouldn't intimidate us, although we always need to identify the *authentic* source of truth as the Bible. After all, it's possible to use nothing but logic, reason, and observation of the world to conclude that an all-powerful God must exist. In fact, according to Romans 1:20, people are without excuse for not knowing there is a God, because physical creation displays His invisible attributes.[150] This obviously doesn't mean that people who have never heard the gospel or anything from the Bible will achieve perfect doctrine and theology by merely looking at the world around them. If that were the case, there would never have been a need for Jesus' followers to spread Christianity throughout the ancient world. All it means is that a person can get some of the basics correct (such as, yes, there is an afterlife), yet to understand the details of those basics (such as Jesus is the only way to Heaven), a person needs to hear or read it from the Christian perspective, which requires the Bible and/or someone teaching from the Bible. With this in mind, we should *expect* other religions to get certain matters correct, meaning that we never need to be threatened by this fact. Instead, we should continue to hold up the Bible as the only reliable source of accurate information relating to spirituality, salvation, and the afterlife.

Too often, present-day readers forget that, although the Bible is the inspired Word of God, the human writers of Scripture were still influenced by their cultural surroundings. It is easy to misinterpret the meaning of the Bible based on where and when literal application is used. For example, certain passages are meant to be taken literally—for example: "Thou shalt not steal" (Exodus 20:15). Other verses, however, are of a narrative nature, designed to convey *an idea* (often regarding moral conduct or integrity), thus must be interpreted by *their essence*, not *their literal language.*

One instance of this occurs in Ezekiel 11:19, when the Lord says, "I will take the stony heart out of their flesh, and will give them an heart of flesh." He is not *literally* saying that some human beings have rocks in their chests and will receive a heart transplant, being given the flesh version of the same organ. Rather, the Lord is outlining a change—a softening, rather—of the thought process of His people toward Himself. Ben Witherington clarifies an important distinction regarding some of the poetic passages found in the Bible:

> The Bible talks frequently about the human heart as if it were the control center of the human personality—the center of thoughts, feelings, and will. So, for example, we hear a prayer "cleanse the thoughts of my heart." From a scientific point of view [this is inaccurate], hearts do not have thoughts—brains do. A heart is simply a blood pump.[151]

The same author later adds:

> Let me be clear that I am not saying that the Bible teaches us wrongly about such subjects. I am simply saying it doesn't intend to teach us anything [anatomically] about such subjects. We have ancient persons speaking in normal colloquial ways, common in their day and in their universe of discourse.[152]

Essentially, despite language and cultural barriers that span the centuries, Bible authors *intended to teach*: (1) history as it pertains specifically to salvation, (2) theology specific to God and His relationship with mankind, and (3) ethical Christian behavior.[153]

Author Carl Gibbs further elaborates on the cultural barriers faced by modern Bible readers:

> Living in such a vastly different historical and cultural setting from that of the Bible authors is one of the great handicaps the modern-day Bible student must overcome.... The truth communicated in the Bible is distorted if we do not understand the

culture of the writer and the historical events that are the backdrop to his message. Beyond this, we come to the Bible with the biases of our own backgrounds and culture.... Since God did not remove the Bible writers from their historical and cultural circumstances, we can assume that the interpreter must reduce the "distortion" with a careful study of the times and culture of the Bible writer.[154]

Bearing in mind the cultural influences upon the Old Testament era will help us have a balanced perspective on pagan terms as they're used in the Bible.

Ancient Israel

Father Abraham had many sons. Many sons had Father Abraham...

Many people remember singing this song in church as a child. Before it's over, most participants are standing, swinging both arms, nodding their head, and lifting each foot alternately until they "turn around, [and] sit down!" But many are surprised when they read details of the culture that Abraham, this great father of faith, emerged from. Many claim that before his name was changed to Abraham, Abram came from an idol-worshiping, pagan culture. However, this statement is technically inaccurate, since during his time, the term "pagan" referred to the rural demographic of an individual, and it wasn't until later (during the Roman reign) that the context of the word was moderated to designate those who worshiped a god other than the Christian God.[155]

Many people claim that in the early chapters of his life, Abram was an idolater. However, we're not completely sure of this. Abram's *father* is mentioned as having been such in Joshua 24:2: "Your fathers dwelt on the other side of the flood in old time, even Terah, the father of Abraham, and the father of Nachor: and they served other gods." The following verse (Joshua 24:3) also states that the Lord brought Abraham "from the other side of the flood...led him throughout all the land of Canaan...multiplied his seed, and gave him Isaac." The Bible is unclear on when the conversion from other gods to the One True God came, or through which man (Terah/Abram) it originally came. Regardless, these individuals had been exposed to, by modern terms, a pagan society with a belief structure that was not built upon the principles of godly faith.

Abraham was exposed to this nation's moral code, spiritual concepts, and even their views of afterlife. Genesis 11:31 establishes that Abram's father, Terah, took his family to Ur of Chaldees. During the years preceding, a drought and famine had caused many to migrate into the Mesopotamian cities for survival. Thus, the culture of these towns became of significant influence to all people therein via the ripple effect. The ancient Mesopotamian way of life was so influential that it affected the belief system of the surrounding geographical area even after the city was conquered by invaders. Ur of Chaldees was progressive and advanced, having such sophisticated features as waterways and "drains, indoor plumbing, ziggurats and...harbor[s]."[156] Ur was likewise a city mapped out in "rectangular blocks, with suburbs radiating in all directions."[157] Structures featured both kitchen and bathroom plumbing, and streets were paved with water runoff channeled through a city drain system.

The industrial nature of these cities was advanced, reflected through their "progressive" belief system centered around non-Christian gods. Beliefs about the afterlife were well developed and included such practices as speaking the name of the dead so as not to forget them. It was thought that the deceased continued to exist in the underworld, the location the soul moved into once the body in this world had expired. Speaking the names of the departed was said to assure that they would live on within this after-realm.

In addition, this belief system called for the living to provide food and drink for the dead. In the era of the Mesopotamians and even into the age of the Hebrews, people buried their dead in the floors of their homes, and it was the duty of the living to care for the dead. In fact, Derek Gilbert explains, "Your well-being in the afterlife *depended* on the faithfulness of your descendants to perform certain rituals...the eldest son inherited the responsibility [of] the care and feeding of the dead."[158] If there was no male heir, families had to get creative in order to find someone to care for the departed in the afterlife—a vital role that, left unfilled, meant death *truly* was the end. Some without direct heirs resorted to recruiting concubines for the tasks; others adopted female children as male heirs or even "hired out" their afterlife duties to people who contracted monetarily to care for people upon departure from this world.[159]

Derek Gilbert explains further:

Once a month, on the night of no moon...[during the darkest night of the month, it was believed] that the veil between the worlds [of the living and the dead] was the thinnest. They would summon the ancestors through a ritual that had several parts: a communal meal, then the calling of the name, where... ancestors [of up to three generations were called upon]. Then, they would provide the drink for them by pouring out the water [onto their graves]. In the Amorite culture, scholars have said—it's an odd saying—but unlike our modern society where you have cemeteries in the center of town, family cemeteries, plots on family land, [or] church cemeteries, we have not found community cemeteries for the Amorite culture, which dominated...from the time of Abraham to the time of David. [This was] because they buried their ancestors under the floor of the house...sometimes they would even install a tube in the floor that led to the mouth of the corpse.[160]

The son or other individual with the responsibility of caring for the deceased was at times referred to as the "son of the cup," or the "cupbearer."[161] Some scholars have even suggested that the lack of an heir to fulfill such duties contributed to Abram's anxiety over having no children, and even to his willingness to take matters into his own hands with Hagar (his wife's servant) at her request (Genesis 16). Ishmael was born from this union, and it wasn't until thirteen years later—when Ishmael was approaching the age at which he would claim heirship—that the Lord appeared to Abram, changed his name to Abraham and his wife, Sarai's name to Sarah, and promised to give them a son, Isaac, stating that Abraham's seed would multiply across the earth. Through this, God made His covenant with Abraham and established a vast bloodline of descendants for Abraham, but He also showed him that God had provided for him in both this life and in the afterlife on *His terms*, not man's.

Later, in Genesis 22, where we read that Abraham was instructed by God to sacrifice Isaac, we see that Abraham began to follow these instructions. Many people wonder why he would do such a thing. Understanding more about this idolatrous culture's influence at the time provides some insight. In Ur of Chaldees and the surrounding area, the Amorite gods that were revered often required child sacrifice, so it is likely that Abraham wasn't surprised by this demand. However, in Genesis 22:8, when Abraham acknowledged that *God* would be the One to provide the sacrifice, he made the statement out of faith, knowing that he served a higher Being than those worshiped by surrounding peoples. Furthermore, we're told in Hebrews 11:19 that Abraham was willing to sacrifice Isaac because he believed that God would raise him from the dead. God answered this declaration of trust in Genesis 22:11–13, where we read that an angel appeared to Abraham and a ram was provided to be offered as a sacrifice. Throughout these stories, God rectified any doubt on Abraham's part that He was/is *the* God—and the provider—of both the living *and* the dead.

To a person who lived in Abraham's day, however, the belief that the dead weren't really gone was common. Those who were departed were thought to merely transfer into an unseen realm, or underworld.

This belief system, along with causing the living to speak the names of the dead and "water" them, motivated the living to visit burial places of the ancestors (which was easy, since they were typically laid to rest, as stated earlier, in the floor of the home) and even leave offerings at the grave. Items such as foods, precious oils, or ornamental stones or jewelry were often placed at the sight of interment with the notion that the departed could them in the afterlife, either for consumption or bartering through the nether regions. Additionally, many of these religious beliefs hold that those who are well cared for in the afterlife can cast good fortune upon those providing for them from the living world, while those who are unhappy with their care may haunt or torment their unfaithful descendants. These concepts have morphed throughout the ages, but are still alive today, handed down through generations. We see remnants of these practices throughout many Chinese, Japanese, and African religions—in areas where ancestors are venerated.[162] Even in countries with multicultural spiritual influences or no religion at all, it is still common to hear people refer to the dead as "watching over us" or "living on," as long as they are remembered. These are diminished traces of early beliefs that have lasted through the centuries.

What the Egyptians Believed

The ancient Egyptian religious system was partly animistic and partly mythological, with the worship of spirit as the main focus.[163] Immortality was a central theme, and it was believed that each person had a divine counterpart who lived past death in the afterworld. To Egyptians, death was a mere interruption of a continued lifespan.[164] There were, however, conditions to obtaining life after death. One stipulation was that the body of the deceased person must be perfectly preserved in this world; otherwise, he or she wouldn't be able to survive the next. This belief served as motivation for the Egyptians' perfected art of mummification.[165] For Egyptians, preserving the body would keep the soul connected, ensuring that the spirit would return to it.[166] Next, the soul of the departed individual had to navigate the Egyptian version of hell before entering the final destination. However, for the deceased to stand any chance of maneuvering through the afterworld, preparations had to be made before death. In other words, those who procrastinated or neglected to make preparations in this life had very low odds of success in the next.

First, funerary items needed to be purchased for placement in the tomb upon burial. This included a variety of objects, ranging from small, precious materials such as jewelry to furniture or even expensive coffins.[167] Some things, such as amulets, were selected as a means of protection and guidance in the afterworld, while others, such as food or clothing, were intended for sustenance during the perilous journey.[168] In addition, funerary texts were purchased and placed in tombs to act as guides for the soul attempting this postmortem quest.

Shabtis were included in preparation for the afterlife as well. These were small, funerary statuettes inscribed with an invocation that would bring them to life so that they could labor on behalf of the deceased. Egyptians believed that in the afterlife they would be granted a small piece of land, but that they were responsible for maintaining it. Carrying *shabtis* enabled the individual to own a type of "servant" who would make the afterlife easier for them.[169]

Coffins and tombs were etched and painted with pictures, spells, and prayers that served to guide the deceased through the underworld and to protect the body's preservation in order to facilitate the journey as well. In similar fashion to the funerary items placed *within* the tomb, these elements were chosen, purchased, and designed according to a person's wealth, status, and desires for the afterlife. A well-designed, well-built tomb, it was believed, even had the power to restore life to the person buried there.[170]

Once these preparations were made, there were rituals to be performed on the mummy as well. The first was called the "Opening of the Mouth" ceremony, wherein priests burned incense and performed an anointing incantation while touching the mummy's body with ritual objects in an effort to stimulate the five physical senses for the soul in the afterlife.[171]

Because the afterworld was regarded as a place of peril and those who could not successfully navigate it would perish, causing death to be final, these funerary provisions were literally a matter of life and death to the Egyptians. Consider the following description of the afterworld:

> Travelling on a solar bark, the mummy passed through the underworld, which was inhabited by servants armed with long knives, fire-spitting dragons and reptiles with five ravenous heads. Upon arriving in the realm of Duat (Land of the Gods), the deceased had to pass through seven gates, reciting accurately a magic spell at each stop. If successful, they arrived at the Hall of Osiris, the place of judgment.[172]

This judgment contained the "Weighing of the Heart" ceremony, which was overseen by Anubis, the god of embalming, and it was recorded by the god of writing known as Thoth.[173] In conjunction with this ceremony, forty-two gods would entertain the confessions of the deceased, whose heart was then placed on a scale, weighed in comparison to a feather belonging to the goddess Ma'at, goddess of truth and justice.[174]

Because Egyptians believed that our hearts hold a complete record of all the deeds we carry out during our life on earth, only those whose hearts didn't outweigh the feather of Ma'at were granted immortality.[175] The heavy (or guilty) heart was eaten by the goddess Amemet, goddess of the underworld.[176] Hence, the person wasn't granted immortality, and perished permanently. However, a person with the right amulet had a chance of surviving this ceremony, or "cheating death," regardless of guilt, as long as the adequate preparations had been made.

Amulets, in consideration for the deceased, held special meaning for Egyptians in two ways: significance and position on the body:

Significance: Each amulet had a particular significance. Some were for direction for the soul's journey; others were for protection, or fortune, etc.[177]

Position on the body: The amulet, or charm, was placed on a certain part of the body during the wrapping process of mummification, with the location directly connection with the amulet of choice and its relationship to the desires of the deceased.[178] The most commonly used amulet was a heart scarab, which was placed on the deceased's heart to keep it connected to the individual in the underworld.[179]

The amulet contained an incantation recited during the "Weighing of the Heart Ceremony," which would cause the heart to pass the test of weighing regardless of an individual's worthiness.[180] When a pharaoh survived this judgment, it was believed that he became one with the god Osiris, god of the dead and ruler of the underworld.[181]

On Top of the World

Anyone who has read the story of Joseph would certainly agree that he overcame great obstacles and escalated to one of the highest points of power in the world during his era. After telling his brothers of his dreams, which incited them to jealousy, he was overpowered and sold into slavery to the Ishmaelites, who carried him to a foreign land. As a slave, Joseph proved himself to be a man of quality work and integrity, and he eventually found himself in a place of power. However, after being unjustly accused, he was imprisoned—until a chance meeting involving dream interpretation provided him an opportunity for an audience with the Pharaoh. Seeing Joseph's unique intuition, Pharaoh placed the young man in charge of much of Egypt's administrative operations. Through subsequent years, Joseph's wisdom and shrewd leadership skills provide a place where he and his reunited family were able to live out their remaining years with many luxuries.

Yet, just before his death:

> Joseph said unto his brethren, I die: and God will surely visit
> you, and bring you out of this land unto the land which he
> sware to Abraham, to Isaac, and to Jacob. And Joseph took an
> oath of the children of Israel, saying, God will surely visit you,
> and ye shall carry up my bones from heaven. So Joseph died,
> being an hundred and ten years old: and they involved him, and
> he was put in a coffin in Egypt. (Genesis 50:24–26)

It would seem that, after all the obstacles Joseph had faced in life,
such an accomplished final resting place would have sufficed. However,
this gesture illustrates Joseph's unique perspective toward the afterlife
among his Egyptian peers. While he knew that, temporarily, he would
be embalmed and placed in a tomb, he declared his final resting place
based on his childhood faith in the God of his fathers. By this time,
Joseph would have been well aware of the Egyptian beliefs about the
afterlife, and that was not the burial he wanted. His last statement was
to remind his family of God's promise to return them to the land that
had been promised to Abraham, Isaac, and Jacob. Joseph's final words
served as a reminder of this, as a charge to remain faithful to the God of
Abraham, and as an assurance that they would not remain in this land
forever. Furthermore, when they were returned to the land of promise,
he wanted his bones to be there as well.

What the Greeks Believed

The ancient Greek culture held that as a person passed on, Thanatos, the
Greek god of death, took a lock of his or her hair. The individual's soul,
or shade,[182] then separated from the body and was led to the River Styx
by Hermes, the messenger of the gods. The River Styx, the entrance-
way to the underworld, could only be crossed if the traveler had the

fare, which was typically provided to the deceased by the living placing coins inside their mouth. If the person could pay to cross, the ferryman, Charon, often portrayed as an emaciated skeleton,[183] would take them across the Rivers Styx and Acheron.[184] Those who could not pay the toll were denied entrance to the underworld and were forced to wander forever.[185] These spirits were said to roam until they eventually would join with Melinoe, an underworld goddess, whose ghostly company would terrorize the living throughout the night.[186]

Those able to pay the fare and cross the rivers would reach the bank on the opposite side, where they would encounter Cerberus, the guardian dog of the underworld. This beast was said to have three heads and served to keep souls from wandering into and out of the underworld.[187] The next phase of their journey was to approach and drink from the River Lethe, which flowed around the cave of Hypnose.[188] When consumed, these waters would cause a soul to forget about their lives on earth, their deeds, and earthly memories. The individual must then be judged by Minos, Aiakos, and Rhadamanyths, who decided based on a person's deeds whether he or she would be permitted to enter the beautiful land of Elysium (a reward for good deeds during life), sent back to dwell in the Asphodel Fields (a mundane place for those whose deeds were neither good nor bad), or sent to Tartarus for punishment.[189]

Some legends of Tartarus exist today. One tells the story of Tantalus, son of Zeus, who was invited to the table of the gods. However, he committed several offenses: He revealed divine secrets to mortals, stole nectar and ambrosia from Heaven and gave them to mortals, and even attempted to test the intelligence of the gods by inviting them to a dinner whereupon he served his own killed and cooked son, Pelop, to the gods in attendance. (Tantalus' entire audience except one, Demeter, abstained from eating.) As punishment, Zeus placed Tantalus in Hades, in a river where he is eternally unable to drink the water, near fruit that is carried away by the wind anytime he tries to eat.[190]

Another legend of punishment within Tartarus is the Greek mythological story of Sisyphus, king of Ephyra. According to legend, the god of the underworld, Hades, came to collect Sisyphus for the afterlife, but he wasn't ready to die. He managed to trick Hades into handcuffing himself, after which Sisyphus stowed Hades in a closet. After some time, Hades was released, but Sisyphus quickly performed other trickery against another god, Persephone, in an attempt to further cheat death. Finally, he was taken to Hades to be judged for his antics against the gods. His punishment was to spend eternity rolling a giant boulder to the top of the hill, only to have it repeatedly come crashing down again.[191]

In similar fashion to the Egyptians, Greeks believed that placing expensive or rare items upon a loved one's tomb would give the departed resources in the afterlife. Some families would continue to continue to visit a tomb, bringing new gifts to the deceased years after death.[192]

In Greek mythology, Hades encompasses three distinct regions once the entrance fee has been paid, boundary rivers have been crossed, and judgment has been faced: Elysium, Asphodel Fields, and Tartarus.

What the Romans Believed

There are a lot of similarities between ancient Roman and Greek thought. In regards to twenty-first-century Western culture, both have been incredibly influential on our philosophical and spiritual understanding. Yet, as we will see, there are a couple of key differences.

The Romans had a clear belief that when people died, they reunited with their dead ancestors; it was the job of a son to sift through the ashes of his father's funeral pyre, locate a bone, and exclaim that his father had now joined the divine spirits—in other words, his ancestors.[193] Romans also believed that a select few of their founders actually became gods, such as Aeneas and Romulus. The Roman Senate (similar to the Greeks, but not going as far) reached the point at which they were deifying prominent individuals after their death, starting with Julius Caesar.[194]

Much like the Greeks, Romans believed in an afterlife consisting of three parts: a place that was neither good nor bad, Tartarus (place of eternal torment), and Elysium (a place of eternal bliss).[195] Some Romans even believed in a kind of reincarnation that, at times, provided for souls in Elysium to reincarnate to new, physical bodies on earth.[196]

One difference between the Greeks and the Romans was that Romans believed it wasn't the Greek Charon, but the messenger god Mercury, the son of Jupiter, who escorted the recently deceased to the River Styx through Avernus, a cave believed to be the entrance to the Underworld.[197] Apart from that, many Roman beliefs about the afterlife were borrowed from Greek teachings and were thus similar or identical. It wasn't until Christianity came into the picture that the Romans began drastically altering their original view of the afterlife in favor of a Christian one. Some of the basic views were kept, such as the existence of a type of Heaven and Hell, and some were abandoned, such as reincarnation and how one attains eternal life in Heaven.

Terminology

The Hebrew Sheol

The Hebrew word *shĕ'owl* is equivalent to Hell, the underworld, or the Greek Hades. It is also sometimes used interchangeably with the terms "pit" and "grave." An example of this is in Numbers 16, where we read that Moses warned Korah and his comrades to stop behaving irreverently toward the Almighty, but their attitudes remained rebellious. Verses 30–33 sum up Moses' warning and God's wrathful response:

> But if the Lord make a new thing, and the earth open her mouth, and swallow them up, with all that appertain unto them, and they go down quick into the pit [Sheol]; then ye shall understand that these men have provoked the Lord. And it came to pass, as he had made an end of speaking all these words, that the ground clave asunder that was under them: And the earth

opened her mouth, and swallowed them up, and their houses, and all the men that appertained unto Korah, and all their goods. They, and all that appertained to them, went down alive into the pit [Sheol], and the earth closed upon them: and they perished from among the congregation. (Numbers 16:30–33)

Ezekiel 31 relays a prophetic word that Ezekiel was sent to tell Pharaoh that he was the subject of God's judgment and wrath, and that although he had been mighty throughout the land, God would tear him down.

I made the nations to shake at the sound of his fall, when I cast him down to hell [Sheol] with them that descend into the pit [location in the ground]: and all the trees of Eden, the choice and best of Lebanon, all that drink water, shall be comforted in the nether parts of the earth. (Ezekiel 31:16)

In this particular, the word "pit" is taken from the Hebrew *bowr*, which refers to a location within the ground upon the earth.[198] However, the term is directly connected to the statement that the." For example: "O Lord, thou hast brought up my soul from the grave [Sheol]. Thou hast kept me alive, that I should not go down to the pit" (Psalm 30:3). The Bible assures us that God will not leave His own in Sheol, however: "For thou wilt not leave my soul in hell [Sheol]; neither wilt thou suffer thine Holy One to see corruption" (Psalm 16:10).

So, how is it that we can have assurance that we will be delivered from this final destination? The Lord has told us that He will deliver us:

Because ye have said, We have made a covenant with death, and with hell are we at agreement; when the overflowing scourge shall pass through, it shall not come unto us: for we have made lies our refuge, and under falsehood have we hid ourselves: Therefore thus saith the Lord God, Behold, I lay in Zion for a foundation a stone, a tried stone, a precious corner stone, a sure foundation: he that believeth shall not make haste. Judgment also will I lay to the line, and righteousness to the plummet: and the hail shall sweep away the refuge of lies, and the waters shall overflow the hiding place. And your covenant with death shall be disannulled, and your agreement with hell [Sheol] shall not stand; when the overflowing scourge shall pass through, then ye shall be trodden down by it. (Isaiah 28:15–18)

I will ransom then from the power of the grave [Sheol]; I will redeem them from death: O death, I will be thy plagues; O grave [Sheol], I will be thy destruction: repentance shall be hid from mine eyes. (Hosea13:14)

Though they dig into hell [Sheol], thence shall mine hand take them; though they climb up to heaven, thence will I bring them down. (Amos 9:2)

Hadēs

In biblical writings, *hadēs* is the Greek equivalent of *shĕ'owl,* and refers to the "dark region of the dead."[199] Biblical use of the word *shĕ'owl* occurs in a several different contexts, a few worth noting here:

And I say also unto thee, That thou art Peter, and upon this rock I will build my church; and the gates of hell [Hades] shall not prevail against it. (Matthew 16:18)

Because thou wilt not leave my soul in hell [Hades], neither wilt thou suffer thine Holy One to see corruption. (Acts 2:27)

Surprisingly, this term is occasionally personified, as in the following passages:

O death, where is thy sting? O grave [Hades], where is thy victory? (1 Corinthians 15:55)

(And I looked, and behold a pale horse: and his name that sat on him was Death, and Hell [Hades] followed with him. And power was given unto them over the fourth part of the earth, to kill with sword, and with hunger, and with death, and with the beasts of the earth. (Revelation 6:8)

And the sea gave up the dead which were in it; and death and hell [Hades] delivered up the dead which were in them: and they were judged every man according to their works. And death and hell [Hades] were cast into the lake of fire. This is the second death. (Revelation 20:13–14)

While the last passage in this list may seem vague as far as its reference to a *location* or an *entity*, it stands to reason that this could be a personified reference, or even hint at a living location. Some find it odd or even confusing that one word can refer to both a being and a location, but "hades" is a prime example of a term that originally pinpointed an entity, but became generalized through centuries of translations. Thus, many places in the Bible that state Jesus conquered "death," "hell," or the "grave," it is likewise asserting that He has taken victory over *not only the location*, but over entities ruling these regions.

Tartarus

Tartarus was described in *The Four Socratic Dialogues of Plato* as the final location of the irreparably damned.[200] Greeks believed that those who died were judged according to their deeds and then were sent to one of three locations: a place where they would rectify negative deeds, a place where they would be rewarded for living a good life, or to Tartarus, which was designated for those whose deeds were so heinous that there was no hope of ever righting such wrongs. Some people believe Tartarus and Sheol should be used interchangeably, but there originally was a discrepancy between the two terms. Over time, the context of the term "Tartarus" has shifted. According to an article in the *Encyclopædia Britannica:* "Tartarus, originally denoting an abyss far below Hades and the place of punishment in the lower world, later lost its distinctness and became almost a synonym for Hades."[201]

The original Greek term for "Tartarus" is *tartaroō*, originally defined as "the deepest abyss of Hell."[202] The original word is only found once in the King James Bible, in 2 Peter 2:4: "For if God spared not the angels that sinned, but cast them down to hell [Tartarus], and delivered them into chains of darkness, to be reserved unto judgment."

Understanding that this word originally referred not only to a negative place in the afterlife, but to the lowest, most "damned" location therein, gives it a special status of holding the evilest entities at the very bottom of Hades.

Possible Tartarus Influence in the Bible

An interesting point about the afterlife comes up when we look at the well-known but commonly brushed-over account of the rich man and Lazarus. Recall that, as Jesus told it, both the rich man and Lazarus had died, Lazarus received a reward, and the rich man gained something far less desirable (see Luke 16:19–31). According to the original writer of the Gospel of Luke (traditionally understood to be Luke himself; however, the earliest manuscripts are anonymous, causing some to challenge the traditional claim[203]), Jesus describes the afterlife as comprising two places, one good and one bad, separated by a great chasm that cannot be crossed. There is a noticeable similarity between the structure of the afterlife as described here and that of the Greek understanding. Add to that the possibility that Luke himself was a Hellenic Jew[204] (though not all scholars agree[205]), and it causes some to wonder whether there was perhaps some Greek influence in play in this under-standing of the afterlife—and if so, what does that say about biblical authenticity?

To many Christians, the initial reaction to this possibility is to deny it. It almost comes off as a threat to say that the Bible might have been influenced in any way by outside religions. Some even bring up the fact that this is a parable and, since Jesus was speaking symbolically, we can cast away any literal interpretation of the passage. That might be true; however, an equally compelling case can be made for this being a literal interpretation. What if this isn't merely a metaphorical lesson but is, in fact, a true account? Must we reject this possibility because it might mean that Greek thought influenced the Bible in some way?

Many would say outside influence on the Holy Scriptures is impos-sible. However, we do know that polemics in the Bible exist. A polemic is a way of writing that directly criticizes differing religious or politi-cal views that are seen as erroneous by the writer.[206] Specifically in the Bible, polemics are a type of Scripture written as a direct reaction to the surrounding ancient Near East religions. For example, Jesus refers to Himself as the One riding on the clouds (Mark 14:6). This refers to Daniel 7:13, which in itself is a polemic of Ba'al. In ancient surround-ing Ugaritic beliefs, Ba'al was referred to as the cloud rider, or one who rides on the clouds.[207] By taking this title and attributing it to Jesus, the writer is basically saying that, no, it is not Ba'al who's in charge. It's not Ba'al who is the supreme being—or in other words, it's not Ba'al who is riding on the clouds. Ba'al has no real power or authority. All power and authority belong to Jesus, not Ba'al.[208] That is the point of biblical polemics: to correct faulty theology from surrounding religions and give proper authority to the God of the Bible.

Because of this, we know that other religious views, at least in some ways, have also had some sort of influence on what the biblical writers expressed, even if only reactionary. We also must recognize that "influence" doesn't necessarily mean "wrong" or "not authentic." If you are a Christian, then you know that all truth originates from God. Yet, how He decides to reveal that truth is up to Him and can vary depending on His will. Therefore, while as Christians we know the Bible is absolutely true, the way God chose to lead the original writers to those truths may not be so apparent. It is entirely possible that God could have providentially led a person to a piece of the truth about, for example, the afterlife, through a different religion that had a lot of other things wrong. This may sound strange to modern-day Christians, but consider how much other religions (on a general level) have in common with Christianity. Other religions believe in the existence of a spirit world. Many, if not all, other religions believe in spirit beings. Many believe in the existence of some sort of life after death. Therefore, it's entirely possible for a person to come from another religion, convert to Christianity, and carry over some original views (for example, those concerning the existence of an afterlife and spirit beings) while radically changing others (such as *how* to get to Heaven, an element of Christianity that is unique in that it is not works-based). In other words, when we compare the Bible to ancient Greek thought, the Greeks get a lot of stuff wrong. However, it is possible they might have certain beliefs that are correct. As Christians, we can only take that principle so far. No serious Christian would advocate the adoption of all Greek teachings on the afterlife, as many of those beliefs conflict with the Bible. The farthest we can take it is only as far as the confines of biblical truth will allow us to go; that is our safe area. Beyond that, we're either in unknown territory or territory that directly conflicts with biblical teaching. Again, it's entirely possible that the writer of Luke, though he was quoting Jesus, had a certain understanding of the afterlife that originated from Greek thought, and certain aspects of his understanding might have been correct while others were not. That's why we can accept the words of Christ as true despite the fact that there might be some commonalities with other ancient religious teachings.

Gehenna

The term "Gehenna" derives from the Greek *Geenna*, which is simply defined as "hell."[209] *Geenna* (pronounced *ge'-en-nä*) is a Greek adaptation of the Hebrew *ge-Hinnom*, in reference a location where trash was dumped in the Valley of Hinnom.[210] In early Jewish times, this valley was located south of Jerusalem and was where some idolaters went to sacrifice their children to the ancient deity Molech.[211] When this ritual later ceased, the site became a place where locals would dispose of or burn trash or other discarded items, including "the bodies of criminals, carcasses of animals and all sorts of filth."[212] The valley was deep and, from above, it appeared to have an endless stream of rising smoke and pungent odors. It yielded such offenses as swarming flies, maggots, and worms. Because of all this, the word became symbolic of how people imagined hell must be. Although some debate that the location of the refuse heap that inspired the name "Gehenna" was actually located in the Kidron Valley,[213] the lore surrounding the concept and its influence remained. Essentially, this image of such a valley—always burning, with smoke ever-billowing into the air above it, emitting the scent of rotting flesh, and overrun with maggots and worms waiting to ravenously consume anyone cast inside—served as a constant reminder to the living of what awaited them if, at the end of their days, they were judged as having wrongfully lived their lives. Many believe this is the setting that inspired the concept of Hell referenced in Mark 9 with a phrase that is quoted verbatim in two verses: "where their worm dieth not, and the fire is not quenched" (verses 46 and 48).

"Gehenna" shows up in the Bible in multiple places, and it always refers to a final destination of the condemned and a place to be warned about, as in the following:

And fear not them which kill the body, but are not able to kill the soul: but rather fear him which is able to destroy both soul and body in hell [Gehenna]. (Matthew 10:28)

But I will forewarn you whom ye shall fear: Fear him, which after he hath killed hath power to cast into hell [Gehenna]; yea, I say unto you, Fear him. (Luke 12:5)

John Calvin referred to this location, explaining Jesus' mission to restore God's children to His kingdom, thus recovering them from a fate in Gehenna:

What the Mediator was to accomplish was…to restore us to God's grace as if to make the children of men, [into] children of God; of their heirs of Gehenna, heirs of the Heavenly Kingdom. Who could have done this had not the selfsame Son of God become the Son of man, and had not [carried our sin Himself] as to impart what was his to us, and to make what was his by nature ours by grace?[214]

Abraham's Bosom

Luke 16 features a story of a wealthy man and a beggar named Lazarus. Most people are familiar with the general account, but its details include many points of debate. It paints an interesting picture of the afterlife, wherein those who "fared sumptuously" (Luke 16:19) but show no concern for the impoverished and forgotten find themselves in jeopardy of severe pain and suffering after death. The wealthy individual is described as having enjoyed a lavish life, while the beggar Lazarus is said to linger at the gate of the wealthy man's earthly abode. The context paints Lazarus to be a man in deplorable health; in fact, his skin was so riddled with sores that local dogs came and licked his wounds. Furthermore, the mournful man was so impoverished that he longed for "the crumbs which fell from the rich man's table" (Luke 16:21). Upon the beggar's death, angels carried him into a wonderful place called "Abraham's bosom" (an element, if you'll remember, seems to parallel modern NDE stories, wherein the recently deceased are embraced with love, surrounded by light, and invited to a final destination of peace). The wealthy man, on the other hand, apparently had no such welcome to the afterlife. We are told that when he died, no angels were waiting to carry him to a final destination. The narrative states only that he was buried, after which he suddenly found himself in Hell. There, he suffered insurmountable torture, and as he saw that Lazarus was in Abraham's bosom, he cried out for mercy. He petitioned Abraham to send Lazarus to ease the pain of the fire by dipping one fingertip in water and touching his tongue. However, he did not receive what he requested; instead, he was reminded that during life on earth he had received good things, yet provided no relief for Lazarus.

Notice the contrast in the transition of each individual entering the state of death. Lazarus was carried by angels to Abraham's bosom, but the wealthy man was merely buried. Furthermore, Lazarus' name is repeated several times in this story, while "the wealthy man" isn't even given a name. Recall our previous discussion about the necessity of speaking the name of the dead to ensure that they were not forgotten. This parallels the thinking of the time: If speaking the deceased person's name causes that person to be remembered, and vice versa, we can gather that, regardless of material wealth, it is our deeds that decide our status in the afterworld. The complete omission of the wealthy man's name appears to be a final condemnation of his selfish, unconcerned nature, making this a story of justice.

At first glance, this passage appears relate a fairly simple accounting of reciprocity, but a closer look raises many questions. For example, where exactly is "Abraham's bosom"? And what is Luke 16:26 referring to when Abraham states: "Beside all this, between us and you there is a great gulf fixed: so that they which would pass from hence to you cannot; neither can they passed to us, that would come from thence"?

One theory about these questions is that Hades is a zone with many layers, and those who are suffering are able to see those who are not. As ancient Greek mythology perceived Hades to be divided into three regions—the good, the bad, and the neutral (mentioned earlier)—it is likewise a popular belief that the punishment of those who were condemned to live forever in the "bad" zone was fortified by their ability to see the pleasure of those enjoying their reward. Under this theory, Abraham's bosom is a location; furthermore, many who believe this theory consider it to be the same location as the "paradise" Jesus referred to in Luke 23:43.

Others believe Abraham's bosom is a place of honor and status, rather than location. In an interview with authors and biblical scholars, Derek and Sharon Gilbert, Sharon clarifies:

> Lazarus goes to Abraham's bosom, which means that he is brought into nearness to where Abraham is…. It isn't that Lazarus is brought to a geographical location with the title of Abraham's bosom, it's the fact that he is been brought to a position of honor.[215]

Furthermore, regarding the concept that in this multidimensional afterworld, those who are being punished can to observe those who are not, she states:

> If you look at it beyond the physical and go into the metaphysical, it gives this chilling idea that when you *do* go into the afterlife, you have the perception into the other side. [This] is terrifying—tormenting—[and it] explains the wailing and gnashing of teeth…that a person can see what they miss because of their choices.[216]

Additionally, the wealthy man was obviously aware that he could not leave the location he was condemned to. Instead of asking for permission to take his own leave, he asked Abraham to send someone on his behalf.

Marley's Inspiration?

The account of the beggar Lazarus and the wealthy man doesn't stop at the sufferer's plea for a touch of cool water upon his parched tongue, but includes yet another dimension—one that might have been inspiration for Jacob Marley's visitation to Ebenezer Scrooge in Charles Dickens' classic *A Christmas Carol*. In this fictional story, Jacob Marley, a deceased, wealthy man who did not care for his fellow man during his life on earth, returns to warn former (and still alive) business partner, Ebenezer Scrooge, of his punishment in the afterlife for disregardingthe needy:

> "Business!" Cried the Ghost, wringing its hands again. "Mankind was my business. The common welfare was my business; charity, mercy, forbearance, and benevolence, were, all, my business. The dealings of my trade were but a drop of water in the comprehensive ocean of my business!"[217]

After further conversation, the ghost reveals his reason for appearing to Ebenezer Scrooge: "I am here to-night to warn you, that you have yet a chance and hope of escaping my fate."[218]

Sadly for those who, in the nonfictional, *real* world, such warnings are not biblically guaranteed. In fact, the Luke account shows that such requests made from beyond the grave on behalf of the living are not granted. Luke 16:27–31 outlines the gloomy conclusion of this story, wherein the wealthy man asked Abraham to send Lazarus to his father's house to warn his brothers of their impending doom, should they make the same mistakes in their own lives. Sadly, Abraham refused, explaining that Moses and the prophets had left sufficient direction for the living to find the righteous path for their life. He stated: "If they hear not Moses and the prophets, neither will they be persuaded, though one rose from the dead" (Luke 16:31). This reinforces the concept that the deceased do not intervene in our daily lives, and that we do not receive guidance from the spirits of the dead, but instead, are to look at the insight God has provided for us through Scripture.

Purgatory

In Roman Catholicism, the doctrine is held that many of the souls of the deceased are sent to Purgatory for a time of purification before they are allowed to enter Heaven. There are some exceptions to this: martyrs, those who qualify for sainthood, and those who otherwise hold some kind of outstanding religious status. The basis of this doctrine was sealed earlier than the Council of Trent (a series of meetings held amongst Roman Catholic leadership in response to the Protestant upsurge between the years of 1545–1563), and was included in the conversation that took place during these appointments. Because Catholics are baptized as infants, their salvation is believed to be secured very early on in life. The pertinent issue regarding sin then becomes that of sins committed after baptism. These must be confessed to a priest to alleviate impending punishment for such sins in Hell. However, the lingering guilt upon the soul for sins committed must still be paid by the individual, which can take place by means of penance or fasting (a means by which a priest could prescribe to an individual a means for pardoning their sins by saying a number of repeated prayers or going without some pleasure for an instructed period of time in order to compensate for wrongful deeds), among other things. Those who happen to die before making such compensation for sins will be punished in Purgatory before being allowed to move on to Heaven.[219] The length of time spent in Purgatory and the severity of one's punishment there depends on the types of sins the person has yet to pay for. Two kinds of sins exist, according to Roman Catholicism: venial and mortal. An individual who dies with a mortal sin outstanding will go straight to Hell, with no opportunity to enter Purgatory. A venial sin, however, will be punished in Purgatory, thus purifying the individual so that he or she can enter God's presence. This doctrine is pulled from

Revelation 21:27, which says nothing unclean can enter Heaven. Time in Purgatory, according to this doctrine, can be shortened by the living participating in masses or bestowing gifts or services to the Church, or by the prayers of priests on behalf of the dead.[220] The Catholic Church has spent a great deal of time differentiating between what constitutes a moral and venial sin. Sins outlined in such passages as Galatians 5:19–21, Romans 1: 29–32, Corinthians 6:9–10—including adultery, fornication, lasciviousness, idolatry, witchcraft, heresy, murder, drunkenness, maliciousness, spitefulness, covetousness, and showing hatred toward or intentionally provoking God—are all considered mortal sins. Those who have not confessed and paid for their sins will go to hell upon death. Sin considered by the Catholic Church to be a grave matter, committed intentionally, deliberately, and with full knowledge—by an individual in his or her right mind—constitutes a mortal sin. Less severe infractions, those committed without full knowledge or intent, or those considered less substantial than moral sense are categorized as venial and are said to weaken the soul, despite the fact that the individual hasn't likely intentionally turned his or her back on God's grace.[221]

Catholic foundation for the doctrine of Purgatory is found in a variety of places. In the extrabiblical document, 2 Maccabees (chapter 12), we read of Judas taking his army to the city of Adullam to assist allies at war. After a battle, Judas, along with his comrades, gathered the dead for burial. However, they were surprised to find that "under the tunic of each of the dead they found ambulance sacred to the idols of Jamnia, which the law forbids the Jews to wear. So it was clear to all that this was why these men had fallen." Shortly, Judas concluded that these soldiers had perished under circumstances of idolatry. The response follows:

> They all therefore praised the ways of the Lord, the just judge who brings to light the things that are hidden. Turning to supplication, they prayed that the sinful deed might be fully blotted out. The noble Judas exhorted the people to keep themselves

free from sin, for they had seen with their own eyes what had happened because of the sin of those who had fallen. He then took up a collection among all his soldiers, amounting to two thousand silver drachmas, which he sent to Jerusalem to provide for an expiatory sacrifice. In doing this he acted in a very excellent and noble way, inasmuch as he had the resurrection in mind; for if he were not expecting the fallen to rise again, it would have been superfluous and foolish to pray for the dead. But if he did this with a view to the splendid reward that awaits those who had gone to rest in godliness, it was a holy and pious thought. Thus he made atonement for the dead that they might be absolved from their sin. (2 Maccabees 12:43–45)[222]

Additionally, Augustine (early fifth century AD) was said to have propagated the concept of purgatory in his work, *City of God*, by stating:

Temporal punishments are suffered by some in this life only, by some after death, by some both here and hereafter; but all of them before the last and strictest judgment. But not all who suffer temporal punishments after death will come to eternal punishments, which are to follow after that judgment.[223]

Furthermore, Augustine's teaching in the same work conveyed the idea that the living could help to achieve atonement for the sins of the dead:

The prayer either of the Church herself or of pious individuals is heard on behalf of certain of the dead; but it is heard for those who, having been regenerated in Christ, did not for the rest of their life in the body do such wickedness that they might be judged unworthy of such mercy, nor yet lived so well that it might be suppose it that they have no need for such mercy.[224]

The idea of Purgatory is highly debated between Catholics and Protestants, with Catholics stating that since nothing unclean can enter the presence of God, and that suffering is a part of Christianity, suffering for and paying for our sins is part of our pathway into Heaven. Protestants, on the other hand, say that Jesus accomplished everything necessary for us to be able to enter the gates of Heaven; His blood has cleansed us so that, as we enter, we are not defiling the presence of the Lord because of our purification through Jesus Christ. The debate has remained heated throughout the centuries, with each side citing Scripture as reinforcement. On one hand, those who believe in Purgatory point to 1 Corinthians 3:15: "If any man's work shall be burned, he shall suffer loss: but he himself shall be saved any: yet so as by fire." The "fire" in this statement, as argued by some, represents a purification that will take place between the time of death and the time of entrance to Haven. Another argument for Purgatory is found in Matthew 12:32, where Jesus explains that a person who speaks a word against the Holy Spirit will not be forgiven, "neither in this world, neither in the world to come," insinuating that someone not forgiven in this world can somehow obtain forgiveness in the next. This particular point of argument was defended by Gregory the Great (540–604), who took the teachings of purgatory a step further by writing about souls of Purgatory in his work, *Dialogues*. One deceased monk discussed in this work, Justus, had apparently "sinned against the vow of poverty, because he had kept for himself three gold coins…without permission of the superior."[225] Gregory set out to assist the expired friar's state in Purgatory by offering "the Holy Sacrifice of the Mass for 30 consecutive days,"[226] by which, upon the final day, the spirit of the monk Justus appeared to his (still-living) brother, explaining to him that on that very day he had been received into the "Communion of Saints in Heaven."[227] Out of this occurrence, the practice of Gregorian Masses (a catholic practice wherein the living can make penance for the sins of the dead) was initiated.[228]

Others, however, claim that the "fire" referred to in Corinthians

3:15 is a refinement encountered in this life by those who are seeking to live righteously:

> And he shall sit as a refiner and purifier of silver: and he shall purify the sons of Levi, and purge them as gold and silver, that they may offer unto the Lord and offering in righteousness. (Malachi 3:3)

Those who support the position fortified by the passage in Malachi explain that the opportunities for righteousness that present themselves here on earth are lost upon death; there is no purging of sin after that. Furthermore, many who believe in Purgatory cite Ephesians 2:8–9, which states that people cannot "earn" their way into Heaven.

In explaining the teaching of Purgatory, sometimes referred to as Limbo, the Catholic Church believes:

> [For the departed, the Bible refers to a]...third condition [beyond Heaven or Hell], commonly called the limbo of the Fathers.... These people thus were not in heaven, but neither were they experiencing the torments of hell...[if this location is not technically] purgatory, its existence shows that a temporary, intermediate state is not contrary to Scripture.[229]

While some within the Catholic Church see Limbo and Purgatory as the same location (with the purpose of each having shifted slightly after the crucifixion), others maintain that these places are very different. The phrase "Limbo of the Fathers" was a term used to refer to the part of Hades where the righteous souls who died went to wait until Jesus' blood purchased their admission into Heaven. When Christ died, those who had been waiting in Limbo were released into Heaven, thus negating the continued need for such a region. Purgatory, however, according to Catholicism, continues to be necessary for the purification of dead followers of Christ who need cleansing for venial sin and is a destination visited by most righteous souls on their way to heaven.

Much debate remains on the topic of Purgatory, some of which centers around the moment on the cross when Jesus told the man being executed alongside Himself, "Today shalt thou be with me in paradise" (Luke 23:43). Some claim this connects to 1 Peter 3:19:18–22, wherein Jesus spoke to "spirits in prison." The case made here by proponents of the concept of Purgatory is that Jesus would have gone to some sort of temporary holding place to preach to the spirits of the dead. And in this place, there certainly *must have been* deceased individuals who were eligible to respond to His message. After all, for Jesus to preach in Heaven would literally be Him "preaching to the choir," while those condemned to Hell surely suffer an irreversible sentence. Thus, this doctrine asserts a third waiting place where Jesus went to preach, which is the "Paradise" that He said He would enter on that day—"today." The repentant sinner would likewise be eligible to enter that "Paradise" upon his death (which would be presumably close to the same moment of Jesus' death). According to this theology, Jesus wasn't promising the man that he would "enter Heaven" on that day, but rather was confirming the man's eligibility to enter Purgatory rather than be condemned to Hell, as a result of his repentance.[230]

Those who disagree with this doctrine, as stated before, maintain that upon Jesus' death, the "waiting place" was opened, allowing all souls therein to ascend to Heaven, and that *this* is what Jesus promised the man when he told them that very day they would be together in Paradise. A third collective holds the position that the righteous have always gone immediately to Heaven upon death; there are not now, nor have there ever been, locations such as Limbo *or* Purgatory. Scriptural basis for this is derived from Old Testament passages such as 2 Kings 2:1, which states: "And it came to pass, when the Lord would take up Elijah into heaven by a whirlwind." An even more compelling passage for this argument is Genesis 5:24, which tells us that "Enoch walked with

God: and he was not; for God took him." This Scripture alludes to the concept that, without need for purification, Enoch literally walked in the presence of God. Furthermore, the fact that Jesus Himself, in the story of a wealthy man and the Lazarus, referred to Abraham being in Heaven *before His own crucifixion*, serves to many people as proof that Old Testament believers went straight to Heaven without the need for a "waiting place."

What to Do with Similarities

As we looked at before in the account of Lazarus and the rich man, there are certain similarities between ancient thoughts on the afterlife and Christianity. We should expect there to be some commonality in Greek and Roman thought when compared to the New Testament of the Bible since they were contemporaries, but there are even interesting parallels found in ancient Egyptian beliefs, some in common and some conflicting. For example, the Egyptians believed the physical body was all-important and had to exist in order for the soul to have intelligence or to be judged by the guardian of the underworld,[231] yet the Bible teaches that our physical bodies will die, be raised, and changed to something incorruptible (1 Corinthians 15:53). Both ancient Egyptian beliefs and modern Christianity require preparations to be made in physical life before death in order to attain the desired destination. The difference is that Egyptians, like most people of ancient religions, taught a works-based salvation to be completed during life, while Christianity teaches a faith-based salvation in Christ, which also must be attained during physical life. In fact, Egyptians believed you needed something, such as a heart scarab amulet, to cover your sins and make you blameless. In Christianity, of course, this covering comes from the shed blood of Jesus Christ two millennia ago. Going further, it would appear in Egyptian belief that souls are meant to conquer Hell; however, Christianity teaches that Jesus Christ already did that for us.

There seems to be something in every person throughout time that compels him or her toward the truth. Other religions were able to get the basic ideas correct, but missed the mark with the particulars. The Bible teaches that eternity is set in the heart of man (Ecclesiastes 3:11), which seems to indicate that a vital part of being human is knowing there is more to life than that which physical space and time can contain. If the Bible is true and every human being has this inner knowledge, then again, we should *expect* other religions to have these similarities. The fact that these likenesses exist lends further evidence that the Bible is true and all other religious teachings are false. What other religions lack is an explanation through ancient teaching as to *why* similarities exist between them. What is it about mankind that explains how we seem to know in our hearts that there is an existence beyond what we can sense? Only the Bible admits this and provides an answer. This is the great strength of Christianity that often goes overlooked. It is so frequently overlooked, in fact, that even people trying to disprove the Bible will use this fact as their main attack. All it takes is a slight shift in perspective to realize that what many Christians wish to ignore is one of our most powerful tools in cutting to the heart of man and showing nonbelievers the eternity found within. The basic understanding is already there; all it needs a bit of cultivating and refining.

chapter four

Jesus' Teachings and the Early Church

Early Christian Views of Death

The beliefs held by the early Christian church regarding death are found in the Bible; thus, they resound with the views of the authors of this book. Where, however, the views of the first members of the Body of Christ differ from modern views of death aren't necessarily found in doctrine, but in the cultural context and severity of scriptural interpretations about death—specifically martyrdom.

After the crucifixion of Jesus, the apostles went about carrying out the Great Commission (Matthew 28:16–20) —spreading the Good News about Jesus' birth, death, and resurrection—with a fervor that changed the world. A new church emerged, the good word was spread, and the conviction of these men meant that most of them would die for their faith. Persecution of believers was a very real threat, and as the books and letters of the New Testament were written, a recurring theme became the concept of self-denial. In modern times, self-denial is often read as the willingness to forego certain conveniences or thrills for the betterment of one's relationship with God. But in the first couple centuries AD, after the life of Christ, the call for self-denial had an entirely different context.

"And he said to them all, If any man will come after me, let him deny himself, and take up his cross daily, and follow me" (Luke 9:23). This is a regularly quoted verse of Scripture, and others that nearly match it word for word are Matthew 16:24 and Mark 8:34. When these words were written to the early church, they were meant and received as a literal message: to live for Christ, believers must be ready to carry their cross and face their own execution regularly. It was simply part of the lifestyle of following Him. Other verses challenged the persecuted believers to own their sufferings with a sense of purpose: "We are troubled on every side, yet not distressed; we are perplexed, but not in despair; Persecuted, but not forsaken; cast down, but not destroyed," (2 Corinthians 4:8–9).

For the early church, to live *truly* meant that they were to emulate Christ, and if this meant being persecuted until death, then their attitude was that to die was "gain" (Philippians 1:21). For these individuals, the cost of following Christ was everything, and the public spectacle of dying for this cause was and honor, because this was the consummation and testimony of how truly converted one was; how absolutely core-deep their conviction ran, and their willingness to perish served as a final declaration of their belief that Jesus would keep His word and receive them into Heaven. Consider the words of Ignatius, Bishop of Antioch as he traveled to Rome, knowing full well that he was about to be martyred for his faith:

> I want all men to know that I die for God of my own free will.... Let me be given to the wild beasts, for through them I can attain to God.... Entice the wild beasts, that they may become my sepulcher and may leave no part of my body behind.... Then shall I truly be a disciple of Jesus Christ, when the world shall not so much as see my body.[232]

For a member of the early church, death was an invited privilege that sealed one's testimony and ministry, simultaneously reuniting them with the One whom they loved most.

But what is God's response to the martyring of His saints? For centuries, people have been persecuted until death for their faith, and sadly, it happens even today. For some people, the question becomes: "Where is God in the midst of these disasters? Doesn't He care that His followers are put to death?"

Consider the words of John:

If the world hate you, ye know that it hated me before it hated you. If ye were of the world, the world would love his own: but because ye are not of the world, but I have chosen you out of the world, therefore the world hateth you. (John 15:18–19)

This passage explains that because Jesus is hated by the world, then His followers are likewise despised as well. *He* was the first to be treated with animosity, and the more closely we follow in His footsteps, the more closely we will experience a similar reaction from the world to what He knew during His time here. Jesus Himself was put to death for His own heavenly cause, and those who are martyred walk the same path that He walked.

Jürgen Moltmann, a WWII prisoner of war in Belgium and Britain from 1945–1948, came to know Christ during his imprisonment and has spent his remaining years writing and teaching theology. One of his most notable works is his 1972 *The Crucified God*, wherein he outlines God as a compassionate Being who suffers alongside His creation, though He never changes in response to anguish. Simultaneously, God is not the *victim* of mankind's cruelties—and in fact, He could even relinquish obligation toward sharing in our sorrows—but because of His great love for us, He *voluntarily* feels pain when He witnesses our heartache. Moltmann wrote of the misery God surely felt during the persecution of His people which occurred during the Holocaust:

> The SS hanged two Jewish men and a youth in front of the whole camp. The men died quickly, but the death throes of the youth lasted for half an hour. "Where is God? Where is he?" someone asked behind me. As the youth still hung in torment in the noose after a long time, I heard the man call again, "Where is God now?" And I heard a voice in myself answer: "Where is he? He is here. He is hanging there on the gallows."[233]

Jesus experienced the dread of one who faced being put to death, as we see from His time spent in the Garden of Gethsemane. When He moved through the Garden, instructing disciples to sit in one area while He moved farther in, we are told that He felt "sorrowful and heavy" (Matthew 26:37). We see a few verses later that Jesus "went a little farther, and fell on his face, and prayed, saying, O my Father, if it be possible, let this cup pass from me: nevertheless not as I will, but as thou wilt" (Matthew 26:39). Jesus faced—with courage—the task that lay before Him, ultimately surrendering to God the Father's will. But even Jesus prayed that if the same work could be accomplished another way, it would be provided. Ultimately, Jesus' sacrifice was the only way to accomplish this task, and He gave Himself willingly: "Who his own self bare our sins in his own body on the tree, that we, being dead to sins, should live unto righteousness: by whose stripes ye were healed" (1 Peter 2:24).

Many people quote this verse as it pertains to physical healing, but many forget that the *healing* purchased by Jesus that day was of a *spiritual* nature. Certainly, God has the power to heal our physical bodies as well, but that was within Jesus' power *before* the crucifixion. Furthermore, if the healing obtained by Jesus' stripes (the marks left on His beaten body during His torment before crucifixion) had referred only to physical healing, then all of His followers could claim healing of all physical ailments at all times—right? Have you ever wondered why some people receive miraculous healings and others don't? Like the situation regarding martyred saints, when a friend is diagnosed with a terminal illness and doesn't receive miraculous intervention, the question comes to many people's minds: "Where is God right now?"

It helps to have a perspective on what specific healing Jesus' stripes accomplished, and that is a healing in the spiritual realm. Even when God chooses not to heal a person who suffers from a terminal illness, we have the peace of knowing that if that person is in Christ, he or she is in a better place (Heaven) and is pain-free—and we know we'll see that person again. The essential thing to remember when someone is suffering a terminal illness is this: Jesus has bought that person a beautiful future, whether He chooses to miraculously heal him or her in this life or whether that healing will be manifest in the departure from the currently ailing body.

Regardless of the nature, it is difficult to accept deaths that seem unjust—such as the death of the suddenly terminally ill; the young, abrupt, and tragic demises that we have no time to prepare for; and situations of martyrdom challenge the faith of even the strongest Christians at times. For those who believe in God, these feelings are no less real, but we have the assurance that we will someday, in the next life, understand what we do not now: "For now we see through a glass, darkly; but then face to face: now I know in part; but then shall I know even as also I am known" (1 Corinthians 13:12).

We also have assurance that God will not leave us in our hour of need, even though sometimes His presence feels as though it is silent:

For the LORD will not cast off his people, neither will he forsake his inheritance. But judgment shall return unto righteousness: and all the upright in heart shall follow it. Who will rise up for me against the evildoers? or who will stand up for me against the workers of iniquity? Unless the Lord had been my help, my soul had almost dwelt in silence. When I said, My foot slippeth; thy mercy, O Lord, held me up. In the multitude of my thoughts within me thy comforts delight my soul. (Psalm 94:14–19)

Fear thou not; for I am with thee: be not dismayed; for I am thy God: I will strengthen thee; yea, I will help thee; yea, I will uphold thee with the right hand of my righteousness. (Isaiah 41:10)

I will never leave thee, nor forsake thee. (Hebrews 13:5)

Did the Apostle Paul Have an NDE?

Claims of near-death experiences abound throughout society and across the world, and while many of them include similar elements, some do not align with all the others. Furthermore, some people come back from "the other side" with claims of witnessing things that don't line up with Scripture. How do we rectify such discrepancies? Does the Bible describe such encounters?

Many biblical scholars maintain that the apostle Paul had such an experience. Consider the following passage:

And there came thither certain Jews from Antioch and Iconium, who persuaded the people, and, having stoned Paul, drew him out of the city, supposing he had been dead. (Acts 14:19)

A little more than fourteen years later, Paul recounted the incident:

It is not expedient for me doubtless to glory. I will come to visions and revelations of the Lord. I knew a man in Christ above fourteen years ago, (whether in the body, I cannot tell;

or whether out of the body, I cannot tell: God knoweth;) such an one caught up to the third heaven. And I knew such a man, (whether in the body, or out of the body, I cannot tell: God knoweth;) How that he was caught up into paradise, and heard unspeakable words, which it is not lawful for a man to utter. (2 Corinthians 12:1–4)

Paul's testimony is that what he saw and heard was beyond awesome. However, despite the fact that his teaching about spiritual matters including the afterlife is powerful and authoritative, he was limited as to what he could tell about the experience.

The Sign of Jonah

An evil and adulterous generation seeketh after a sign; and there shall no sign be given to it, but the sign of the prophet Jonas: For as Jonas [Jonah] was three days and three nights in the whale's belly; so shall the Son of man be three days and three nights in the heart of the earth... Behold, a greater then Jonas [Jonah] is here. (Matthew 12:39–41)

As Jesus was being questioned by the scribes and Pharisees who wanted Him to give them proof of His Messiahship, Jesus called them out. He took them back to the historical story of Jonah, who, having run from God, found himself in the belly of a great fish. But was Jonah *literally* in the belly of a fish, or did he go somewhere else? Was he alive for this duration of time, or did he die and later resurrect?

Many who read the story of Jonah accept the tale literally: He was cast into the sea and swallowed by a fish, hung out in the belly of a large sea animal for three days, and then, miraculously, was spat out on the shore near Nineveh and told by God to carry on with his mission. Others, however, believe the passage in Matthew 12 hints at something more supernatural. In addition, the comparison made between Jonah and Christ in this Scripture makes a person wonder if there is more to the story than initially meets the eye.

There appears to be two schools of thought concerning what happened to Jonah during the three days and nights that he was detained by the fish. The first is the literal interpretation mentioned previously, while the other states that Jonah's experience was a death and resurrection. Furthermore, the second line of thinking also holds that while Jonah's experience foreshadowed the time Jesus spent in the tomb after His crucifixion, the future return of Christ will take place after yet another symbol: the "sign of the Son of Man in heaven" (Matthew 24:30). Each interpretation has compelling arguments.

In the early part of chapter 1 of the book of Jonah, we see that God ordered the prophet to go to Nineveh and preach to the people there regarding their wickedness, but Jonah was disobedient and fled, boarding a ship headed for Tarshish instead. The Lord sent a great wind that caused a storm so terrible that the ship nearly perished. Once it was determined that Jonah's defiance against the Almighty had caused this turn of events, Jonah allowed himself to be thrown overboard—into the raging sea—so the storm would subside and allow the ship to safely finish its course.

Jonah 1:17 tells us that the Lord prepared a great fish to swallow Jonah, and that he was in the belly of this animal for three days and nights. In this verse, the word "belly" is taken from the Hebrew word *me'ah*, a term referring to an *anatomical* location of the fish's body.[234] However, Jonah 2:2 states that Jonah cried to God "out of the belly of hell." In this case, the word "belly" derives from the Hebrew word *beten*, which in some cases still notes a physical location within the body, but also refers to the depth of Sheol.[235] The word "hell" in Jonah 2:2 is taken from the Hebrew word *Shĕ'owl*, which, as noted earlier, is a direct translation to the underworld or the grave.[236] So, the argument in this case is that Jonah was in the underworld when he cried out to God for help.

Furthermore, Jonah 2:3–7 describes a series of events that many claim to be a description of Jonah's drowning and dying:

> For thou hadst cast me into the deep, in the midst of the seas; and the floods compassed me about: all thy billows and thy waves passed over me. Then I said, I am cast out of thy sight; yet I will look again toward thy holy temple. The waters compassed me about, even to the soul: the depth closed me round about, the weeds were wrapped about my head. I went down to the bottoms of the mountains; the earth with her bars was about me for ever: yet hast thou brought up my life from corruption, O Lord my God. When my soul fainted within me I remembered the Lord: and my prayer came in unto thee, into thine holy temple.

Recall that Jonah 1:4 states the storm was so extreme that the ship Jonah had boarded to Tarshish would have been broken by the tumultuous waters. Here, the prophet describes being tossed amidst the waves of the same raging sea. The waters enveloped him "even to the soul," while plant matter wound about his head. Jonah sank further down until he reached the "bottoms of the mountains" and his "soul fainted."

Interestingly, the phrase, "the earth with her bars was about me forever," comes from the Hebrew phrase *'erets běriyach 'owlam*, which, translated into modern language, means "the earth's city gates, fortress, or prison of long duration and antiquity perpetually held me."[237] Bearing this in mind, many scholars believe that it was actually Jonah's corpse that the fish swallowed. They make the argument that Jonah likely would never have survived the dark, internal condition of such a creature, submerged in stomach acids and deprived of oxygen. Instead, they claim that Jonah was resurrected when he was vomited out onto the shore.

Those who believe that Jonah didn't die during this experience compare the use of the word *sheol* to a poetic statement regarding the trauma of his episode. It is believed and accepted that, since God had prepared the fish (Jonah 1: 17), the creature had been somehow miraculously conditioned in such a way that a person could survive being swallowed by it. Jonah was alive and was sustained in the belly of the great fish for three days and three nights. He was conscious and aware of his surroundings, despite being subjected to total darkness for the duration. As for the question of his exposure to the animal's digestive tract, stomach acid, or other factors that *should* have killed him, the scholars have a simple answer: It was *the Lord* who had prepared the great fish to swallow Jonah. Ensuring survival isn't a problem for the Creator of the universe. Furthermore, many who believe that Jonah never died during this experience reinforce their position using the final moments of the story, found in Jonah chapter 4, when he dramatically struggled with his own humanity. At this point in the story, Nineveh had repented and would not be destroyed. However, rather than rejoicing that the rebellious city made a righteous decision and would be spared, Jonah was angry. In fact, he even played a game of "I told you so!" with God (verse 2). He traveled outside the city on the anticipated date of the city's destruction, and perched himself in a location with a good view. He was frustrated, knowing in advance that the show of obliteration he *would like* to see would not happen. Despite God's intervention by supplying a small shade-gourd for him to sit beneath, he remained obstinate toward God's forgiveness for the remainder of the story. Many who see this attitude on behalf on Jonah cannot believe that he died, stating that had he *truly* been brought back from death, or had he *really* seen the afterworld, his perspective would have been more mature during these final moments of the account.

Regardless of whether Jonah physically died, there is an undoubted connection to Jesus, as stated in Matthew 12:40: "For as Jonas was three days and three nights in the whale's belly; so shall the Son of man be three days and three nights in the heart of the earth." As we know, Jesus was raised from the dead on the third day (Luke 24:7).

We are told that on the very day of Christ's death, He gave up the ghost, His soul was separated from His body, and, in the Spirit, He entered Paradise. His body was dead, but His spirit was alive and well. Jesus spent three days and three nights in the belly of the earth, just as Jonah spent three days and three nights in the belly of the great fish. Jesus, being put to death physically, was very alive spiritually—and, quickened by the Holy Spirit, He preached to the spirits held captive in death's prison:

> For Christ also hath once suffered for sins, the just for the unjust, that he might bring us to God, being put to death in the flesh, but quickened by the Spirit: By which also he went and preached unto the spirits in prison. (1 Peter 3:18–19)

For many, regardless of whether Jonah actually died, it is easy to accept the connection between Jonas and Jesus. However, the link to prophetic events often escapes the same crowd. There are more than two instances in the Bible of a resurrection on the third day. One of these events takes place in the future.

> And I will give power unto my two witnesses, and they shall prophesy a thousand two hundred and threescore days, clothed in sackcloth…. And when they shall have finished their testimony, the beast that ascendeth out of the bottomless pit shall make war against them, and shall overcome them, and kill them. And their dead bodies shall lie in the street of the great city, which spiritually is called Sodom and Egypt, where also our Lord was crucified. And they of the people and kindreds and tongues and nations shall see their dead bodies three days and an half, and shall not suffer their dead bodies to be put in graves…. And after three days and an half the spirit of life from God entered into them, and they stood upon their feet;

and great fear fell upon them which saw them. And they heard a great voice from heaven saying unto them, Come up hither. And they ascended up to heaven in a cloud; and their enemies beheld them. And the same hour was there a great earthquake, and the tenth part of the city fell, and in the earthquake were slain of men seven thousand: and the remnant were affrighted, and gave glory to the God of heaven. (Revelation 11:3, 7–9, 11–13)

When these witnesses arrive on the scene in the end times, they will be hated by the world. Only those who belong to God will not loathe them. In fact, the animosity toward these will be so extreme that when they die, they will not be given a burial; rather, their corpses will be left on the ground while the people of the earth celebrate. When they rise again and ascend into Heaven, the judgments of mankind begin to speed up. The Day of the Lord will approach quickly thereafter:

The great day of the Lord is near, it is near, and hasteth greatly, even the voice of the day of the Lord: the mighty man shall cry there bitterly, That day is a day of wrath, a day of trouble and distress, a day of wasteness and desolation, a day of darkness and gloominess, a day of clouds and thick darkness … And I will bring distress upon men, that they shall walk like blind men, because they have sinned against the Lord: and their blood shall be poured out as dust, and their flesh as the dung. Neither their silver nor their gold shall be able to deliver them in the day of the Lord's wrath; but the whole land shall be devoured by the fire of his jealousy: for he shall make even a speedy riddance of all them that dwell in the land. (Zephaniah 1:14–15, 17–18)

If the sign of Jonas (Jonah) is a sign of the Son of Man (Jesus), then the final reign of Jesus could be foreshadowed by such a sign as well.

Between the three stories we see the similarities of death, a three-day burial or detainment, followed by a resurrection. Thus, future parallels of the Jonah story could indicate the fulfilling of prophetic events and the consummation of the Kingdom of God.

In all of these accounts, God shows that He is the authority over death.

Jesus Paved the Way for Our Afterlife

This is the Son of the carpenter, Who skilfully made His cross a bridge over Sheol that swallows up all, and brought over mankind into the dwelling of life. And because it was through the tree that mankind had fallen into Sheol, so upon the tree they passed over into the dwelling of life. Through the tree then wherein bitterness was tasted, through it also sweetness was tasted; that we might learn of Him that amongst the creatures nothing resists Him. Glory be to Thee, Who didst lay Thy cross as a bridge over death, that souls might pass over upon it from the dwelling of the dead to the dwelling of life! (Homily on our Lord 4).[238]

The Bible tells us that after we die, there is a judgment. For that very reason, Jesus Christ came to earth and was offered before God the Father to carry the burden of our sins. Because He was the ultimate sacrifice, we have the ultimate opportunity for eternal life. However, because Jesus was the *One* perfect sacrifice, we are offered *one* life during which we must choose to live for Him. Once a person has passed on, there is no opportunity for "do-overs," nor is there a chance for reincarnation. "And as it is appointed unto men once to die, but after this the judgment: So Christ was once offered to bear the sins of many; and unto them that look for him shall he appear the second time without sin unto salvation" (Hebrews 9:27–28).

According to the Bible, life after death is taught not only as a reality, but as a certainty. Jesus imparted that there was more to life than just this moment in time. He clearly spoke of the soul's existence after the death of the body for both the saved and the lost:

> Verily, verily, I say unto you, He that heareth my word, and believeth on him that sent me, hath everlasting life, and shall not come into condemnation; but is passed from death unto life.... The hour is coming…when the dead shall hear the voice of the Son of God: and they that hear shall live. For as the Father hath life in himself; so hath he given to the Son to have life in himself; And hath given him authority to execute judgment also, because he is the Son of man…the hour is coming, in the which all that are in the graves shall hear his voice, And shall come forth; they that have done good, unto the resurrection of life; and they that have done evil, unto the resurrection of damnation. (John 5:24–29)

This passage explains a few important things to us about Jesus' authority over death. First, those who believe in Jesus and follow His word will have everlasting life. Second, a day will come when those who are dead in Christ will rise again. Third, the Father who has the power to breathe the breath of life has shared that life-instilling authority with Jesus. Fourth, Jesus has been given the right to judge the dead, which He will also do in that day.

The apostle Paul explained to the Corinthian church that the resurrection of Jesus provides proof that doctrine found in the Bible—about the afterlife and other scriptural matters—are also true:

> But if there be no resurrection of the dead, then is Christ not risen: And if Christ be not risen, then is our preaching vain, and your faith is also vain. Yea, and we are found false witnesses of

God; because we have testified of God that he raised up Christ: whom he raised not up, if so be that the dead rise not. For if the dead rise not, then is not Christ raised: And if Christ be not raised, your faith is vain; ye are yet in your sins. Then they also which are fallen asleep in Christ are perished. If in this life only we have hope in Christ, we are of all men most miserable. But now is Christ risen from the dead, and become the firstfruits of them that slept. (1 Corinthians 15:13–20)

The resurrection of Jesus, according to Paul, is proof that physical death is not the end of the existence of the soul. Furthermore, His resurrection, in proving the concept of the resurrection of the saints, thereby adds credibility to *all* scriptural doctrine; otherwise, as the passage states, we would be "miserable."

The sole purpose of Jesus Christ's coming to earth, being born of a virgin, living among men a perfect, sinless life, and then being wrongly convicted, brutally beaten, and publicly crucified was foretold by the prophets of old. His purpose was to provide for mankind the way of escape from eternal punishment for sin. He took our sins, nailed them to His cross, and paid the penalty for sin so that in the afterlife we could live with Him forever in His glorious heavenly home.

But he was wounded for our transgressions, he was bruised for our iniquities: the chastisement of our peace was upon him; and with his stripes we are healed...and the Lord hath laid on him the iniquity of us all...he is brought as a lamb to the slaughter.... He was taken from prison and from judgment...he was cut off out of the land of the living: for the transgression of my people was he stricken...because he hath poured out his soul unto death...and he bare the sin of many, and made intercession for the transgressors. (Isaiah 53:5–12)

Words from Christ about the Afterlife

Jesus, the only begotten Son of God, came on mission from Heaven to live on the very earth He had created, dwelling among mankind which He created, because He knew that there is more to this life than just living in this moment. His intent was to provide real life in this world and an eternal home with Him in heaven. Jesus tells us in John 10:10 that He has come to provide life that is more abundant than what we can experience on earth without Him, but this "abundant" life includes the hope of an eternal life. Likewise, He explained that there is a place in the next world that is prepared for those who love Him—a place we can be assured we will be taken to in the next life:

> In my Father's house are many mansions: if it were not so, I would have told you. I go to prepare a place for you. And if I go and prepare a place for you, I will come again, and receive you unto myself; that where I am, there ye may be also. (John 14:2–3)

Even as Jesus was hanging on the cross, He promised the one thief who believed in Him that on that very day they would be in Paradise together, assuring the criminal that he would receive life after death. This showed that His command, even under conditions of human conviction and scorn, was authoritative and instant in the spirit realm.

> And one of the malefactors which were hanged railed on him, saying, If thou be Christ, save thyself and us. But the other answering rebuked him, saying, Dost not thou fear God, seeing thou art in the same condemnation? And we indeed justly; for we receive the due reward of our deeds: but this man hath done nothing amiss. And he said unto Jesus, Lord, remember me when thou comest into thy kingdom. And Jesus said unto

him, Verily I say unto thee, To day shalt thou be with me in paradise. (Luke 23:39–43)

Through the victory that Jesus obtained via His sacrifice on the cross, He purchased our atonement and made it so that corrupt man could take on incorruption, and paved the way for death to be swallowed up in victory. Before this occurrence, we were bound to the Law, which we could never live up to. This is why men in the Old Testament had to periodically make sacrifices for their sins. All that changed when Jesus went to the cross in our place:

> So when this corruptible shall have put on incorruption, and this mortal shall have put on immortality, then shall be brought to pass the saying that is written, Death is swallowed up in victory. O death, where is thy sting? O grave, where is thy victory? The sting of death is sin; and the strength of sin is the law. But thanks be to God, which giveth us the victory through our Lord Jesus Christ. (1 Corinthians 15:54–57)

Since Jesus is the Word who has been since the beginning (John 1:1), who existed in eternity past and was active in every part of creation, He knows both life and death intimately. He has the power over death, hell, and the grave. Thus, His teachings on the afterlife hold final authority on the subject. As Jesus Himself said, "I am he that liveth, and was dead; and, behold, I am alive for evermore, Amen; and have the keys of hell and of death" (Revelation 1:18).

Paul confirms this in Romans 6:9: "Knowing that Christ being raised from the dead dieth no more; death hath no more dominion over him," and again in Romans 14:9: "For to this end Christ both died, and rose, and revived, that he might be Lord both of the dead and living."

It would then be wise for us to hear and adhere to the teachings of Jesus on this and every subject. He has the final word.

Physical Death and Spiritual Death

> Jesus said unto her, I am the resurrection, and the life: he that
> believeth in me, though he were dead, yet shall he live: And
> whosoever liveth and believeth in me shall never die. Believest
> thou this? (John 11:25–26)

Jesus speaks of two kinds of death: physical death, which is separation from the physical body, and spiritual death, in which the soul is separated from God's presence for eternity. Those who follow the Lord—come what may—until the end of their lives on earth will reap the reward of this steadfastness in the next life:

> He that overcometh shall inherit all things; and I will be his
> God, and he shall be my son. But the fearful, and unbelieving,
> and the abominable, and murderers, and whoremongers, and
> sorcerers, and idolaters, and all liars, shall have their part in the
> lake which burneth with fire and brimstone: which is the second
> death. (Revelation 21:7–8)

People Jesus Raised from the Dead

Jesus was known to some as a great teacher; to others, He was a great prophet, and yet multitudes followed Him because of the many miracles He performed. He turned water into wine, He made the blind to see, He caused the lame to walk again, He healed a withered hand, He fed thousands with only a few fish and several loaves of bread, and He even cured the awful disease of leprosy in ten men at one time. But of all the miracles Jesus performed, one of His most notable is raising someone from the dead. And, He did it on more than one occasion.

The Son of the Widow from Nain

As Jesus was entering the city of Nain, a little town southwest of Capernaum, He came upon a funeral procession. A young man, the only son of his widowed mother, was being carried out of the city to be buried. Luke tells the story as follows:

> And it came to pass the day after, that he went into a city called Nain; and many of his disciples went with him, and much people. Now when he came nigh to the gate of the city, behold, there was a dead man carried out, the only son of his mother, and she was a widow: and much people of the city was with her. And when the Lord saw her, he had compassion on her, and said unto her, Weep not. And he came and touched the bier: and they that bare him stood still. And he said, Young man, I say unto thee, Arise. And he that was dead sat up, and began to speak. And he delivered him to his mother. And there came a fear on all: and they glorified God, saying, That a great prophet is risen up among us; and, That God hath visited his people. And this rumour of him went forth throughout all Judaea, and throughout all the region round about. (Luke 7:11–17)

Jesus Christ was able to speak to a dead man and command him to rise from the dead, even while the man's body was being carried in a funeral procession. The passage indicates that some of the people responded with fear, stating that God Himself had visited the people. This is due to the fact that the crowd knew no other source could have possibly held such authority over death. As the only begotten Son of God, the Creator of the universe, for Him to call to a man who is physically dead, separated from his body, and bring him back to that body, fits completely within His power.

The Daughter of Jairus, Ruler of the Temple

Mark records another incident in which Jesus was called upon to heal a young child. This time it was the daughter of one of the rulers of the synagogue. The little girl was sick and near death. Jesus immediately went with him, and a great crowd followed:

> And, behold, there cometh one of the rulers of the synagogue, Jairus by name; and when he saw him, he fell at his feet, And besought him greatly, saying, My little daughter lieth at the point of death: I pray thee, come and lay thy hands on her, that she may be healed; and she shall live. And Jesus went with him; and much people followed him, and thronged him. (Mark 5:21–24)

The crowds swamped Jesus and made it very difficult for Him to get to his destination. Before they arrived at the location of the ill child, news arrived that it was too late: the girl had already died. Imagine this father's hopes and dreams that were destroyed in that moment, and the emotions that must have flooded his heart. Certainly, he must have been thinking, "It's too late; my daughter is dead and gone. All is lost."

But, remember who we are talking about: Jesus Christ—the One whom has been given all power in heaven and earth (Matthew 28:18), the Almighty Word who holds the keys to hell and death (Revelation 1:18).

The story continues: Jesus heard the announcement that the man's daughter had perished—they were too late to save her. He instructed the man to believe, and took only Peter, James, and John the brother of James. As he entered the home of the synagogue ruler, he saw those mourning the loss of the child, and challenged them by asking why they wept. He stated that she wasn't dead, but was sleeping. His proclamation was met with laughter and scorn. Jesus sent these people out of the house and took the girl's father and mother into the chamber where she lay. Jesus took the girl's hand, and spoke: "*Talitha cumi*," He said, which means, "Damsel, I say unto thee, arise" (Mark 5:41). Immediately, the girl awakened and began to move about.

It is interesting to note that Jesus always works in direct connection to the faith of those around Him. When His announcement that the girl merely slept was met with disbelief, He emptied the house of those who lacked faith. While Jesus has supreme authority over death and the grave, He does not force miracles on those who will not place their trust in Him.

Lazarus, a Close Friend of Jesus

Jesus had a close friend named Lazarus who lived in Bethany with his two sisters, Mary and Martha. One day, these two women sent word to Jesus, telling Him that His beloved friend Lazarus had fallen ill and asking Him to come quickly. Jesus' response was to explain that the sickness would not lead to death, but would instead provide opportunity for God's glory to be known (John 11:4). Jesus understood that while there would be a temporary separation from the body on Lazarus' part, it would not be permanent. Jesus knew that the life of Lazarus would be restored. Because of this, he didn't hurry to Lazarus' side, but rather continued His present mission until two days later, when He finally began to make the journey (John 11:6). By this time, Jesus was aware that His friend had already died, saying, "Our friend Lazarus sleepeth; but I go, that I may awake him out of sleep" (John 11:11). It is obvious from Jesus' statements that He had a plan for bringing glory to God. There is no lingering question that He waited out of insensitivity, or because He was so preoccupied that He couldn't make time for His friend. We see from the resurrection of the daughter of Jairus that Jesus can state that someone in a different location is alive and that person will be. So, even if Jesus hadn't been able to make the journey to Lazarus' home, He certainly could have healed his friend from wherever He was when He received the news that Lazarus was sick. Jesus' delay was *deliberate*.

He knew that a miracle would be worked in order to glorify God. The confrontation with Martha and Mary yielded little or no faith and literally drove Jesus to tears. Now, there are some who say that Jesus was being empathetic with the sisters and broke down and wept. Others says that He was overcome by the whole scene of the weeping, wailing, and mourning, and because of His love for Lazarus, He too wept. But from the beginning of the account in John's Gospel, Jesus told the disciples that something great was going to happen. In John 11:15, Jesus told His disciples that He was glad He hadn't been there to heal Lazarus, because what was ahead would help them to believe. People in some ancient Jewish cultures believed that the soul lingered over the deceased body for three days, while a war between good and evil fought for the soul of the departed. John 11:17 tells us that by the time Jesus arrived at Lazarus' home, he had already been in the grave for four days. Because of the fact that Jesus knew in advance that He would raise Lazarus from the dead, some believe that He also *intentionally* waited until Lazarus had been dead for *four* days, so that those in His culture would not assert that Lazarus' soul had been hovering near his body and waiting for an opportunity at re-insertion, but instead recognize Jesus' authority over death and the grave. Jesus Himself reminded those around Him of this authority when, before raising Lazarus from the dead, he stated: "I am the resurrection and the life: he that believeth in me, though he were dead, yet shall he live" (John 11:25). At the utterance of three words: "Lazarus, come forth" (John 11:43), death was again overcome and Lazarus walked among the living.

> Jesus therefore again groaning in himself cometh to the grave. It was a cave, and a stone lay upon it. Jesus said, Take ye away the stone. Martha, the sister of him that was dead, saith unto him, Lord, by this time he stinketh: for he hath been dead four days. Jesus saith unto her, Said I not unto thee, that, if thou wouldest believe, thou shouldest see the glory of God? Then they took

away the stone from the place where the dead was laid. And Jesus lifted up his eyes, and said, Father, I thank thee that thou hast heard me. And I knew that thou hearest me always: but because of the people which stand by I said it, that they may believe that thou hast sent me. And when he thus had spoken, he cried with a loud voice, Lazarus, come forth. And he that was dead came forth, bound hand and foot with graveclothes: and his face was bound about with a napkin. Jesus saith unto them, Loose him, and let him go. (John 11:38–44)

Even though Lazarus had died physically in that his soul had separated from his body, Jesus said he was still in existence as though he were sleeping. Jesus, by His God-given power and authority, called Lazarus to rejoin the soul with the body that had been in the grave for four days, and he indeed came forth out of the grave, still bound by the grave clothes.

If death were termination of existence, there would be no returning of the soul to the body after death. In the three aforementioned cases of resurrection, these people were dead—their souls were separated from their bodies, yet they still were able to rejoin their physical bodies. This is additional proof that death doesn't mean termination of existence. Physical death is only a separation of soul and body, and Jesus Christ is Lord over death, hell, and the grave!

Later, the religious leaders wanted to silence the crowds coming to see Jesus, along with Lazarus, whom Jesus had raised from the dead.

Much people of the Jews therefore knew that he was there: and they came not for Jesus' sake only, but that they might see Lazarus also, whom he had raised from the dead. But the chief priests consulted that they might put Lazarus also to death; Because that by reason of him many of the Jews went away, and believed on Jesus. (John 12:9–11)

The religious leaders didn't know who they were dealing with that day. Jesus could have again and again raised Lazarus, because Jesus *is* the resurrection and the life.

The Transfiguration

On the mountain where Jesus prayed, His face became as bright as the sun, and Moses and Elijah appeared there with Him (Matthew 17). Both these men had long been "dead" for hundreds of years, with their souls separate from their bodies, yet both physically appeared and held a conversation with Jesus on this mountain. Though the three disciples—Peter, James, and John—who were with Jesus had never seen these men, they recognized and identified both. Initially, Peter suggested that tabernacles be built for these visitors, but immediately a supernatural light shone brightly, and a voice out of Heaven said, "This is my beloved Son, in whom I am well pleased; here ye him" (Matthew 17:5). At this, the disciples realized that temporal accommodations would not be necessary for these heavenly visitors. The disciples fell down, prostrate in fear, until Jesus came and, touching them, said "Arise, and be not afraid" (Matthew 17:7). When they looked up, only Jesus stood before them.

This account reinforces the previously made point that if death were truly the end, those who were deceased would not be able to revisit this earth. Yet, there before the disciples stood Moses and Elijah, men who had been dead for centuries. This is another instance that confirms that God's departed servants still exist in His afterworld realm.

Jesus' Death Tore the Veil of the Temple

In the Gospel of Matthew, we are told that, about the ninth hour while He was on the cross, Jesus cried out with a loud voice and gave up the ghost. Physical death had come upon the only begotten Son of God. The penalty for sin had been accomplished: "without shedding of blood is no remission" (Hebrews 9:22), and the great wall separating God and man was torn down.

> Jesus, when he had cried again with a loud voice, yielded up the ghost. And, behold, the veil of the temple was rent in twain from the top to the bottom; and the earth did quake, and the rocks rent. (Matthew 27:50–51)

The curtain or veil of the temple was considered a barrier, an obstruction blocking man's access to God. Since the time when Adam and Eve, in the Garden of Eden, had sinned against God and given in to the temptation of the serpent, all mankind was separated from God. Jesus' sacrificial death on the cross as the perfect Lamb of God made way for mankind to approach God once again. Having paid the ransom for sin, mankind could now, through the door of Christ, have access to God the Father: "For there is one God, and one mediator between God and men, the man Christ Jesus Who gave himself a ransom for all, to be testified in due time" (1 Timothy 2:5–6).

When Jesus died, supernatural activity rocked the natural world… the earth quaked, the rocks tumbled and broke apart, and Jesus, the Son of God, traveling through the unseen realms, electrified the graves there in Jerusalem:

> And the graves were opened; and many bodies of the saints which slept arose, And came out of the graves after his resurrection, and went into the holy city, and appeared unto many. (Matthew 27:52–53)

So, after the resurrection of Christ Jesus, these "sleeping saints" were raised up and were seen by a host of people in Jerusalem. We don't have a biblical record of how many saints were resurrected or how long after this event they remained alive on the earth. Perhaps they went to Heaven when Jesus ascended, or maybe they continued to live in the natural realm until they died a second time (not to be confused with the second death discussed in Revelation). However, we understand that this event was part of what set apart the early church from all false religions that had thrived up until this point. The living resurrected provided *proof* that Jesus was who He had claimed to be: One who held all authority over life and death. This event, found in Matthew 27:52–54, became notorious throughout the land as evidence that Christianity had something unique that other religions could not boast of: a Deity who had walked upon the land, proving Himself to His followers through His compassion and love, and who had publicly conquered the grave.

We have some of the early Christian fathers' writings about the event:

Ignatius to the Trallians (AD 70–115): "For says the Scripture, 'Many bodies of the saints that slept arose,' (Mat[thew] 27:52) their graves being opened. He descended, indeed, into Hades alone, but He arose accompanied by a multitude."[239]

Irenaeus (AD 120–200): "He [Christ] suffered who can lead those souls aloft that follow His ascension. This event was also an indication of the fact, that when the holy soul of Christ descended [to Hades], many souls ascended and were seen in their bodies."[240]

Clement of Alexandria (AD 155–200) " 'But those who had fallen asleep descended dead, but ascended alive.' Further, the Gospel says, 'that many bodies of those that slept arose,'—plainly as having been translated to a better state."[241]

Many believe that Lazarus, as well as the other two whom Jesus raised from the dead, eventually died again and therefore were buried by their families. It could likewise be reasoned that these "awakened saints" also at some time later died again and were then buried again. We are told in Scripture that a similar event will take place in the future:

Marvel not at this: for the hour is coming, in the which all that are in the graves shall hear his voice, And shall come forth; they that have done good, unto the resurrection of life; and they that have done evil, unto the resurrection of damnation. (John 5:28–29)

One everyone can be certain about: We all have to face death one day. Furthermore, each of us must make choices that direct the pathway to one of two final destinations, Heaven or Hell. Remembering that death is *separation,* not *termination,* we define physical death as separation of the soul from the body, whereas spiritual death is the separation of the soul from the presence of God.

As the passage from John 5 indicates, those who have placed their faith in Jesus Christ have chosen wisely. On the other hand, those who do not believe on Jesus are condemned already, and to them is the resurrection of damnation. Jesus promised us:

For God so loved the world, that he gave his only begotten Son, that whosoever believeth in him should not perish, but have everlasting life. For God sent not his Son into the world to condemn the world; but that the world through him might be saved. He that believeth on him is not condemned: but he that believeth not is condemned already, because he hath not believed in the name of the only begotten Son of God. (John 3:16–18)

The fact that there is both "the resurrection of life" and "the resurrection of damnation" (John 5:29) should motivate us to seek Jesus and become His followers. The idea that there is a resurrection of damnation drives us to some further examination.

Resurrection of Damnation

Damnation, according to Scripture, is defined as existence after physical death wherein the soul is separated from the presence of God. But would this be eternal torment (burning in Hell forever) or annihilation (soul and body destroyed in the Lake of Fire and therefore ceasing to exist entirely)? Some scholars assert that the second death, spoken of in Revelation, refers to the concept that once all human souls have reached their final destination, those who are in Hell will be annihilated, citing God's compassion as a motivation for destruction over eternal, irreconcilable torment. God "is longsuffering to us-ward, not willing that any should perish, but that all should come to repentance" (2 Peter 3:9).

Annihilation

The Merriam-Webster dictionary defines "annihilation" as "the state or fact of being completely destroyed or obliterated."

> And the sea gave up the dead which were in it; and death and hell delivered up the dead which were in them: and they were judged every man according to their works. And death and hell were cast into the lake of fire. This is the second death. And whosoever was not found written in the book of life was cast into the lake of fire. (Revelation 20:13–15)

Some contend that casting all those who died without faith in Christ Jesus, both great and small, along with death and Hell, into the Lake of Fire, spoken of as the "second death," is a picture of final annihilation. They believe that, beyond separation from God for eternity, this is the final termination of the existence of the soul. Reinforcing this concept is that while the Bible speaks of eternal life, the Bible does not use the term "eternal death": "For the wages of sin is death; but the gift of God is eternal life through Jesus Christ our Lord" (Romans 6:23). According to this thought, the suffering in Hell of those who die without Christ is forever terminated they are when cast into the Lake of Fire. Though this sounds ruthless, the other possibility sounds exceedingly cruel, and if it were not in Scripture, would almost be unbelievable.

Eternal Torment

Jesus made it perfectly clear when He told the story of the rich man and the beggar Lazarus that those who do not live according to His law will be sent to Hell and tormented while the righteous will be sent to an eternal reward. Plenty of other passages in Scripture state that followers of Christ will rest, while others will suffer for rejecting Him.

> Seeing it is a righteous thing with God to recompense tribulation to them that trouble you; And to you who are troubled rest with us, when the Lord Jesus shall be revealed from heaven with his mighty angels, In flaming fire taking vengeance on them that know not God, and that obey not the gospel of our Lord Jesus Christ: Who shall be punished with everlasting destruction from the presence of the Lord, and from the glory of his power; When he shall come to be glorified in his saints, and to be admired in all them that believe (because our testimony among you was believed) in that day. (2 Thessalonians 1:6–10)

The Lake of Fire was not intended for man. God doesn't want anyone to perish, which is why He sent His Son to die for our sins. Furthermore, the origin of deception of many will likewise be cast into the Lake of Fire: "And the devil that deceived them was cast into the lake of fire and brimstone, where the beast and the false prophet are, and shall be tormented day and night for ever and ever" (Revelation 20:10).

We also find that those who worship Antichrist and receive his mark are destined to the same fate as the devil himself:

> And the third angel followed them, saying with a loud voice, If any man worship the beast and his image, and receive his mark in his forehead, or in his hand, The same shall drink of the wine of the wrath of God, which is poured out without mixture into

the cup of his indignation; and he shall be tormented with fire and brimstone in the presence of the holy angels, and in the presence of the Lamb: And the smoke of their torment ascendeth up for ever and ever: and they have no rest day nor night, who worship the beast and his image, and whosoever receiveth the mark of his name. (Revelation 14:9–11)

Some believe that the resurrection of damnation is taught throughout Scripture to be everlasting, day and night forever and ever. Others state that it equals a total annihilation of those sent to the Lake of Fire, who subsequently will cease to exist. Both concepts are terrifying, as each represents permanent and eternal separation from God.

Resurrection of Life

The Bible is replete with references to eternal life, everlasting life, and spending eternity in the presence of Jehovah God. The concept is forever awesome! Eternal life begins the moment you believe Jesus, trust in Him to forgive your sins and give you eternal life. Jesus said, "The thief cometh not, but for to steal, and to kill, and to destroy: I am come that they might have life, and that they might have it more abundantly" (John 10:10). If you are a believer, you don't have to wait until Heaven to experience the abundant and eternal life Jesus promised.

Jesus promised His followers that He was going to prepare a place for them and that He would come again to gather them together to live with Him. The promise of the resurrection of life brings hope and expectancy that we will be in the presence of the LORD forever and forever.

For the Lord himself shall descend from heaven with a shout, with the voice of the archangel, and with the trump of God: and the dead in Christ shall rise first: Then we which are alive and remain shall be caught up together with them in the clouds, to meet the Lord in the air: and so shall we ever be with the Lord. (1 Thessalonians 4:16–17)

Wherever He is will be gloriously magnificent, and His promise is that we will be with Him for eternity.

At the last part of the Bible, we find God's people rejoicing in their never-ending heavenly home that's out of this world. But we also find that those who have rejected God's offer of love through His Son, Jesus Christ, will be separated from God and be cast into outer darkness and into the lake of fire that was prepared for the devil and his urchins.

Final Eternal Home: Heaven or Hell?

Let's make some sense of what the Bible says about our final eternal home. We've discussed some of the terms used throughout Scripture referring to the afterlife: Sheol, Hades, Tartarus, Gehenna, the Lake of Fire, as well as Paradise, Abraham's bosom, and Heaven. Often in modern culture, these concepts are generalized as either Heaven or Hell.

Hell

The English word "hell" is used fifty-four times in the King James Version. Adding the references to Tartarus, Hades, Gehenna, and Sheol, and other terms that translate into the modern English word "hell," we find that there are more than 150 references in the New Testament alone that warn of this place. Furthermore, many of these references were uttered by the Lord Jesus Christ Himself. There are many who object to the concept of Hell by saying, "A loving God would not send billions of people to a horrible hell; a compassionate God would be more tolerant." However, recall that 2 Peter 3:9 states that God doesn't want people to perish. Jesus paid a high price to offer us the opportunity of salvation, and He makes this precious prospect available to everyone in the world.

Any who reject His offer are choosing for themselves an eternity separated from the presence of God.

Why Does God Send People To Hell?

As mentioned previously, the question of why God would send people to Hell if He is indeed a loving and compassionate being is ever-recurring. The answer usually goes like this: "God doesn't *choose* to send people to Hell; they choose it for themselves by rejecting Him." While this may deescalate the general argument, many individuals walk away from such a conversation with lingering questions: questions which, if left unanswered, often call an individual to steer away from a God they feel waives a stick of wrath and judgment.

However, understanding the nature of salvation, why it was necessary, and how it was purchased helps us understand this matter with greater depth, and alleviates frustration left by information gaps that the aforementioned statements do not fill. Some people find the answers to these questions in Scriptures such as Psalm 5:4, which states that no evil can dwell with God, thus, people who haven't accepted Him can't dwell in Heaven with Him, because they have evil that hasn't been covered by the blood of Jesus. Others refer to 1 Timothy 2:4, which reminds us that God does not want *any* to perish; if this is true, then why wouldn't God force all people to accept His forgiveness—or even forgive them despite their refusal of the gift? If He did this, everyone could go to Heaven, which would be wonderful! Surely a loving God could conduct forgiveness this way if He wanted to, couldn't He?

A vital, yet commonly misunderstood point in all of this is the fact that salvation is a *transaction*: one that Jesus made while on the cross. Anselm, a renowned Christian philosopher of the eleventh century whose work has withstood the test of time, clarified this convoluted topic for upcoming generations of churches during a time when such doctrine was under debate, by presenting his work on the nature of atonement, *Cur Dos Homo* ("Why God Became a Human Person").[242] In this thoughtful, pragmatic work, Anselm explained that sin committed by humans is an insult to God's superiority. Because God is the Supreme Being, His standard for justice must be immaculate and unwavering. Anything less than the utmost would likewise be indicative of an inferior being. Thus, the ultimate price must be paid for an insult against the character of the ultimate being. However, because mankind is an inferior being, created *by* God and *for* God, we already owe Him everything that we have, meaning that even in a state of perfection—were it possible to achieve—we would only reach the "expected" status in the eyes of the Most High God. Once sin entered the scene, the lowliness of humanity stooped even farther into the regions of inadequacy. Since our very best would only render us barely acceptable in the first place, adding sin to this dilemma placed us in a deeper state of debt that our very best could never elevate us out of.

The quandary then becomes this: In order for retribution to be made at a standard high enough to appease the justice necessitated by and due to the Most High God, a being of higher rank than a human had to pay the price. In fact, any being inferior to God Himself who attempted to pay such a price would not be able to offer adequate retribution on our behalf, because God's criteria can only accept God-standard levels of payment. However, in order for the transaction to be valid for creatures as lowly as human beings, the penalty had to reach the depraved depths of the realm from which that sin originated: the human, physical realm. For the payment to be *applicable* to humans, it had to descend to the state wherein human sin dwells.

The existence within the physical realm of a perfect God/man Being—Jesus—manifested in a life without sin, and was followed by a sacrificial death, paying the price needed to recreate the pathway between humans and God. In His sacrificial death, Jesus paid the price for our evil deeds. But where does this payment go? Anselm explains that "since God needs nothing, the reward is transferred to sinful humanity; thus God's honor is restored, sin is forgiven, and atonement is achieved."[243]

Many people who ponder a God who "sends people to Hell" often wonder why, if He doesn't want "anyone to perish" (1 Timothy 2:4), He doesn't throw some all-covering "blanket of forgiveness" across all the individuals who would otherwise be condemned to suffer for eternity, inviting them to Heaven (despite their rejection of Him) out of his vast love for all of humanity. The problem with this thinking is this: God has *already* done this very thing—because of His love for humanity—when Jesus (a Being of superior enough rank to pay a price meeting the standard of retribution that God must require) descended to earth and took on human, fleshly form (thus adopting commonality with the lowly, depraved state of humanity, where sin dwells) and then lived a perfect life and gave Himself as a sacrifice, taking on punishment for our sins (thus providing payment and atonement that could reconnect sinful, humankind with the ultimate most high). Salvation obtained or offered by anything other than a perfect blend of God and man would neither be worthy of offering to God nor applicable to man.

While many might initially view God's forgiveness of man as an emotional connection, the transaction Jesus completed on our behalf was actually technical. Thus, there are rules involved. Because the Most High God had to descend to the lowest low (the human, physical realm) in order to purchase salvation for mankind, humans must likewise choose God while they are in the lowest realm (human) in order to join Him at the highest realm (Heaven).

For mankind to reconnect with God and ascend to where He dwells once we enter the spirit realm, we must have first chosen to instate the purchase price, which was made by Jesus in the physical realm while we were *still in the physical realm.*

Once we leave the corporeal jurisdiction (once we are deceased), it is too late to change our position regarding this transaction, because it must be initiated within the corporeal division, just as Jesus' payment was.

Imagine visiting a store to shop the momentous sales offered on the Black Friday, the day after Thanksgiving. On the way in, you see a store employee handing out coupons saying you can "buy one get one free" of certain popular items. The store's layout is structured so that once you are inside, you can't go back out to revisit the woman. In other words, if you don't accept the coupon on the way in, you won't have another chance to get one. Those who turned down the offer will find themselves in line for the purchase, responsible for the full cost of the items with no discount. This is similar to the situation for those who have refused Jesus' offer of atonement. Contrary to what some may claim, the situation isn't that God sends those He loves to Hell, it is that *despite His sacrifice of love*, many choose not to accept His gift. Worse, once we've left the physical realm, we'll never be able to pay for our own atonement, but become permanently ineligible to receive assistance for our salvation. We lock ourselves outside of the transaction by not accepting the "coupon" while we were eligible for it. God will not usurp our will by forcing this salvation on us, because the payment is a gift. This is why, despite the fact that God isn't willing for anyone to perish, *still* some do. He wants us to accept this coverage as a bestowment of His love and generosity while we are living. However, it is no longer a *gift* if it is forced upon us, meaning that unless we accept freely what has been given freely, the forgiveness cannot be attached, negating the gift. Unfortunately, this is why if we deny Him *in this life*, He must deny us *in the next* (Matthew 10:33).

What Hell Is and Is Not

Matthew 25 tells the parable of the sheep and the goats—a tale wherein Jesus explains how people will be judged according to their deeds at the end of the world. He explains that believers and unbelievers will be separated by the testimony of their deeds. (As a side note, this doesn't mean that deeds or the lack thereof is what decides a person's final destination—as Jesus' point in this parable is that His followers should be compelled to *action* as a testimony of their relationship with Him). When the damned are sent to their final destination of punishment, Jesus' words are: "Depart from me, ye cursed, into everlasting fire, prepared for the devil and his angels" (Matthew 25:41).

The concept that the Lake of Fire was actually prepared not for human beings, but for "the devil and his angels," is a concept propagated by the works of Enoch, whose writings are referred to by several New Testament authors. Many ideas handed down throughout the centuries resemble notions found in the book of Enoch. In the Old Testament, however, mention of "Sheol" or "Hades" do not usually emphasize the inferno that became a more commonly referenced theme throughout the New Testament. It is possible that common acknowledgment of *Gehenna* brought the fiery aspect to the forefront of concepts of Hell.

Isaiah 14:12 says: "How art thou fallen from heaven, O Lucifer, son of the morning! how art thou cut down to the ground, which didst weaken the nations!" We understand through this text that Lucifer (Satan, the devil) was cast from Heaven for his rebellion against God. Alongside the fiery theme portrayed in conjunction with Hell, we understand that evil entities exist there, and that this location is the place of their eternal punishment.

Michael Heiser's Connection Between Hell and Enoch[244]

Michael Heiser, a highly respected scholar of Old Testament and Christian theology, is outspoken on matters of Heaven and Hell. He draws a connection between the book of Enoch and the condition of Hell, explaining that the afterlife for sinners is a direct link to the earliest sources of corruption brought upon humanity by the fallen angels of Genesis. According to Heiser, Enoch sheds light on how this malevolent influence upon early mankind initiated the wrath that brought about the Flood of Noah, the evil spirits being cast into Hell, and the sins that separate man from God:

Then said the Most High, the Holy and Great One spake, and sent Uriel to the son of Lamech, and said to him: "Go to Noah and tell him in my name 'Hide thyself!' and reveal to him the end that is approaching"... And again the Lord said to Raphael: "Bind Azâzêl hand and foot, and cast him into the darkness: and make an opening in the desert, which is in Dŭdâêl, and cast him therein. And place upon him rough and jagged rocks, and cover him with darkness, and let him abide there for ever, and cover his face that he may not see light. And on the day of the great judgement he shall be cast into the fire...[and by flood the earth will be purified of] all the secret things that the Watchers have disclosed and have taught their sons. And the whole earth has been corrupted through the works that were taught by Azâzêl: to him ascribe all sin."... And the Lord said unto Michael: "Go, bind Semjâzâ and his associates who have united themselves with women so as to have defiled themselves with them in all their uncleanness. And when their sons have slain one another, and they have seen the destruction of their beloved ones, bind them fast for seventy generations in the valleys of the earth, till the day of their judgement and of their consummation, till the judgement that is for ever and ever is consummated".... In those days they shall be led off to the abyss of fire: and to the torment and the prison in which they shall be confined for ever. And whosoever shall be condemned and destroyed will from thenceforth be bound together with them to the end of all generations. (1 Enoch 10:1–15)

We see from this passage that all sin taking place in the world at that time had been introduced by these evil entities, who came to corrupt mankind. Because of this, these malevolent beings have been cast to a place of punishment within the center of the earth. This establishes that the source of sin being introduced to mankind was negative supernatural influence. Thus, they were banished to a place of imprisonment in the center of the earth, and mankind who succumbs to their influence is subject to similar punishment. Also noteworthy are certain phrases in this passage that suggest the existence of territorial division between varying regions of this realm. Even some terminology used throughout Scripture insinuates that through the navigation of locations, we establish rule from one realm to another. For example, *Heaven* is the throne room of God, and is therefore His dominion. We also understand that since God created all things, and ultimately all things fall under His authority, He is the ruler of all things, beings, and locations. However, within certain realms of God's creation, we likewise understand that there are territories set aside for the banishment of the rebellious; these zones fall under the rule of those malevolent spirits. *When, where* and *to what extent* these evil beings have authority is still subject to God's final say: "Woe to the inhabiters of the earth and of the sea! for the devil is come down unto you, having great wrath, because he knoweth that he hath but a short time" (Revelation 12:12). This passage shows that even though there is a designated time and place for Satan to freely roam the earth, God has set an expiration date on his reign. Furthermore, among these zones throughout creation, there is no indication that any of these territories remains unclaimed. In other words, if you're not occupying God's jurisdiction, you walk on the turf of some other entity.

This, consequently, is why dabbling in areas of paranormal contact can be a dangerous game. If we're operating outside the realm of what Scripture has instructed, we're in the presence of some other entity and as a result are extending an invitation for contact or potentially worse interaction. Scripture reinforces the idea of regional context through passages that explain that the soul changes location upon departure:

Therefore we are always confident, knowing that, whilst we are at home in the body, we are absent from the Lord.... We are confident, I say, and willing rather to be absent from the body, and to be present with the Lord." (2 Corinthians 6 and 8)

Being "with the Lord" means we will achieve eternal life, because this has been promised:

For God so loved the world, that he gave his only begotten Son, that whosoever believeth in him should not perish, but have everlasting life. (John 3:16)

On the other hand, those who die who did not "believe on Him" are to be separated from God and will experience death, having not been granted the eternal life promised to those who chose Him. This means they will be sent to the location of the damned.

Scripture gives lengthy descriptions of Heaven, but not as much about the Hell. The book of Enoch, however, provides some insight:

And I proceeded to where things were chaotic. And I saw there something horrible: I saw neither a heaven above nor a firmly founded earth, but a place chaotic and horrible. And there I saw seven stars of the heaven [angels cast out of Heaven] bound together in it, like great mountains and burning with fire. Then I said: "For what sin are they bound, and on what account have they been cast in hither?" Then said Uriel, one of the holy angels, who was with me, and was chief over them, and said: "Enoch, why dost thou ask, and why art thou eager for the truth? These are of the number of the stars [of Heaven], which have transgressed the commandment of the Lord, and are bound here till ten thousand years, the time entailed by their sins, are consummated." And from thence I went to another place, which was still more horrible than the former, and I saw a horrible thing: a great fire there which burnt and blazed, and the place was cleft as far as the abyss, being full of great descending columns of fire: neither its extent or magnitude could I see, nor could I conjecture. Then I said: "How fearful is the place and how terrible to look upon!" Then Uriel answered me, one of the holy angels who was with me, and said unto me: "Enoch, why hast thou such fear and affright?" And I answered: "Because of this fearful place, and because of the spectacle of the pain." And he said [unto me]: "This place is the prison of the angels, and here they will be imprisoned for ever." (Enoch 21).

We see in 2 Peter 2:4 that angels were indeed delivered into a place of imprisonment:

God spared not the angels that sinned, but cast them down to hell, and delivered them into chains of darkness, to be reserved unto judgment. (2 Peter 2:4)

We observe through the passage from Enoch that there are different territories within this realm of the underworld, some which are worse than others:

And those two men led me up on to the Northern side, and showed me there a very terrible place, and [there were] all manner of tortures in that place: cruel darkness and unillumined gloom, and there is no light there, but murky fire constantly flaming aloft, and [there is] a fiery river coming forth, and that whole place is everywhere fire, and everywhere [there is] frost and ice, thirst and shivering, while the bonds are very cruel, and the angels [evil spirits] fearful and merciless, bearing angry weapons, merciless torture, and I said: "Woe, woe, how very terrible is this place." And those men said to me: "This place, O Enoch, is prepared for those who dishonor God, who on earth practice sin against nature, which is child-corruption…, magic-making, enchantments and devilish witchcrafts, and who boast of their wicked deeds, stealing, lies, calumnies, envy, rancour, fornication, murder, and who, accursed, steal the souls of men, who, seeing the poor take away their goods and themselves wax rich, injuring them for other men's goods; who being able to satisfy the empty, made the hungering to die; being able to clothe, stripped the naked; and who knew not their creator, and bowed to the soulless [and lifeless] gods, who cannot see nor hear, vain gods, [who also] built hewn images and bow down to unclean handiwork, for all these is prepared this place among these, for eternal inheritance." (2 Enoch 10)

This explains the basis for man's judgment, giving a list of sins committed by the condemned. These were introduced to humanity through the influence of the fallen angels who turned their deviant ambitions toward the destruction and condemnation of humanity. This is why Jesus came to die for our sins, so that these could be covered by His blood, granting us entry to Heaven despite our deviant human ways.

While the book of Enoch has not been accepted into the canonical Scripture, it is still a good source of information that we know influenced the views of ancient biblical and religious writers. Whether or not the works of Enoch were divinely inspired, we can still see the correlation between Scripture and information gleaned from this resource. Second Peter 2:4 states specifically that angels who were cast from Heaven were bound in Tartarus, confirming the validity of Enoch's statement that there is a prison holding such entities. Furthermore, valuable correlations are made when considering the insight offered by Enoch: fallen angels rebelled against God and were cast to the earth, where they taught corruption and rebellion to mankind. Subsequently, these entities were imprisoned in a fiery, chaotic, and miserable place; those people who practice the sins of these evil ones will pay a similar penalty unless they seek redemption through Christ.

Heaven and Hell Often Misrepresented

Modern pop culture draws many ideas as to what Hell is like. While some try to depict it as an eternal party where all your strange desires are met by Satan and his imps, others picture it as a place where the devil rules and doles out punishment to all those who end up imprisoned there. Some people, who imagine Heaven to be a place where lazy angels sprawl on clouds all day long while playing harps, think that Heaven must be boring, so they *opt* for Hell as a preferable eternal destination. Surely, these individuals have no understanding of what they're actually signing on for. Sadly, for these deceived people, many will find out too late that they made the wrong decision in this life.

For some, if information doesn't come straight from Scripture, they hesitate to embrace it as truth, even concerning ancient texts such as the book of Enoch. This is understandable, and it's always wise to be wary when about such matters. After all, the ancient fallen ones who corrupted mankind at the beginning of humanity were at work in earliest times, weren't they? Looking at extrabiblical sources such as Enoch should only be considered supplemental to examining Scripture—a way of filling in gaps when the insight gleaned *does not* contradict the truth of the Bible. However, Scripture does give us some information about Hell. We know that it will have an unquenchable fire (Matthew 3:12; 13:41–42; Mark 9:43), which creates insatiable thirst (Luke 16:24); there will be anguish and pain (Matthew 13:42; 24:51); and it will be an everlasting punishment (Matthew 25:46), where those therein will feel awareness and remorse (Luke 16:19–31) and suffer torment forever (Revelation 14:10–11).

Likewise, the Bible describes Hell as a place where God's wrath and indignation (Revelation 14:10) will manifest in everlasting punishment (Matthew 25:46) and destruction (2 Thessalonians 1:9) that rages on in an eternal fire (Matthew 25:41).

Hell was designed for the devil and his angels (Matthew 25:41), along with the ungodly, the unjust, unbelieving, liars, murderers (Revelation 21:8); it was also for the Beast, his false prophet, and his worshipers (2 Peter 2:4–9; Revelation 14:11, 19:20).

It is clear from Scripture that the final, eternal home for those who reject Christ's offer of salvation is the Lake of Fire:

> Then shall he say also unto them on the left hand, Depart from me, ye cursed, into everlasting fire, prepared for the devil and his angels. (Matthew 25:41)

We're told that one day there will be a great judgment. Every human who ever walked the earth will be subjected to this accounting of our beliefs and deeds:

> And I saw a great white throne, and him that sat on it, from whose face the earth and the heaven fled away; and there was found no place for them. And I saw the dead, small and great, stand before God; and the books were opened: and another book was opened, which is the book of life: and the dead were judged out of those things which were written in the books, according to their works. And the sea gave up the dead which were in it; and death and hell delivered up the dead which were in them: and they were judged every man according to their works. And death and hell were cast into the lake of fire. This is the second death. And whosoever was not found written in the book of life was cast into the lake of fire. (Revelation 20:11–15)

Whether you believe in total annihilation or eternal torment, each of these comes at the greatest expense: everlasting eternal separation from the presence of God. Consider this, on the other hand: We have God's offer of salvation and eternity in His presence in Heaven.

Heaven

As mentioned before, the other side of the afterlife is Paradise or Abraham's bosom, Heaven, and the New Jerusalem. After Jesus' sacrificial death for the sins of the world, He traveled to Hades, or as some call it, the "city of death." There He preached to the disobedient spirits who were imprisoned, and reclaimed the keys to Hell and death: "I am he that liveth, and was dead; and, behold, I am alive for evermore, Amen; and have the keys of hell and of death" (Revelation 1:18)

What does it mean to say that Jesus preached during the time after His crucifixion and before His resurrection? Let's take a closer look:

> For Christ also hath once suffered for sins, the just for the unjust, that he might bring us to God, being put to death in the flesh, but quickened by the Spirit: By which also he went and preached unto the spirits in prison; Which sometime were disobedient, when once the longsuffering of God waited in the days of Noah, while the ark was a preparing, wherein few, that is, eight souls were saved by water. (1 Peter 3:18–20)

Just as Jesus promised the repentant thief on the cross beside Him, He went to Paradise (Abraham's bosom) and set free the righteous Old Testament saints. Then, at some point after His resurrection, He led those saints victoriously into the heavens where God dwells. From that point on, we find references to Paradise as being in the presence of God. This deviation from the word "Paradise" to "being in the presence of God" alludes to the concept that until the supreme sacrifice had been paid (Jesus' suffering for our sins), even the righteous departed saints were unable to stand in the presence of God. However, Jesus repaved the path from mankind to the Almighty God.

Misconceptions about Heaven

Many today believe that, at death, anyone and everyone gets to go to heaven—regardless of their belief in God. Many state that people are generally good, so God wouldn't send them to hell. Some even believe that this fallen world is so bad that we are in hell already, and that conditions will only improve from here. Some also believe that our departed loved ones become our guardian angels and are watching over our every movement,[245] a concept that *directly contradicts* the afterlife plan outlined by the Bible. Some say that going to Heaven means that we will spend eternity floating on clouds, playing harps, as pictured in many cartoons and caricatures.

Heaven: Owned and Operated by God

In the first verse of the Bible, we're told that God created Heaven: "In the beginning God created the heaven and the earth" (Genesis 1:1). The psalmist confirms this with the words: "When I consider thy heavens, the work of thy fingers, the moon and the stars, which thou hast ordained" (Psalms 8:3). Isaiah takes this a step farther by explaining that God made Heaven *purposefully*, with the intention of it being a dwelling place:

> For thus saith the LORD that created the heavens; God himself that formed the earth and made it; he hath established it, he created it not in vain, he formed it to be inhabited: I am the LORD; and there is none else. (Isaiah 45:18)

Not only did God create this place for habitation, but he made it His throne, from where He would rule the rest of creation:

> The LORD hath prepared his throne in the heavens; and his kingdom ruleth over all. Bless the LORD, ye his angels, that excel in strength, that do his commandments, hearkening unto the

voice of his word. Bless ye the LORD, all ye his hosts; ye ministers of his, that do his pleasure. Bless the LORD, all his works in all places of his dominion: bless the LORD, O my soul. (Psalms 103:19–22)

Jesus Is Preparing a Place for His Followers

In Colossians 1:16, we are told that Jesus Christ created all things, whether in Heaven or earth, visible or invisible. All things were created by Him, and for Him. He also promised us that He is preparing a place for us with many mansions, and that He will someday take us there to be with Him (John 14:1–3).

Did you catch that? In six days, He created the heavens and the earth (Exodus 20:11), but for about two thousand years He has been preparing a place for His followers. It must be *awesome!*

> But as it is written, Eye hath not seen, nor ear heard, neither have entered into the heart of man, the things which God hath prepared for them that love him. (1 Corinthians 2:9)

After Jesus made the promise to prepare a place for His followers, He left earth to return to His home in Heaven. Again, He conquered the grave: He left this earth on *His own miraculous terms*, and not by succumbing to death:

> And when he had spoken these things, while they beheld, he was taken up; and a cloud received him out of their sight. And while they looked stedfastly toward heaven as he went up, behold, two men stood by them in white apparel; Which also said, Ye men of Galilee, why stand ye gazing up into heaven? this same Jesus, which is taken up from you into heaven, shall so come in like manner as ye have seen him go into heaven. (Acts 1:9–11)

New Heaven, New Earth, and the New Jerusalem

When Adam and Eve sinned against God, corruption and death entered the world. Paul tells us in Romans that this opened the door for sin and death to impact all of mankind: "Wherefore, as by one man sin entered into the world, and death by sin; and so death passed upon all men, for that all have sinned" (Romans 5:12).

Likewise, we understand that "the wages of sin is death; but the gift of God is eternal life through Jesus Christ our Lord" (Romans 6:23). The result of sin is death, decay, and destruction, but one day, as Peter tells us, the day of the Lord will happen when we do not expect it. We are to "according to his promise, look for new heavens and a new earth, wherein dwelleth righteousness" (2 Peter 3:13). Thankfully, the day of the LORD, when the heavens and the earth pass away, is not the story of doom and gloom for those who follow Christ. As Peter testified, there will be new Heaven and a new earth.

The apostle John tells us of a beautiful new beginning that awaits us in the presence of God:

> And I saw a new heaven and a new earth: for the first heaven and the first earth were passed away; and there was no more sea. And I John saw the holy city, new Jerusalem, coming down from God out of heaven, prepared as a bride adorned for her husband. And I heard a great voice out of heaven saying, Behold, the tabernacle of God is with men, and he will dwell with them, and they shall be his people, and God himself shall be with them, and be their God. And God shall wipe away all tears from their eyes; and there shall be no more death, neither sorrow, nor crying, neither shall there be any more pain: for the former things are passed away. And he that sat upon the throne said, Behold, I make all things new. (Revelation 21:1–5)

How Does the Bible Describe This New Heaven?

Revelation 21 describes the new heaven as a beautiful city, enveloped by the glory of God, illuminated with a light as clear as crystal. It is surrounded by twelve gates for each of the twelve tribes of the children of Israel, and at each gate is stationed a majestic angel. The city has twelve foundations, each named in honor of the twelve apostles of Christ. The wall and foundations are built of precious stones such as jasper, sapphire, chaldecony, emerald, sardonyx, sardius, chrysolite, beryl, topaz, chrysoprasus, jacinth, and amethyst. The city itself is like pure gold as clear as the clearest glass. Each city gate—of which are twelve—is made of pearl. The streets are pure gold. And here is the best part: There is no temple, because the Lord God Almighty dwells there, and He *is* the temple. Likewise, the city has no sun or moon, because the glory illuminating from the Son of God is all the light this beautiful city will ever need. This wonderful place will know no night, nor sorrow, nor corruption, nor sadness, nor fear; God Himself will wipe the tears from our eyes and tell us that we will no longer know the pain of the fallen world (Revelation 21). What a beautiful thought: The image of standing before our Creator, who finally, permanently, removes all our sickness, pain, and sorrow, and who cares enough to *personally* wipe the tears from our eyes, welcoming us to this new home He has created for us to dwell in with Him.

PART THREE

MODERN TAKE ON LIFE AFTER DEATH, AND WHAT LIES AHEAD

chapter five

Popular Modern Concepts

With more than 4,200 religions in the world, there are, understandably, many varying afterlife beliefs. While discussing each one would be impossible here, this chapter will cover a few theories of some of the world's major religions.

The interesting thing about afterlife beliefs is that, like all spiritual matters such as God, angels, Heaven, and Hell, it seems acceptable to make them *personal* matters. Rather than saying what "is," some shop around for an afterlife theory until they find one that is the most appealing. Sometimes these views are based on nurturing and culture, while other times, it's just a matter of scratching the "itching ear" (2 Timothy 4:3). In other words, rather than searching for the objective truth concerning the afterlife, many people find themselves choosing a subjective preference.

Exhaustive studies are obviously available, but the information on the following pages should offer at least a working knowledge of some of the more prominent views on life after death.

Muslim (Islamic)

Muhammad (AD 571–632), founder of the Islamic faith, grew up in the seventh century learning of Christianity. At a certain point, though, he separated himself and chose his own path, one that an estimated 1.7 billion people follow today.[246] In fact, some believe it is the fastest growing religion in the world. "the Prophet," as Muhamad is called, is believed to be second only to God ("Allah") Himself.

Muslim beliefs are based on the Qur'an and Muhammad's teachings. It is said that Allah began dictating the Qur'an to Muhammad through the archangel Gabriel, also referred to as "Jibril," in AD 609, when the Prophet was forty years old. Muhammad is said to have transcribed the words of Allah for twenty-two years, until his death in AD 632.

All beings are created by God, the Muslim believes, and all return to Him after death. As in Christianity, the Islamic faith holds that, when the body ceases to exist, the soul lives on. Beyond that, however, the similarities between the two faiths seem to be few and far between. While Muslims believe that varying levels of Heaven and Hell exist, there are three major differences.

First, they say that the soul waits in the grave for "Judgment Day," when Allah will not only mete out eternal reward or punishment based on one's deeds, thoughts, and actions in life, but will also destroy the world as we know it.

The Qur'an teaches that there are many levels of heaven—normally referred to as "Paradise"—and Hell. One has a brief time after death to see future blessings or punishment, but then the soul returns to the grave to await Judgment Day. The only souls allowed to skip this waiting period are martyrs, who are given seventy-two beautiful virgin women for their "offering" to Allah. Everyone else, it's said, receive a visit from two angels, named Munkar and Nakir, on the eve of their death. The angels will ask each soul the following questions:

1. "Who is God?" The proper response is, "God is Allah."
2. "Who is your Prophet?" to which one must reply, "My prophet is Muhammad."
3. "What is your book?" The correct answer to this would be, "My book is the Qur'an."
4. "Who is your imam [main prayer leader in a mosque]?" In response, one would relay the imam's name.
5. "Which is your *qiblah* [the direction of Mecca, toward which Muslims pray five times per day]?" The only proper reply is, "My direction of prayer is toward Mecca."

Some Muslim funeral processions are led by a religious leader reciting the questions and the correct answers in an attempt to help the deceased person respond correctly. If the proper responses are given, the soul is allowed a grave overlooking Paradise. Souls bound for Paradise are "roomy," allowing them room to sit up and view their future reward. If incorrect answers are offered, though, the angels become tormenters, and the soul is placed in a cramped grave, lying down, just within view of Hell.

Correct beliefs and actions are believed to be the factors Allah assesses to determine where one spends eternity. Unlike Christians—who believe justification, redemption, and eternal life are obtained by a belief that Jesus Christ is the Son of God, seeking forgiveness of sins and following Christ's teachings—Muslims are judged *solely* on their good deeds, thoughts, and intentions. The belief that one must earn his or her own redemption is the second major difference between Muslims and Christians views of the afterlife.

The third difference is that the Islamic faith holds to the belief that no eternal abode is permanent. One can always work hard and earn his or her way from one level of Paradise or Hell to the next. Paradise is thought to be a perfect existence, with no more pain or suffering, and consisting of beautiful locales, often compared to the Garden of Eden. This Paradise is dissimilar to the Christian's view of Heaven, however, because Muslims believe there will be pleasures of *all* kinds, including sexual.

Within the Christian faith, sex is allowed in marriage, but doesn't exist once the soul has transcended to spend eternity with the Lord, because the realm in which this activity takes place is the physical, in conjunction with man's order to reproduce and fill the earth with inhabitants (Genesis 1:28). When Jesus was asked about this subject, He stated there is no marriage in Heaven; rather, all will be like family. That said, Christians will still be "known as we are known," and we will be fully aware of familial ties.

Buddhism

While experts say there are anywhere from 200 to 500 million Buddhists in the world today, most agree that number is around 350 million.[247] Buddhists don't believe in the "soul," as Christians think of it, but rather, that the mind (some say "desire" or "spirit") is eternal. It has existed before the housing body existed, and will continue long after death.

To the Buddhist, the aspects of us that remain after death—mind, spirit, desires, etc.—enter the *santana*, or "chain of being." This chain appears to refer to a constant "life loop," like a music playlist set on "repeat" for eternity. Upon death, the part of us that remains is reborn into another being, not necessarily a human. The belief is that the form taken in the new life depends upon the deeds carried out in the previous one. This is referred to as *karma*, which Webster's Dictionary defines as "the force generated by a person's actions to perpetuate transmigration and it its ethical consequences to determine the nature of the person's next existence."[248]

Buddhists believe living is a process, but furthermore, that it is a "vast process of becoming."[249] The goal is to live a virtuous and upright life filled with good deeds. The thoughts and actions of this life are the sole deciding factors for the state of rebirth. If good deeds and "enlightenment" make up this life, one will be reborn in a higher state. The opposite holds true for those who are "evil" or who dedicated themselves to carrying out evil acts. Death can be experienced countless times, the goal being to rid oneself fully of all evil desires. The current life is full retribution for the manner in which the last one was lived, whether good or evil, on this journey to *nirvana.*

While some have attempted to correlate nirvana with the Christian Heaven, the comparison is inaccurate. The goal of a Buddhist is to escape the constant cycle of living and dying to obtain a perfect place of spiritual peace. Nirvana is only attained, the belief goes, by learning and growing over a plethora of lifetimes.

While Christians have at least a vague physical description of Heaven (the "streets of gold" and "crystal clear stream" of Revelation chapter 21), exactly what nirvana *is* seems to remain unclear, even to the Buddha (567–487 BCE) himself. He placed the emphasis not on reaching nirvana, but on preforming good deeds and attempting to transcend the suffering of this life.

According to the Buddha, life *is* suffering. In the first sermon he delivered, he said, "The Noble Truth of Suffering is this: Birth is suffering; aging is suffering; sickness is suffering; death is suffering; sorrow and lamentation, pain, grief, and despair are suffering."[250]

Within the writings of the Dhammapada (147:51), he spoke more boldly about suffering:

Behold this beautiful body, a mass of sores, a heaped up lump, diseased, much thought of, in which nothing lasts. Truly, life ends in death…(e)ven ornamented royal chariots wear out. But the Dhamma [or "Dharma," which speaks of the road traveled on the way to Nirvana] of the Good grows not old. Thus do the Good.[251]

Buddhists believe that once they have escaped the cycle of life and death, there is a transition from being *followers* of the Buddha to *becoming* Buddha. When "Buddhahood" is obtained, freedom is gained from this reality, and oneness with the eternal is discovered. As stated, no specific definition of "nirvana" has ever been given, although it's been likened to a generic sense of "higher enlightenment."

Setting aside the idea of reincarnation, the most glaring difference between Buddhism and Christianity is, as is the case in many religions, that what we *do* or *don't do* ends up determining how we spent eternity. Whether the next life is a blessing or curse solely depends upon what we *did*, what we *said*, and what we *thought*. If good deeds outweigh bad deeds, a "higher life form" is gained on the way to someday becoming "fully enlightened."

Christians, however, understand that we are, at our core, fallen creatures in need of a Savior. Salvation and eternal life are both gifts we can *never* earn. This takes the pressure off of believers in Christ to try to achieve "perfection," instead concentrating on following Christ. While we're obviously urged to perform good deeds and have clean thoughts and words, eternal redemption is given by the covering of our sins by Jesus' blood.

Hindu

Though Hindus may argue that their religion is "timeless" (similar to the belief Christians hold about the existence of God), scholars put the creation of Hinduism between 2300 and 1500 BCE. There are some nine hundred million Hindus, and, like Buddhists, they also believe in the "continuous life cycle" of reincarnation. For some Hindus, there is no Heaven or Hell, only the never-ending circle of living and dying, with the quality of each life based on how the last was lived. For example, someone who was a poor philanthropist in this life might be "reborn" into a wealthy family in the next.

Sects of Hinduism vary greatly, however, and others believe in a series of heavens and hells, as with Buddhism. While Brahman is the primary god of the Hindus, it is believed he shows himself by being embodied in some *thirty-three million* other gods and goddesses. The ways to attain "heaven" depend on the sect of Hinduism, and ranges from praying to the rights gods and goddesses to practicing yoga and meditation. The ultimate goal for most, it seems, is releasing oneself from the selfishness of this world and moving into a state of knowledge and enlightenment.

Upon death, Hindus are cremated, so that four of the five elements believed to make up the human body—fire, earth, water, and air—can be returned to the earth. The fifth element, which they refer to as the "soul," "void" or "ether," travels around after death before returning to the world and being reborn—unless, that is, "full enlightenment" has been reached, in which case one reaches nirvana. As in Buddhism, the exact nature of this paradise varies greatly, with some likening it to becoming "one drop in the ocean." While the descriptions sound as if one is losing his or her individuality, some Hindus think of it more as an adjoining to the higher enlightenment.

The idea of multiple levels of heavens and hells may sound contra-dictory to the theory of reincarnation, but in the Hindu theology, nei-ther Paradise nor torment is permanent. One may rise to Heaven if one's karma was good, but the stay would be short-lived before returning to earth to be reborn in another body or situation presumably better than the last. Likewise, if a soul (or "void," or "ether") had more evil deeds than good ones ("bad karma"), it might be sent to any one of a varying number of levels of Hell. While there, he or she would be tortured by horrific demons for an undetermined amount of time.

After a certain period that only the gods can measure, though, the soul would be returned to earth, again, to be reborn. The belief is that, if a soul had received a sentence in Hell, whether short or long, the rebirth would be a step *down* from the last one. Thus, if one was a human in a previous life, and bad karma sentenced that person to a limited time in

Hell, then he or she might be reborn as an animal, a plant or even an insect.

As stated in the section regarding Buddhism, the Christian world-view holds that only Jesus can offer the gift of eternal salvation. This redemption is not based on works, as with the formerly discussed belief systems. Also, concerning multiple gods and goddesses, the Bible clearly states, "No one comes to the Father (God) except by Jesus (John 14:6)." This eliminates the theory of there being "many paths to God (or enlightenment)," as in so many other religions.

"Ghosts" and the Witch of Endor

The idea of ghosts or specters, displaced souls remaining on earth after death, has been around for centuries. For some, a "ghost story" is merely an eerie tale to be told 'round the fire. Many others fully believe, however, that the spirits or souls of humans will hang around long after their death. Sometimes, the theory goes, ghosts are merely "spirits with unfinished business." This unfinished business may come in many forms: homicide victims whose killers have not been brought to justice, children or youth who passed away unexpectedly and don't understand they are actually dead, people who had a strong love for another and "refuse" to accept their fate, and on and on.

One of the first notable ghost stories is from the first century, reported by noted Roman lawyer, author, and magistrate Pliny the Younger. Pliny wrote about a long-bearded ghost, an elderly fellow who rattled chains, haunting his Athens home. A few hundred years later, in AD 856, a "poltergeist," a specter that makes itself known by making loud noises or physically moving or throwing objects, was said to haunt a German farmhouse.[252]

When spinning tales of specters, though, some point to the story of Saul, king of Israel and David's predecessor, as having been a part of one of the first ghost stories. This fascinating story can be found in First

Samuel chapter 28. While he once walked in favor with God, by this time, King Saul had fallen out of the Lord's good graces. The prophet Samuel, who anointed Saul when he was a strapping, young lad, had remained one of the king's most trusted advisors, but had recently passed away. Having relied on God's guidance, many times spoken through Samuel, the king grew desperate to hear from the Lord. He had been told that he and his sons would fall at the hands of the invading Philistines, but understandably, was looking for a more positive report. When the army set up camp on his doorstep, Saul grew terrified and gathered his own army. He asked the Lord for guidance, but alas, the heavens were silent. Additionally, he sought peace by asking God to speak to him through dreams or prophets, but again, received no word, no peace.

Desperate, he sought out a person who was practiced in the art of witchcraft to reach into the "spirit world" for him. Now, understand that Saul himself had banned sorcery from the land and driven out all witches under penalty of death. He was told there was a witch in the city of Endor, so the king, along with two of his men, disguised himself and paid her a visit. The paraphrased version of the story goes this way:

"Consult a spirit for me," he told the woman, "and bring up for me the one I name."

But the woman said to him, "Surely you know what Saul has done. He has cut off the mediums and spiritists from the land. Why have you set a trap for my life to bring about my death?"

In another move that probably didn't win him in any favors with God, Saul swore to her by the Lord, "As surely as the Lord lives, you will not be punished for this."

Then the woman asked, "Whom shall I bring up for you?"

"Bring up Samuel," he said.

When the woman saw Samuel, she was afraid for her life, and cried out at the top of her voice to Saul, "Why have you deceived me? You are Saul!"

The king said to her, "Don't be afraid. What do you see?"

The woman said, "I see a ghostly figure coming up out of the earth."

"What does he look like?" he asked.

"An old man wearing a robe is coming up," she said.

Then Saul knew it was Samuel, and he bowed down, prostrate, with his face to the ground. Some translations say the king "perceived" it was Samuel, leading some scholars to believe the "ghost" of Samuel didn't actually appear, but rather, that Saul just *thought* it was his most trusted advisor. In the next verse, however, this rumor seems to be dispelled, as the Word of God relates that Samuel "said" to Saul, "Why have you disturbed me by bringing me up?"

The verse does not say, "The witch spoke for Samuel" or "Saul *perceived* Samuel said," but that Samuel literally "said." While the New Testament records the stories of both Lazarus and Jesus rising from the dead, this seems to be the only biblical account of the "soul" of a deceased person coming back to earth. Rather than adhere to the idea of spiritists being able to "bring up" the souls of the dead, some Christian scholars believe God allowed Samuel to visit Saul to reinforce what the Lord Himself had already told the king.

"I am in great distress," Saul told the Samuel. "The Philistines are fighting against me, and God has departed from me. He no longer answers me, either by prophets or by dreams. So I have called on you to tell me what to do."

Samuel replied (in modern terms), "Why do you consult me, now that the Lord has departed from you and become your enemy? The Lord has done what he predicted through me. The Lord has torn the kingdom out of your hands and given it David. Because you did not obey the Lord, He has done this to you today. The Lord will deliver both Israel and you into the hands of the Philistines, and tomorrow you and your sons will be with me. The Lord will also give the army of Israel into the hands of the Philistines."

Understandably shaken, Saul collapsed to the ground, filled with fear because of Samuel's words. The next day, the prophecies came true, and the king and his sons died on the battlefield—Saul at his own hands when he fell on his sword.

This account brings up some interesting questions. Does this mean the Bible promotes the belief in ghosts? Are ghosts mentioned in other parts of Scripture? If ghosts were part of normal beliefs during biblical times, why does modern mainstream Christianity by and large condemn believing in the existence of ghosts?

There is actually a rich history to the question of ghosts addressed in the Bible. Taking a look at it can help us further understand some of the more ghostly events we examined in the first part of this book. Believe it or not, ghosts are in fact mentioned in other parts of the Bible, providing evidence that their existence was recognized in ancient Jewish thought. Isaiah 29:4 states:

And you will be brought low; from the earth you shall speak, and from the dust your speech will be bowed down; your voice shall come from the ground like the voice of a ghost, and from the dust your speech shall whisper.

The Hebrew word translated to the English "ghost" in the ESV ("familiar spirits" in the KJV) is *ob*, typically pronounced as *ove*. Matthew 14:26 says, in describing the reaction of the disciples when they first saw Jesus walking on water (though clearly not yet recognizing it was Him):

But when the disciples saw him walking on the sea, they were terrified, and said, "It is a ghost!" and they cried out in fear.

Thus we see that there was clearly a belief in ghosts in the times of the Bible. This brings us back to the witch of Endor.

We must remember, levitical law dictated that witches, or mediums and necromancers, were to be put to death. According to the Lexham English Bible:

And a man or a woman, if a spirit of the dead [*ob*] or a spirit of divination [*yiddeoni*] is in them, they shall surely be put to death; they shall stone them with stones—their blood is on them. (Leviticus 20:27, LEB)

This can help us understand what a witch or a medium was at that time. A medium in communion with a spirit of the dead—in other words, a ghost. Clearly, for someone to be in communion with something, that something must first exist. It seems illogical to believe that God would pass down laws pertaining to matters that are impossible. If it was impossible to be in communication with a ghost because ghosts do not exist, why did God prohibit it? Some may speculate that it is because people would believe it is a ghost when in reality it is a demon deceiving them. Yet, if that were true, why would God continue in that deception by referring to them as *ob*? Why wouldn't He clear up the misunderstanding and simply explain that these are not truly ghosts, but are lying spirits, and thus must be avoided at all costs? Why didn't God correct the terminology used by Samuel, Isaiah, and the disciples? Surely, it would have been a simple thing to do and would have made things easier to understand—that is, unless, ghosts are real and the text means exactly what it says.

The work of Flavius Josephus gives us a bit more information, as he explained a Jewish belief: "For this sort of necromantic women that bring up the souls of the dead, do by them foretell future events to such as desire them."[253] If this is what the Bible teaches, why are many mainstream Christians uncomfortable about the subject today?

The main reason is it is difficult to align this with our current view of the afterlife. Many Christians believe in an afterlife where you either go to Heaven or Hell at the moment of death and there is no escape. In Heaven, people are completely and perfectly obedient to God, meaning they would not go outside of His wishes and visit someone through a medium or necromancer who is still physically alive. The only disobedient ones who are dead would be locked in Hell, without the ability to escape, so they cannot fulfill the role of a "ghost," either. Therefore, according to mainstream Christianity, ghosts do not exist, and anything presenting itself as a ghost can only be a demon because, of the spiritual beings to select from, they are they only candidates left.

The truth is, however, far more complex than that. As it is famously said, "all shallows are clear,"[254] meaning if you are looking at an issue and it seems clear, you're not looking into it deep enough. When you look into an issue more deeply, you realize it's actually murky and complex. The physical world itself, viewed outside of a reductionist lens, is certainly deep, complex, and impossible to understand in its entirety. How much more, then, should we expect the afterlife to be this way? How much more complex is an unseen reality than the physical and perceivable one we interact with during every moment of our physical existence?

Sometimes there just are no easy answers. Unfortunately, rather than admitting ignorance on a very complex issue, many would rather do the issue injustice by reducing it to something shallow and infantile. All we know about the afterlife is what we are told, and it is just a matter of fact that all of the details are not given to us. Comforting, though, is that the things we're told do not contradict one another. If there seems to be any contradiction, we must realize these are only reflections of our own ignorance, and that is perfectly acceptable. We're not required or expected to fully know and understand everything. When we see issues that appear to be incongruent, such as ghosts, we must look farther into the murky depths of the matter to see what's really going on. We know the Bible forbids us to try to contact ghosts. We also know that ghosts are referred to in the Bible in other areas. Perhaps the reason we're not to communicate with ghosts is exactly because we don't understand the spirit world and we very well could become deceived. Perhaps God is protecting us from our own ignorance and our own hubris in thinking we know better than God what we are doing. Perhaps it is the simple fact that

God wants to reveal answers about the afterlife to us and doesn't want us consulting other spirits toward that end. We already have the eternal Father to communicate with; yet many who go after ghosts don't really believe that in the way the Bible describes. That is why you never see "God-hunting" television shows, while ghost-hunting television shows have been a lucrative industry for quite some time.

This only shows the importance of what we looked at earlier. There is one Person who conquered death and came back to tell us about it. Wouldn't it be in our best interest, then, to consult that one Person rather than all who came before and after Him, yet did not return? It seems the obvious choice, if we were going to talk to anyone who had died, the only one who would qualify for a truly insightful conversation, one that could even last a lifetime, would be Jesus Christ.

Theory of Quantum Consciousness

Proposed as early as the nineteenth century by French Nobel recipient and philosopher Henri Bergson, quantum consciousness is an integration of religious and scientific afterlife theories. This idea proposes that the mind, or consciousness, has an existence beyond the bounds of our reality of three dimensions. Theorists liken the mind to a radio receiving energy signals from a cosmic, fourth dimension. Just as a radio is merely a transmitter, relaying information from another source, so this body is with the ethereal consciousness. In other words, the theory states, our current state of being is *receiving* memories, likes and dislikes, ideas, passions, thoughts, and feelings from the eternal "mind," similar to a radio delivering music and news from a separate, outside source.

It must be noted, as we looked at before, when quantum consciousness theorists refer to "the mind," they're not speaking of the physical "brain." They claim the brain is the receptor for the higher "mind," which exists in the cosmos and never truly "dies." This also brings the idea of "past lives" into play, explaining feelings such as *deja vu* as the human brain receiving a signal from the outer consciousness known as the "mind."

This theory attempts to satisfy those who find the idea of eternal life satisfying, without the "confines" or "shackles" of traditional religion. Thus, science, which is constantly evolving and recreating itself, can be intertwined with a hope that death is not the end. After all, eternal life is the most appealing part of religion for many people.

A great number of mainstream scientists seem to balk at the idea of quantum consciousness, due to the very nature of science consisting only of what can be observed and studied. In this line of thinking, quantum consciousness doesn't qualify as "true science." Obviously, as strongly as many feel about their particular beliefs on the afterlife, they are just that: *beliefs*. "Beliefs," "feelings," and "theories" don't quantify as "science." Even more, many interpretations of consciousness get heavily into New Age beliefs. As I (Josh Peck) wrote about extensively in my book with Steven Bancarz, *The Second Coming of the New Age*, the new age movement is founded on subjective beliefs and not objective science. Therefore, since one can only theorize about "what comes next after death," these scientists who believe this theory should be disregarded.[255]

Could there possibly be a basis for a belief in some sort of quantum consciousness, and could the Bible support if such a belief were even proven true scientifically? Theoretically, yes. As with everything else, many different ideas and thoughts fall under the umbrella of "quantum consciousness" belief. As I (Josh) wrote about in *Abaddon Ascending*, which I coauthored with Tom Horn, some versions of quantum consciousness theory merely state that consciousness, on a purely physical level, is just an interaction with a quantum field, just as mass is an interaction with the Higgs field. This (again, on a physical and nonspiritual level) could very well be the case. However, the science is still too young to be able to fully endorse any one view of quantum consciousness.

While there are many fascinating theories of quantum consciousness, we must be careful not to blur the lines between physical science and spiritual belief. A lot of new age spiritual beliefs have to do with quantum consciousness, even if in name only. These beliefs track heavily with issues such as reincarnation and universal salvation, yet the Bible clearly states that "it is appointed unto man [that is, humans] once to die, and after that the judgment." The idea seems to adhere itself to those who long for the eternal, but who wish not to carry the burden of "sin" or of following what they perceive to be merely a set of established rules. That said, there is no biblical or scientific basis for new-age interpretations of quantum consciousness.

Sikhism ("Sikh")

Although thirty million people follow Sikhism, it's definitely one of the lesser-known religions. Sikh leaders are known as "gurus," and the religion was founded in the Punjab region of India by fifteenth-century Guru Nanak Dev, mainly in rebellion to the caste system populated by Hinduism. Interestingly, Sikhism merges the theory of reincarnation with the idea of grace bestowed by "one God," referred to as *Ik Onkar*. The "one God" is also referred to by some followers simply as "Truth."

As in many other religions, Sikhs believe *karma*, or one's actions, thoughts, and feelings, determines the nature of the next life. The only way to escape the life-and-death cycle of reincarnation is to embrace "God" or "Truth" and disregard all self-centeredness. Sikhs liken the cycle of "shedding" this body in death and embracing a new form to a changing of clothing. The belief is that one "changes clothing" many times before attaining pure selflessness, the forms of life housing the soul ranging from humans to animals. Thus, all life, animal and human alike, is sacred to the Sikh.

Followers of Sikhism *do* believe in Heaven and Hell, but whether the soul travels to one or the other, or is reborn in another body, is solely up to "God." It is believed that if one does not live by the *Shabad* ("Word of God"), follow the current guru, and have any comprehension of spiritual wisdom, they may be sent to Hell, or suffer reincarnation as many as *8.4 million* times before attaining enlightenment and earning the right to join God ("Truth") in Heaven. Sikhs hold to the notion that the form closest to God is the human one, and it is their best chance to finally join Him in their Heaven. This belief set holds the notion that the only way to achieve salvation is to abdicate all selfishness and ego.[256]

Thankfully, as Christians, we can never "earn" our way to Heaven; it is solely by the blood of Jesus that we obtain righteousness and eternal life.

Jainism

Originating sometime between the seventh and fifth centuries BCE, followers of Jainism, or "Jains," hold to the notion that their religion has no founder. Estimates put the number of devotees around six million worldwide—with more than five million living in India. At the core of their beliefs is nonviolence and "reincarnation until liberation."[257]

In the never-ending cycle of living and dying that is reincarnation, Jains believe one may have to suffer eight levels of Hell before achieving the next rebirth. Each level grows colder and bitterer, and much suffering may be endured before the next life is earned. The religion holds that liberation from the "life cycle" *is* possible, but it may take many lifetimes for a soul, or *jiva*, to earn a place among "the gods." Since only the gods know how many have obtained liberation, Jainism has a countless number of gods, as opposed to the One True God of Christianity.

As in other previously discussed religions, *karma*, or the thoughts, deeds, and actions carried out over one's lifetime, is the sole determining factor for the quality of one's next life after death. The *jivas* who earn liberation from the life cycle are called *siddhas*. These are bestowed an infinite amount of power, knowledge, vision, and bliss. The transition from *jiva* to *siddha* means the being has, at last, over countless lifetimes, achieved perfection.

Jains hold that the *siddha* has achieved the status of a god, but their "gods" are not viewed in the traditional sense. For example, their gods have no power to create or destroy. Also, it is impossible for a Jain to have a relationship with a god, as the *siddhas* cannot interfere with universal laws. Finally, these gods cannot offer humans any assistance whatsoever, including offering grace or forgiveness of sins.

Thus, the "gods" only serve as inspiration for those who practice Jainism, nothing more.[258]

Thankfully, Christianity teaches that the One True God not only created the universe and the human body, but that mercy can be obtained and sins forgiven by His Son, Jesus Christ. What a joy to know petitions, worries, fears, pain, sorrow, and sin itself can be laid at the feet of Jesus in prayer!

These are just a few of the plethora of religions in the world. While edicts, belief, doctrinal practices, and the like prove to be an interesting study, God's Word teaches there is only *one* path to God, and that is belief in His Son, Jesus. Our God is real and alive, an active participant in the common and ordinary, a fact for which followers of Jesus Christ are eternally grateful.

The God of the Philosophers

The concept of "the philosopher's god" refers to a personalized concept of a higher being obtained by a personal philosopher as a result of his or her own search for god. While many philosophers had ideas which agreed with or reinforced each other's concepts, the essence of the "god of the philosophers" was the individuality by which each individual identified his or her own belief of a supreme being. Interestingly enough, there seems to be a renewed interest in philosophy and how ancient people reasoned their way to God through logic. When we examine the attributes of this philosopher's God, we find out how incredibly similar it is to the God of the Bible. One might reason, in fact, that they are one and the same. When properly explained, this could not only lead someone to a belief in God, but to trust in His Son, Jesus Christ, for the salvation of eternal souls.

Deducing God and the Afterlife from the Physical World

Many in our modern, materialistic world, assume that the most logical conclusion to draw about the afterlife is that it doesn't exist. This is because an afterlife cannot be measured, observed, or experimentally repeated in this physical life. However, could the existence of God and an afterlife be logically proved through things we *can* observe, measure, and reproduce? This was a major question for ancient philosophers, many of whom have been largely forgotten or, at the least, their arguments have been severely reduced to the most basic of straw-man arguments.

According to Scripture, the existence of God, His characteristics, and even the afterlife can be recognized in the world around us. Not only *can* they be recognized, but Scripture says they *are* recognized by even the most unrighteous. This ups the ante in terms of biblical claims, because it not only says believers will be able to appreciate the handiwork of the Creator at some point after their conversion to Christianity, just as a person with an untrained eye can learn to appreciate great works of art by studying more about the discipline. Rather, Scripture says anybody, even nonbelievers and pagans, already do recognize, at least at some level, the Creator for exactly who He is from the physical reality in which we all exist. Even more, Scripture says if the anyone denies there is a Creator, and He is the God of the Bible, that person is actively and knowingly suppressing the truth and will be held responsible for doing so:

> For the wrath of God is revealed from heaven against all ungodliness and unrighteousness of men, who by their unrighteousness suppress the truth. For what can be known about God

is plain to them, because God has shown it to them. For his invisible attributes, namely, his eternal power and divine nature, have been clearly perceived, ever since the creation of the world, in the things that have been made. So they are without excuse. (Romans 1:18–20)

The fact is, the arguments for understanding God and the afterlife through His creation have long since been established by believers and nonbelievers alike. Many Christians are unaware of this because, in mainstream churches across the country, philosophy has been abandoned. Nonbelievers are unaware of this as well, because, in universities, the type of philosophy taught is anti-God, anti-creation, and anti-afterlife. The rebuttals commonly made against philosophers who deduced God from creation are typically based on reductive. Straw-man arguments.

One such argument is a favorite among the scientifically minded among us. They typically use quantum physics and cosmology in an attempt to disprove the "the universe needs a cause and God is that cause" argument. While it is true, the existence of the universe does need a cause and, indeed, that cause is God, to reduce the entire argument in such a way is a gross understatement of the philosophy and even scientific understanding around this idea.

The Linear Series Argument

First, we must be able to agree that change occurs. Every item in the universe is one thing, then at some point in the future, it changes to something else. A common example used to illustrate this is a cup of coffee. At first, the coffee is hot. Later, if left on the counter, it becomes cooler than what it was. Hot coffee changes to room-temperature coffee. If left out even longer, it will eventually change from room-temperature coffee to a microcosm of bacteria. Left even longer still, the entire cup and the liquid within it will change and become dust.

Four types of change can be illustrated with this same example. The coffee cooling down would be a "qualitative" change. If you move the coffee from the kitchen to the living room, this is a "location" change. When you pour coffee into a mug, thereby changing the amount of coffee in the mug, this is called a "quantitative" change. Lastly, if you let the coffee sit for a long time, allowing the coffee to grow bacteria, and letting it sit so long that even the bacteria dies, this is a "substantial" change.

These changes do not occur because the new "thing" (coldness, location, amount, or bacteria) comes from nothing. The ancient Greek philosopher Aristotle (384–322 BC) argued these changes come from *potential* rather than nothing at all; everything has potentiality, and a change is a potential becoming actualized.[259] For example, while the coffee is hot, the coldness of the coffee is not *actually* present, but it doesn't come from nothing, either. Rather, the *potential* for the coldness of the coffee is present in the nature of the hot coffee. Once the coffee becomes colder, the potential has become actualized.

The coffee has many potentials. It has the potential to grow in volume, which would be made actual if you pour more coffee into the mug. It has the potential to give you energy if you drink it. It has the ability to change location if you move it. It has the potential to heat up or cool down. All of these potentials become actuals, given certain and specific conditions. However, there are many potentials the coffee does not have. The coffee does not have the potential to become a lightbulb. It doesn't have the potential to charge your cell phone. It doesn't have the potential to turn into a potion that grants immortality. These would be impossible. Like with anything else, the coffee has a list of potentials and a list of impossibles.

What, then, would we say about nothingness itself? Since it is nothing, it cannot have potentials or actuals, and can only have impossibles. There is nothing onto which to hang potentiality. There is nothing to *change*. Because of that, any change whatsoever would be deemed impossible. The same would be true for the beginning of the universe.

Yet, we know the universe exists—so how does this fit in with Aristotle's potentiality and actuality paradigm?

Many scientists have recognized this problem and have since tried to redefine "nothingness." According to many prominent professors and physicists today, nothing isn't *really* nothing. Empty space isn't *really* empty. Astrophysicist and author Ethan Siegel, displaying a so-called fact commonly taught in academics, said, "Whatever nothingness truly is, we are all *something* right now. And whatever exists right now, it did, at some level, *come* from nothing, no matter how you define nothing."[260] However, this is not true.

Prior to the above quote, Ethan Siegel points out four definitions of "nothingness," which include:

- Ground-state energy, which may have been larger in the past
- A state outside of space and time
- Nothingness of our universe, which might be different than the nothingness of other areas in the multiverse
- A cosmic vacuum, with all virtual energy and is able to change depending what's in it

Clearly, none of these can properly define "nothing," because they all involve "something." A ground-state energy that may have been larger (involving *change*) is not nothing because, conceptually, it can be removed, and nothingness can be considered without it. A state outside space and time is not nothingness, because when we consider this concept, it is in terms of the absence of space and time, not merely the removal of them. If a state can be outside of space and time, that condition would not be nothing. It is something that *exists*. If there was a "nothingness" of our universe, it would not have the potential to be different in other areas of a multiverse, because there is would be no material present to change. Also, "nothing" cannot be true in our universe, because it, itself is "something." To claim this realm devoid of substance in this way would include the denial of space and time, since both are present) in our existing universe, which is illogical. It would be like saying the color of my shirt is so blue that it is green. It is simply an unreasonable statement with no foothold in physical reality. Lastly, a cosmic vacuum, and virtual energy that is able to change are still "things," so they cannot be considered in terms of nothingness.

Rather than overcomplicating the matter or trying to redefine nothingness, we can just say that this condition is the absence of *anything*. If there is an element or property of any kind there, including space and time itself, then it is occupied by *something*. Since "nothing" has no attributes, no characteristics, and no potential, it is 100 percent impossible that our universe came from nothing. In fact, it is ruled out that "nothing" could ever be a reality at all. It is itself an impossibility.

This partly ties in with the attributes of God. For example, how can we know that God is eternal and everlasting? How do we know He always was and always will be? How do we know He just *is* and He exists outside of physical time and space, yet also within it? We can deduce this purely and simply from the impossibility of nothingness. If nothing cannot exist, there must always be something. Time and space had a beginning point, because everything in physical existence has potential and actualization. The existence of time and space are the actualization of some potential, yet nothingness cannot have potentiality. Physical reality requires an actualization of potential that is not bound by time and space; therefore, this actualization would have to be eternal and omnipresent. Just by recognizing very basic truths about how reality around us works, we are able to deduce there is a nonphysical actualization requiring no potentiality that is eternal and omnipresent. These are the most basic attributes of God.

The series of events from potential to actual we just looked at concerns *time*. It is called a *linear* series. We see that in a linear series involving time, there must be a first cause or a first potential. How do we know the universe doesn't just reach back infinitely in time? How do we know time had a beginning at all?

If the universe was infinitely old, all potential would already be actualized. In fact, an infinitely old universe would be pure actualization spurring from all available potentials (not as we looked at before, the existence requires an actualization without potentiality; rather, this would be an actualization from all available potentialities). We would not see change at all. Change is dependent on time, meaning that, for something to occur, there must be a potential, a cause, and a span of time for that change to occur within. Change cannot occur without time. Outside of time, things just *are*. This, by the way, is how we deduce that God is never-changing. He is who He is. God Himself confirmed this when He told Moses, "I am that I am."[261]

If we had an infinite stretch of time behind us with no beginning, the universe would be known as "static," meaning that every change that could occur would have already. Infinity is a difficult concept for us to understand because, like nothingness, it doesn't exist within physical reality. To put this into context, however, imagine a universe that is much older than our own. Imagine a time in the future when all the stars have already burned out. All temperature in the universe is equal and, with no heat sources available, is as cold as cold can get. Go even farther into the future when all particles themselves have decayed. Life, and any kind of physical existence at all, would eventually be impossible. Eventually, all you would have is space and time, nothing else. Even then, time and space could break down, which means you would be left with nothingness. As shown earlier, nothingness is impossible.

Now, try to put that in terms of an infinitely old universe. Not only would this already have happened long ago, but this type of universe would be perpetually static. There would be no creation of it, therefore there couldn't have been a time when change could have existed. Even time and space wouldn't be able to exist because for there to be either requires change (one second to the next, or one location to the other). Thus, we are back to the nothingness problem. A universe of infinite time is a universe of nothingness, which is illogical and, by definition, nonexistent. An infinitely old universe cannot exist.

The Hierarchical Series Argument

We know time must have a beginning and an end, but what about space? The series of events we looked at is linear through time, though there is another kind, called a *hierarchical* series, which concerns *space*. This is a different type of potentiality and actuality that shows not only the impossibility of an infinitely large universe, but also that there is a potential actively holding everything together at every moment in time. Scripture confirms this:

> For by him all things were created, in heaven and on earth, visible and invisible, whether thrones or dominions or rulers or authorities—all things were created through him and for him. And he is before all things, and in him all things hold together. (Colossians 1:16-17)

Imagine again our example of the mug of coffee, only this time, instead of thinking of a series of events, think of it in terms of a single moment of time, like a snapshot from a camera. If your coffee is located on your kitchen counter, it is roughly three to four feet above your kitchen floor. What is holding it up there? The kitchen counter, of course. The coffee has the potential to be three to four feet above the ground, which is being actualized by the kitchen counter. What is holding the kitchen counter up? Your kitchen floor, which is being held up by the foundation of your house, which is being held up by the earth itself, which is held in place (again, we are only looking at a single moment of time, so we are not considering the rotation of the earth), by gravity and other forces, so on and so forth. Eventually, you need an original potential to actualize this hierarchical series, just like you need one with a linear series.

Also, going back to the coffee itself, what is causing that coffee to exist in that moment of time in a hierarchical sense? If we were talking about a temporal, linear sense, we would say that a person has to make the coffee first, then the coffee exists. But what about in a spatial, or hierarchical understanding? In other words, what is keeping the coffee in existence at that moment in time? The coffee in the mug is a combination of water and ground coffee beans, so we could say both need to exist in order for the coffee to exist. Water is made up of hydrogen and oxygen molecules, which both need to exist in a certain combination in order for the water to exist in the same moment of time. Hydrogen and oxygen atoms have the potential to become water molecules if they are arranged in a certain way, which is actualized in the water in the coffee. Atoms themselves are actualized by the potential of certain combinations of subatomic particles. If string theory is correct, subatomic particles are actualized by vibrations of string of energy. Everything is actualized by something else. We can push back these stages as far as we want, but eventually we will need something that can actualize the potential of something else without itself requiring a first potential.

For something to remain in existence at any given moment, something that is pure actualization must exist. This pure actualization would, itself, not be subject to potential; otherwise, the series would just continue another stage. This is the crux of Aristotle's famous "Unmoved Mover" argument. In his book, *Five Proofs of the Existence of God*, Ed Feser calls this the "unactualized actualizer."[262]

Deducing the Attributes of God from His Creation

As we have seen, we can conclude facts about this unactualized actualizer from what is actualized: everything in existence. As we will see in a moment, you can deduce the personhood of God as well. Because God created time, He must be outside of time; He must be eternal. Because God is sustaining everything at every moment of time within space, He must also not be bound by space, meaning He is omnipresent. We can even realize He is perfect from this understanding.

What does it mean to be imperfect or flawed? It means a certain thing is not able or willing to actualize its full potential. If the coffee mug breaks and all the coffee spills to the floor, it is not a perfect mug of coffee because the mug's potential of holding the coffee is not actualized. The mug has an absence of a feature it requires to be complete and have its potential naturally actualized. This means the potential that is inherent in the mug is left unrealized. It is imperfect. If God is pure actualization, then by logic He must be purely perfect, because He would not have some potential that is not being actualized. He has no potential, as you will remember; therefore, it is impossible for there to be unrealized potential. It is impossible for this God to be imperfect. God must be purely perfect.

We can also know that God must be one and not many. For there to be two things, there must be something to differentiate them. There must be something *different* between the two things; otherwise, they would be the same thing. Since the root cause of everything is already purely and perfectly actualized, there would be nothing that could be on the same stature yet different. If there was another unactualized actualizer in existence, it would have to be the very same unactualized actualizer, since there would be nothing to differentiate the two, bringing us back to one.

We can also know this one God is purely and maximally powerful, which is known as *omnipotence*. What does it mean to be powerful? It merely means you can make something happen; you can actualize some potential. Some people can do this better than others in certain areas. They would be considered "more powerful." However, since God is pure actualization, and if the actualization of potential is defined as powerful, then God, who actualizes all potential in existence, would have to be purely powerful. Again, God is omnipotent.

How do we know God is good and not evil? We consider something "good" when it realizes the potential that is natural or inherent within it. We consider something bad when it does not. On a moral basis, we consider something good when it chooses to realize its potential and something bad when it chooses to not. If a person has natural gifts that go to waste by choice (for example, if the person is lazy), we would consider that "bad" or, in extreme cases, "evil." If a person does not waste his or her natural gifts, rather choosing to actualize the potential he or she was naturally born with, then we consider this "good." Now, a pure actualization with no needed potential would be considered as the ultimate good, having absolutely no evil within Him.

This might lead us to ask: How do we know God is intelligent and not just some force? It is all about *choice*. Some things exist while others do not. If an unactualized actualizer was just an impersonal force and it is full actualization, fully powerful, and fully "good" in the sense that it realizes the full potential of what it can actualize, then *all* things would be actualized. Yet, that isn't the reality we see around us. In fact, if it was, we would be back to the infinity problem. For all things to be, you need infinite time and space. Infinity itself would have be real, yet as we saw earlier, in the current certainty we observe around us, this is absolutely impossible. Therefore, for an unactualized actualizer to make certain things and not others, it requires a choice between what will be made and what will not. A choice is really just a selection of preference, meaning this unactualized actualizer would have to pointedly prefer one thing over another. In order to have preference, one must have intelligence. Intelligence is required for a choice to be made, for if there is no intelligent decision, both options would be realized for this unactualized actualizer to be fully and purely actualized. In short, an unintelligent, unactualized actualizer means it cannot be omnipotent, because for there to be a "choice" made without intelligence, it would mean one thing is made instead of another by way of a lack of power rather than an actual choice being made. Since we know God is all powerful, we also know He must be all intelligent, or *omniscient*.

This also explains that He must have free will rather than merely a creative force of nature. Consider how the roots of a tree naturally grow into the ground and bring in nutrients to ensure its survival. The tree is not conscious or intelligent, yet it is able to sustain itself and even grow seeds to create new generations of its species. How do we know God is not like the tree and that His will is free? The reason the tree does all of this is because of something higher than itself; if a thing does not have a choice yet acts in a certain way, an outside force *must* be acting on it in some way. The earth rotates the sun not by free will, but by natural forces of gravity and inertia. The tree grows and reproduces itself not by free will, but by its and the way it was created. Human beings, on the other hand, have free will. We can choose to reproduce or not reproduce. We can decide to live or die based on our own free will. However, because we are created beings, there are matters outside of our control as well. We are not omnipotent. We rely solely on God to keep our existence intact; we cannot exist without or apart from Him. Therefore, on some level, there is still something higher compelling us to exist: God. We have free will to decide what choices in life we will make, but we do not have free will to exist apart from God's actualization of us. This is how we know God's will must be free in all aspects. If God's will wasn't free, it would mean something would exist higher than God, directing Him to make the decisions He makes—and, as we have seen, this would be impossible. God doesn't rely on anything for His existence, yet everything else relies on Him.

One more thing we can look at concerning intelligence is that we never see a lesser potential creating a greater actualization in terms of quality. For example, you cannot pour one cup of coffee into a mug and have a mug of two cups of coffee. You cannot move the coffee two feet and have it displaced by five feet. The potential for the cup to move two feet is actualized by you moving it that distance. We know that, as human beings, we have the potential for intelligence and consciousness, which were actualized when we came into existence. These attributes cannot be created from an unintelligent and unconscious sort, just as the potential of a cup of coffee becoming cold cannot be actualized by adding heat to it. Therefore, we can deduce that not only is God intelligent and conscious, but He is *purely* so.

Given all of this, we can now look at the question of why we call God "He" rather than "She" or "It." First, as we saw before, God must be a personal entity of intelligence and free will rather than a force, so calling God "It" would not be appropriate. Second, we must realize that "He" and "She" are based in biological gender and how we humans characterize humans and animals. God, quite literally, does not fit into any category of biology (save for Jesus, which we will deal with shortly); therefore, from a purely biological sense, God would be genderless. However, there is good philosophical reason to refer to God as "He" rather than "She" based on His nature alone.

God's relationship to His creation, based on everything we looked at, is far more like a father rather than a mother. From what we observe in human biology, a father's role in creating new generations of human beings is far more active than the mother's. A father impregnates the mother while the mother is impregnated by the father. The father plays the active role while the mother plays the passive role, strictly biologically speaking. Also, there is no physiological change to the father after conception occurs, yet there is to the mother. The mother is the one who *changes,* while the father remains *unchanged* in comparison. During this time, the mother typically become far more physically dependent on the father than the father does to the mother. Throughout history, it has not been biologically and traditionally the job of the mother to provide food, water, and other forms of sustenance to the father while she is pregnant; rather, it is the other way around. The father provides while the mother is provided for. If the mother were to leave the father, the father (again, strictly biologically speaking) would not suffer in terms of provision, yet if the father were to leave the pregnant mother to fend for herself, it could be detrimental to the health of the mother and child.

There is a physical connection between the mother and child that does not exist between the father and child. The child would recognize the womb as his home, and the father would be more of a mystery. The child would only hear his voice from time to time and would have no physical connection to him, yet the child is still a part of the father.

While there are parallels we can draw between the notion of a mother and father and the relationship of God and creation, we must realize that the planet we live on is not a conscious and intelligent being the way a mother is, so we can only take the analogy so far. It might even be better to draw parallels between the earth and the womb itself as a physical, unconscious thing. Much in the same way a baby has a connection to the womb/mother, we have a physical connection to the earth, yet we don't have that type of physical connection to God. We can still have a relationship with God, who acts in every way as our Father, but there is a barrier of physicality—a barrier between our world and His, just as in the case of the womb for a child. Also, much like the child who can hear the voice of the father at times, possibly even feeling him if he put his hand on the mother's abdomen, so we, too, can have a relationship with God. He can talk to us in limited ways we can understand. Also, like in the example above, we rely on God for our existence, yet He doesn't rely on us for His existence at all. If God abandoned us, we would cease to exist, yet if the whole universe ceased to exist, God would still exist. Because of all these things and more, traditionally, God has been referred to as "He" rather than "She." These ideas are reflected in Scripture quite often. If we choose to follow Jesus and be reconciled with God, we are referred to as His children (Romans 9:8). Yet, we as believers are also referred to as the Bride of Christ (2 Corinthians 11:2; Revelation 19:7), which falls in line also with the male/female example we looked at.

We see this example further carried out in Scripture:

Wives, submit to your own husbands, as to the Lord. For the husband is the head of the wife even as Christ is the head of the church, his body, and is himself its Savior. Now as the church submits to Christ, so also wives should submit in everything to their husbands. Husbands, love your wives, as Christ loved the church and gave himself up for her, that he might sanctify her, having cleansed her by the washing of water with the word, so that he might present the church to himself in splendor, without spot or wrinkle or any such thing, that she might be holy and without blemish. In the same way husbands should love their wives as their own bodies. He who loves his wife loves himself. For no one ever hated his own flesh, but nourishes and cherishes it, just as Christ does the church, because we are members of his body. "Therefore a man shall leave his father and mother and hold fast to his wife, and the two shall become one flesh." This mystery is profound, and I am saying that it refers to Christ and the church. However, let each one of you love his wife as himself, and let the wife see that she respects her husband. (Ephesians 5:22–33)

Because this passage has been taken out of context in the nonbelieving world many times over, it is important to explain what is going on here and how it relates to the paternal attributes of God. The example given here is twofold. It not only teaches how a relationship between a man and wife operates, but it uses that as an example of how Christ operates with us and how we are to operate with Him. Finally, this question of why we refer to God as a "He" was made evident in Jesus Christ. If God rejected the idea of being referred to as "He," He very well could have set it all up differently and had the Messiah be a woman. Yet, He did not do that. Jesus, fully God and fully man, was born into physical existence as a *male*.

This, of course, does not mean that men have more value than women; that is an argument usually coming from people trying to disprove the existence of a loving God or to justify gratuitous overdomination of males over females. Rather, as Ephesians 5:22–33 states, as far as biological men and women, *both* are *equally* important, yet both thrive in *different* areas. Yet Scripture indicates that this is an example of our relationship to Christ. It doesn't mean we are equal to Christ; that isn't the point at all. The point is that Christ absolutely has a role to play in our lives and, if we properly exercise that, it is more of a relationship than anything else. Christ isn't a tyrant; rather, He allows us to actively participate in the relationship with Him based on our own free will. This is why husbands are not supposed to be tyrants either, yet are supposed to love their wives, with wives showing respect and love to their husbands. God through Christ, leads us perfectly and justly, solely out of love and the desire for our well-being. Husbands should follow that model and treat our wives the same way. We, as believers, follow God through Christ out of love, respect, and trust. As long as God is leading us perfectly in righteousness (which He always does), then it is our responsibility to follow that lead. If a husband is leading perfectly in righteousness (which doesn't always happen, of course, because human beings are flawed and make mistakes), then there should be no difference between the leading of Christ and the leading of the husband. This is why it is the responsibility of every husband to follow Christ as closely as possible daily and to look to Christ as the standard for behavior and leadership.

Believing Facts Is a Choice

Based on all of this information, there is only one God in all of the world religions who fits these requirements: the God of the Bible. Every other god from every other religion is lacking in some way or another; only the Bible describes this God perfectly as we can deduce from the physical reality around us. Because of this, we know we can trust what He says about Himself and the afterlife. We know He must be perfectly good, pure, perfect, and intelligent. God tells us quite a bit about the afterlife and, since we have established that He is the only truly reliable source on the subject, we do well to listen to what He has to say. This is how we know that our main source of information about the afterlife, the Bible, is an accurate one. It is the only text endorsed by this all-powerful, all-good God of truth. Not only that, but this is how we know we can trust His Son, Jesus Christ, who is God in the flesh, to explain the correct way to make sure we have a pleasant afterlife with Him rather than an unpleasant, unending afterlife eternally apart from Him. When we take a logical look at these matters, we come to the stunning realization that all of them point directly to Jesus Christ.

Interestingly, understanding the basics of these concepts doesn't require modern scientific knowledge Just by thinking of a cup of coffee being held up by a counter, existing in a cup, and having a beginning, we can deduce that, eventually, something must have caused all of it in time and actively causes all of it in space without itself having a cause. We really don't need to bring subatomic particles and the universe into the argument. Ancient philosophers who discussed potentiality and actuality had a very limited understanding of the building blocks of the universe or the universe as a whole. Yet, even they were able to conclude these truths from the world around them. So, what is our excuse?

As Scripture indicates, we as human beings already know these things. The knowledge of God is built within us. It is up to us individually if we are going to explore it in the physical world or if we are going to suppress it and not consider the real arguments made by philosophers and believers in the past. We are responsible for this choice (and it is certainly a choice), and we will be judged accordingly.

chapter six

Our Future Bodies

There are, of course, many books about Heaven and the resurrected bodies of people who have given their lives to Christ will receive. However, very few books in mainstream Christianity clearly identify the need for this body and how we can understand the attributes this body will need in order to fulfill the promises of God. Some things are clearly laid out in Scripture, while others require some thought. Some commonly addressed topics are easy. For example, if the resurrection of Jesus is an example of what we can expect, we know our glorified bodies will be able to walk through walls, will have some kind of structure (such as bones), will be able to eat (Luke 24:36–43), can fly (Acts 1:9), and will be immortal (1 Corinthians 15:53–55). However, these are just surface characteristics.

The true purpose and attributes of our resurrected bodies is far more glorious than we could ever imagine, yet that issue is almost never discussed in mainstream Christianity. I (Josh) believe this is because the topic can get very deep and complex. I will try my best to explain these complexities in this chapter. I'll also attempt to explain the same concepts using different examples and methods since, again, they can be a bit difficult.

The Philosophy of Resurrection

Much could be said—and, indeed, has been written—on what the Bible says about the resurrection and our glorified bodies. Any look at the afterlife from a Christian perspective cannot ignore these matters. However, instead of rehashing the common knowledge, I (Josh) want to focus on some lesser-known aspects of eternity, resurrection, and our future, glorified bodies.

The Christian doctrine of resurrection has received a lot of attention from philosophers. Christians believe the resurrection of Jesus serves as a model of what we can expect if we have submitted to Him and have become born-again believers. We believe people who have rejected Jesus will be resurrected as well, but it will be for judgment rather than reward. In Acts 24:15b, Paul says "that there will be a resurrection of both the just and the unjust."

Materialist and immaterialist philosophers have been debating the resurrection for quite some time. In what's been called "the simulacra model," Peter van Inwagen attempts to present a model of resurrection that is compatible with materials and the Christian doctrine of resurrection. The problem for the materialist who is trying to defend resurrection as described by Christianity is that the body begins to break down and becomes destroyed by natural processes after death. Van Inwagen's solution is to propose a model of resurrection in which our physical bodies do not decay, but instead are replaced with a copy called a "simulacrum." He stated: "At the moment of each man's death, God removes his corpse and replaces it with a simulacrum, which is what is burned or rots."[263] Then, at the time of the resurrection, this theory states that God will take the preserved corpse and restore it to life.

There are obvious problems to this, even for materialists. Van Ingwen admits in this article that there is no reason for God to replace a corpse with a simulacrum. God could just as well remove and preserve our corpses and *not* replace them with anything at all. Van Inwagen attempts to answer by saying that if God did not replace corpses with simulacra, there would be widespread and irrefutable proof of the existence of the supernatural. Van Inwagen adds a postscript to his original article:

> I am inclined now to think of the description that I gave in "The Possibility of Resurrection" of how an omnipotent being could accomplish the Resurrection of the Dead as a "just-so story": Although it serves to establish a possibility, it probably isn't true.[264]

Of the immaterialist views on resurrection, Augustine's and Aquinas' are probably among the most popular. Augustine was an early adopter of a form of dualism inspired by Plato and Descartes, which stated:

1. The body and the soul are separate substances.
2. The soul is immaterial.
3. The soul is identical or strongly connected to the mind.

Augustine added to this that the soul is immortal, because it desires perfect happiness, and no happiness would be perfect if one feared losing it at death. Thomas Aquinas held the view that people are a substance that is a blend of both matter and form. This substantial form is the rational soul. This is called the "hylomorphic" view. There was a debate between people who held this view about whether the soul could survive death and, if it could, whether this would ensure a personal resurrection. Aquinas argued that the human mind/soul can exist apart from the physical body. The mind/soul doesn't depend on the physical body for existence. Therefore, instead of ceasing to exist at physical death, when the soul becomes disembodied, it would come to know the world in a different way. This is very interesting in light of the extradimensional near-death experiences we looked at earlier. Aquinas also argued that we can expect a personal resurrection.

This shows that even in ancient times, philosophers, theologians, and religious thinkers understood the importance of a resurrection. But why do we need a resurrection at all? We know that God promises it will happen in the Bible, but if our souls can detach from our physical bodies and live on with God, what need do we have for a resurrection and glorification of the physical body? These are very good questions, with some very complicated answers. The key to the need for resurrection is understanding the need of the spirit for embodiment.

The Need for Embodiment

Here is something interesting to think about that will form the framework of this chapter: Every time God interacts with people or angels, He is embodied to some degree. There is a difference between physical embodiment and spiritual embodiment. God is never described as a disembodied essence. For example, when He interacts with humans or angels, He *speaks*. Why is this?

It is entirely possible that any kind of communion with God is impossible unless it is done through some type of embodiment. Think about what God is. Is He a physical form as Jesus Christ on earth? Yes, though not *entirely*. Is God His heavenly embodiment as the King on the throne? Yes, though again, not *entirely*. Is God truly His Holy essence in whatever that means for Him in His own subjective sense? Yes! This is because God's own *subjective* sense of Himself *is* the ultimate objective reality. No one can truly know that purely objective truth but God Himself, because He is One and there are no others like Him. This means that all of creation, from the highest angel to the lowliest worm, can only interact with God through a means that, in a sense, filters His subjective/objective nature in a way we can understand. But, included with that *is* the embodiment, which is why God is typically understood as a Trinity. God decided to create man, meaning God had a desire that was fulfilled in His creation of us, meaning there would have to be a way for Him to interact and have a relationship with us, meaning the Trinity is necessary. Yet, we know God was/is a Trinity *even* before He created man. Therefore, the means by which God can interact with us, angels, and anything else He created was in place before anything outside of God Himself existed.

This can be confusing and, if we're not careful, can lead someone to believe that all of creation is *equal* to God because of these things, but this is not so, because of one missing element: time. God is eternal and time is His creation. This means God exists both outside of and within time. Eternity is a state of being outside of time. Temporal is a state of being within time. There was a "time" (for lack of better word) before time was created. That statement isn't technically accurate, but it does show the limitations of human language. Naturally, anything God creates would have to be *less* than Him. A creation of God certainly couldn't be greater, because God is the greatest; nothing could be conceived of that is *greater* than God; otherwise, *that* would be God. Nothing can exist without being created by God, as we looked at in the last chapter. No creation of God can be equal with God, because then God would not be One. Therefore, everything God created is less, or more limited, than Him.

Think for a moment of the makeup of a human being. A human is body, soul, and spirit. The spirit is the thing that we really are; it's what animates the rest. The spirit is the subjective understanding of one's own self. God modeled us after Himself, yet we are limited. God, too, has a body (Jesus), soul (Heavenly Father on the throne), and spirit (or Holy Spirit, God's own ultimate subjective understanding of Himself, which is the ultimate truth, because nothing could be truer; therefore, it is also the ultimate objective truth)—and all of these *are* God. It's not accurate to say they are *pieces* of God, because they are all fully God. It is similar to say ice, water, and steam are all fully H2O, yet this isn't a perfect analogy (mainly because there is no such thing as a perfect analogy; they all break down at some point), because these are still different *states* of existence based on temperature.

Because we are lesser, we would never be able to interact with God without the limiting factor of embodiment. I say "limiting" based on just our own perspective, because embodiment doesn't "limit" God, just like it doesn't "enhance" Him, either. God is already the ultimate and the infinite; there is no taking away from or adding to God. Yet, from our own, already-limited perspective, we can see how we cannot fully appreciate God Himself in His entirety without us being equal to God—which, again, is impossible. This is why Jesus Christ is necessary and why everything points back to Him. Without Him, in every sense, we could never truly be reconciled to God.

Going back to time, we must understand that who we are right now, in this moment in time, is not the totality of who we are as a being. In the same way, we are not *only* our body, soul, or spirit. To be truly who we are meant to be the way God intends, we must be all three—but again, not merely all three in one moment of time. We are not who we are today, but we are the totality of who we are in every moment of time—including eternity, if we've given our lives to Jesus. The totality of who we are is body, soul, and spirit in and out of all moments in time. Within the totality of time, we only exist physically in a part of it. However, in eternity, outside of time, we just *are*.

The amazing thing is that the Triune attribute of God preexisted human beings. Yet if God was only spirit, we would have no way to tangibly interact with Him, meaning His desire to create human beings and angels would not be fulfilled, which means He wouldn't be all powerful, and the whole concept breaks apart. However, if God was *already* a Trinity before He created man, the aspects and attributes of His very nature always included the creation of mankind. It means that creating man wasn't merely a desire for God in the way we would think of it. A desire of God's is actually a necessity, because how could an all-powerful God have a desire that does not end up fulfilled? Therefore, because He desired to create mankind, mankind was a necessity by the very nature of God.

I bring this up because human words cannot possible truly explain what God's love for us really means. It goes beyond love. We can't grasp how important we are to God. Neither can we comprehend how important matters like free will, justice, perfection, and others are to God. We can't truly fathom how much of a waste it is to ignore these issues throughout life and reject God entirely. We are not God; therefore, we cannot truly ever *understand* God the way He understands Himself. We can *know* Him, of course, if we don't waste the gift He's given us in Jesus Christ. We can interact with Him. But it is necessary for there, again, to be a means through which we can perceive Him. This means is embodiment. This is why a physical body, a spiritual body, and a physical resurrection of the body, which becomes a glorified body, is needed. Without it, we have no way of perceiving God. We would be disembodied spirits with no possible means through which to interact with God. In other words, we would be completely separated from God in every way imaginable. Without right standing with God, we are just consciousnesses without any kind of housing, blind and deaf, completely separate from the only thing that makes us whole; we are the absolute personification of incomplete. We only know nothing but pain in every sense, because no good can come without God. We are, in a sense, worse than nothing.

To understand this, we can go back to our square and cube examples from early on in this book. Imagine the square is the physical body, the cube is the soul, and the spirit is the mind. Even in this dimensionally reduced example, it is impossible to understand the spirit/mind without a body for it to be housed in. Even in our wildest imaginations, we might think of the mind/spirit as a type of mist that hovers about, but even this would be woefully incorrect. What is the mist made of? Doesn't the mist still just act as a type of body for the mind/spirit? We can never truly understand the spirit without embodiment, because to do so would be to understand God in every way, denoting that we'd need to be equal in power to God, and again, the whole concept of God breaks down at that point.

Physical and spiritual reality are environments that require bodies to operate in, but like the mind of the square, needs a body that's appropriate for the environment, whether it's two dimensional or three dimensional. If he is physically alive in the second dimension, he needs a square body. If his square body dies, meaning his mind is not embodied in a limited, second dimension anymore, he needs a three-dimensional body, which is the cube. Now, let's say that, in this analogy, I am the creator and there are only three dimensions; there is no higher dimension to which to ascend. One can either have access to a three-dimensional body that I can make for him, or one can reject me completely with his own free will, meaning he will not have access to a body. If he rejects me and loses his chance at another body, this would be like a second death, which sounds very familiar to what is described in the book of Revelation concerning those who reject Christ. If a square, out of his own free will, accepts me while he was physically alive, I (valuing free will) would then be permitted to offer him a new body. But wait—he already has access to a cube/soul/three-dimensional body. What is the point of resurrecting and glorifying his two-dimensional square body?

It is because a cube is not really complete without access to a square. A cube (again, being a series of squares stacked on top of each other) cannot be complete without a square of any kind; it is impossible. Yet, what would be the point of giving him a square that will just die again? He must have a square that is not subject to death, meaning it can exist in eternity. His previous square was *confined* to the second dimension because it was subject to death, and as the Bible states, flesh and blood (in other words, a physical body subject to death) cannot inherit the kingdom of God (1 Corinthians 15:50). Otherwise, he would have a body that is once again locked into the second dimension without access to the third. Thus, he needs a new, incorruptible square body that is not *locked* in the second dimension, but that has *access* to the second dimension and can move freely in and out of it.

Again, you might ask, applying this to us humans, why do we need a body that can interact with the physical world at all? Once we're dead, isn't getting to go to heaven enough? The answer is: It is a matter of being "whole" and "restored." You cannot be fully restored if you don't have access to a place you once had access to. Again, a cube cannot truly be a cube without the existence of a square. Without a square, cubes are impossible. This is why the body of the resurrected and glorified Christ was able to move about freely in our three dimensions of space, but was also able to move freely in higher dimensions, which is how He could ascend to the clouds and enter an apparently closed room. Going back to the example of the square having an NDE and realizing that he is a cube, during that time, he is seeing in three-dimensional reality, yet his two-dimensional perspective is lost. He doesn't have access to the two-dimensional way of seeing the world. If he wanted *complete* perspective, he would need access to both his cube perspective and his square perspective. He would need a body that could do both.

This very well might be why a resurrection is required in order for true restoration. Without a glorified and resurrected body, Jesus may not have had the same type of three-dimensional perspective, meaning He may not have been able to interact or communicate with the physical world at all. Consider again people who have experienced extradimensional NDEs: They are unable to communicate with anyone in the physical world. Even more, their perspective has become extradimensional. Their normal, three-dimensional perspective is lost. To be restored, glorified, and have access to all God has created, we need not only an extradimensional soul, but a physical resurrection of the body. This new body is not subject to death, deterioration, or decay, but is immortal.

When Do We Receive Our New Bodies?

Most Christians believe one of two things concerning *when* we receive our glorified bodies. When we die, we are either temporarily in our extradimensional soul awaiting a resurrected body or we are given our resurrected bodies promptly at the time of our death. In either case, you might wonder, why don't we see people who have died interacting with this physical world? For reasons we looked at earlier, it does seem at least possible for that to happen, such as in the case of ghosts. But why is communicating with ghosts forbidden? Why was the glorified Jesus so much different than a ghost? We have to remember that the judgment has not taken place yet. People who have rejected Christ have not yet been consigned to the second death in the lake of fire. It is reasonable to assume, from our perspective as physical beings, that our dead loved ones who accepted Christ do not yet have their glorified bodies. How is this possible; if you can't have a cube without a square, how can you have a dead person in Heaven without a physical aspect to their bodies? Again, it all has to do with *time*.

Eternity is not infinity. Eternity is a state outside of time. It would stand to reason, then, that a person who dies gets pulled into eternity and is immediately standing before God at the judgment. We tend to think of the judgment as a future event, and from our perspective it is, but this is an incomplete way of thinking about it. It isn't that God pulls someone who dies forward in time to a future event. Rather, he is pulled out of time to an event that just *is*, which again, is impossible for us to understand. This might be why God forbids us to speak to what we think of as ghosts. From our perspective, a dead loved one has not yet received his or her glorified body. From their perspective, they have. Therefore, the strange disconnect here is perception and understanding; we have no way to relate in any sensical way to someone who has died until we die, too. If the square tried to communicate with a cube, from the square's perspective, he would be communicating with a cube that has no squares, which is impossible, so it is obvious that the human brain cannot interpret or perceive it correctly. True communication is impossible, and attempting to do so only brings about confusion, which is why it is forbidden. Now, on occasion, God allows events to occur in a tangible way, such as the incident with the witch of Endor, which only shows that God is above all of this and will do as He pleases. It could very well be that the prophet Samuel was already in his glorified body—but, again, time gets really fuzzy when thinking in these terms. We can't say that for sure, but to Samuel, the judgment may have already taken place and he may have already received his reward. Or, it could be that he was in this odd, pre-eternal, in-between place awaiting the Messiah. Perhaps before Jesus came on the scene, time and embodiment worked differently for those who already died. It is difficult to say. Yet, because of how impossible all of this is to understand, it makes sense why God would forbid the living to speak with the spirits of the dead.

Ancient Spirit Doubles

The idea of communicating with the dead bleeds into ancient beliefs across cultures and religions of spirit doubles. German folklore talks of the *doppelgänger* (meaning "double goer").[265] Building upon the ancient, widespread belief that every man and animal has a spirit double, the folklore of the *doppelgänger* says if a person is to meet his own double, it is a sign that his death is coming soon. The Qur'an also speaks of a spirit double called a *qarin,* which means "companion, mate, comrade, or intimate."[266] A *qarin* is spirit being that is believed to be born with every person, yet is born the opposite sex (males have female *qarins,* and vice versa), staying with them throughout their entire lives. On the Last Day, a *qarin* can testify against a person, causing them to be cast into hell (Sura 50:21–32). It is also believed this entity can deceive and cause eternal doom to people (Sura 4:38; 43:36–38). Much like the *doppelgänger,* the *qarin* is thought of as a demonic spirit, though Mohammed believed it was a personal spirit that could be converted to Islam.[267]

There even appears to be an ancient Hebrew belief in a spirit double, though this was more akin to our modern understanding of a guardian angel. Acts 12:12–15 relates that, when an angel let Peter out of prison, some people mistook him for the his double:

When he realized this, he went to the house of Mary, the mother of John whose other name was Mark, where many were gathered together and were praying. And when he knocked at the door of the gateway, a servant girl named Rhoda came to answer. Recognizing Peter's voice, in her joy she did not open the gate but ran in and reported that Peter was standing at the gate. They said to her, "You are out of your mind." But she kept insisting that it was so, and they kept saying, "It is his angel!"

This passage illustrates that even the apostles had a belief in a type of angel that was identical in appearance to the person to whom he was assigned, though we're not told much else about it. Regarding Acts 12:15, the *Faithlife Bible Study* says:

The Greek word used here is not *phantasma*, the typical Greek word for ghost used elsewhere in the NT (Matt 14:26; Mark 6:49) and in other ancient Greek literature. Instead the Greek word used is *angelos*, which is used to describe a heavenly being sent from Yahweh or a messenger. The church's reaction likely testifies to an ancient belief that one's angel was a kind of celestial entity that accompanied a person for his or her welfare (compare Matt 18:10; Heb 1:14).[268]

The *Holman New Testament Commentary of Acts* reads:

What a fascinating idea. Ancient Jews and many modern Christians believe that each person has a guardian angel, though that idea is hardly supported with great weight in the pages of the New Testament. Some years after the New Testament was written, this concept developed into the view that these guardian angels also bore the image of the persons they protected and often appeared immediately after that person's death. Although we certainly do not want to read postbiblical literature back into our interpretation of Acts, it is not difficult to see that notion among these early believers. Did they believe Peter had been delivered and now waited outside in the street? No. They *could* believe, however, he had died and gone to heaven and his look-alike angel stood there![269]

For Christian theologians, this idea is known as a "divine double," though it is not widely known across mainstream Christianity today. I (Josh) recently interviewed theologian Dr. Michael Heiser (author of *The Unseen Realm* and *Angels*) about this question of spirit doubles in the Bible.[270] When I asked about Acts 12:15, Dr. Heiser replied:

It could go two directions; there are two discernible sets of thoughts about this kind of thing in second temple Judaism and in the New Testament era. In the New Testament cultural worldview matrix, the statement could mean that what they were hearing is his departed self. In other words, "his angel" would convey the idea that Peter is dead and now we're essentially getting a visitation by his ghost. There was a belief that when someone died, it wasn't that they became an angel, it's that they could appear to you as a phantom-like creature or entity. Since angels were those kind of entities as well, the two ideas became conflated together. It could also be something that is found in second temple Judaism. There is a doctrine that is spelled out in the Dead Sea Scrolls called the "two spirits" idea. It says there's a spirit among humanity, a spirit of man, and there's two sides to it, one good and one evil. To the ancient people of Qumran, a person either had the evil spirit or the good spirit. So you can see how that idea could glom on to this divine double belief.

Some of the earliest sources of the divine double belief that may have influenced early Christianity can be found from Tatian the Assyrian, who was a Christian author from the second century who believed in a conjunction of each human soul with its divine spirit, and Valentinus, a second-century theologian who believed a type of union exists between us and our angelic counterparts.[271] In his only surviving work, the *Address to the Greeks*, Tatian discusses a version of the divine double belief. This version sees a man becoming reborn as a type of twin, in a sense, of Jesus. In a way, it is similar to the idea we currently have that when we die, go to heaven, and are sinless; we will be similar to Jesus, yet we will not be identical to Him.

Tatian also believed in a stark difference between soul and spirit. He describes how Satan led humans and certain angels astray. These deceived beings (humans and angels) were banished by God, causing each of them to lose their "more powerful spirit."[272] Tatian writes:

> [There are] two different kinds of spirits, one of which is called a soul, but the other is greater than the soul; it is the image and likeness of God. The first humans were endowed with both, so that they might be part of the material world, and at the same time above it. This is how things are.[273]

This sounds similar to our previous example of the cube and mind, in that the cube represented the soul while the mind represented the spirit; however, there are differences. Tatian believed we humans now only have our soul as a spirit. Our actual spirit, the "greater soul," has been lost to us. The other spirit is the image and likeness of God (such as is described in the creation account of the book of Genesis). Without the spirit, humans have no real attachment to the divine, at least not as much as we had prior to the Fall. Without intervention, Tatian believed the soul will dissolve with the body at death.[274]

Valentinus (AD 100–170) was a contemporary of Tatian. According to Irenaeus of Lyons (ca. AD 130–202) in *Against Heresies*, Valentinus believed and taught that the cosmos is organized into an emanating series of male and female pairs. In fact, his whole view of the physical and spiritual world was gnostic in nature, even referring to thirty divinities, or *aeons*, in fifteen pairs that make up the divine realm, called the *Pleroma* or "Fullness." Later Valentinian explanations of the sacraments (such as baptism) included the belief that they affected a union of each individual with his or her angelic counterpart. The Valentinian interpretation of divine doubles was more closely related to Gnosticism than Christianity, which is important to note because there are stark contrasts between the two.

It is strange that cultures and beliefs from ancient times and all over the world had a belief in a type of spirit double. It is as if at one time in human history, long ago, possibly before the Fall, this was common knowledge that became lost throughout time. It seems the cultures who managed to hold on to some kind of belief in a divine double ended up twisting the entire concept around into a vague reflection of the truth. What is the core, absolute truth about divine doubles? We're only given a hint of it in the Bible. However, it does seem that, whatever that truth is, it has something to do with the spirit, soul, death of the physical body, and the afterlife.

Glorified Bodies and Eternity

Is it possible that people have appeared who are already in their glorified bodies? We may see an example of this at the transfiguration of Jesus, where we saw an example of the future, present, and past converging in the same point. Two of God's people who had died long before seemingly appeared—already in their glorified bodies. We even see a glimpse of Jesus in His glorified body prior to His death and resurrection! Matthew 17:1–8:

And after six days Jesus took with him Peter and James, and John his brother, and led them up a high mountain by themselves. And he was transfigured before them, and his face shone like the sun, and his clothes became white as light. And behold, there appeared to them Moses and Elijah, talking with him. And Peter said to Jesus, "Lord, it is good that we are here. If you wish, I will make three tents here, one for you and one for Moses and one for Elijah." He was still speaking when, behold, a bright cloud overshadowed them, and a voice from the cloud said, "This is my beloved Son, with whom I am well pleased; listen to him." When the disciples heard this, they fell on their faces and were terrified. But Jesus came and touched them, saying "Rise, and have no fear." And when they lifted up their eyes, they saw no one but Jesus only.

The transfiguration could have very well been an example of eternity bleeding a bit into normal time as we know it. Jesus began to shine, and His clothes became white. This is similar to the description of Jesus given by John much later in the book of Revelation. As far as Moses and Elijah, we aren't exactly sure if they were already in their glorified bodies as most believe or—which would perhaps be even more interesting—if God was talking to them while they were still alive! We may have a clue here; verse 2 says that the face of Jesus shone like the sun. This same type of thing happened to Moses as recorded back in the book of Exodus:

When Moses came down from Mount Sinai, with the two tablets of the testimony in his hand as he came down from the mountain, Moses did not know that the skin of his face shone because he had been talking with God. Aaron and all the people of Israel saw Moses, and behold, the skin of his face shone, and they were afraid to come near him. (Exodus 34:29–30)

Could it be these describe the same event? When Moses was talking with God, causing Moses' face to shine, could that have been the same conversation Jesus was having with Moses? Jesus is God in the flesh, so could Jesus have been speaking with Moses through the barrier of linear time, back to a time when Moses was alive, the end result being Moses' face shining just like Jesus? Perhaps that is the effect of being in the vicinity of this glimpse through eternity.

It seems, in our eternal bodies, we will no longer be constrained or locked into linear time as we are now, but might possibly be free to move around it. In fact, if there are multiple dimensions of time (as far as we know, there is only one, but there theoretically could be more), not only would we be able to move around in them, but we wouldn't be bound by any of them and would be able to exit them entirely on into eternity. This might help explain one of the most enigmatic verses in the Bible concerning our future with Jesus. Ephesians 2:5–7:

> But God, being rich in mercy because of the great love with which he loved us, even when we were dead in our trespasses, made us alive together with Christ—by grace you have been saved—and raised us up with him and seated us with him in the heavenly places in Christ Jesus, so that in the coming ages he might show the immeasurable riches of his grace in kindness toward us in Christ Jesus.

The clear message here is that God loves us so much. However, there is more. Notice the use of past and future tenses in this passage. Many times, when this passage is interpreted, it is taught that Jesus sees us as if we are already seated with Him. However, the text teaches this principle in past tense, portraying the fact that this has already happened. When we "were dead," He "made us alive together with Christ," and "raised us up," and "seated us" together in the heavenly places in Christ Jesus. If we have accepted Jesus as our Savior, this is already done. How might this fit into our understanding of a glorified body that can move freely through and not be confined by time?

When we look at this passage closely, we realize very direct and literal language is used. We do not see "as if" or "like" anywhere in the passage. It is directly saying that a literal event occurred when you and I accepted Jesus Christ as Savior. We were literally seated in Heaven with Jesus.

The Greek word used for the idea of us being raised together comes from *synegeirō*, meaning:

1. to raise together, to cause to raise together
2. to raise up together from mortal death to a new and blessed life dedicated to God.[275]

From this, we can see that we were, in a sense, born into death, but since we accepted Jesus' gift of salvation, we have been raised and seated in Heaven. Also notice that this happened to all of us together, implicating that it happened within the same instant.

What we're dealing with here is the same event in two different understandings of time: one within and one without. This is why understanding eternity as a state outside of time can help us. In the one linear dimension of time we can experience here on earth, we accept Jesus as Savior and begin our new life. In eternity, this reality just is. The passage seems to be saying that we as Christians are already in Heaven, at least as far as eternity is concerned. Right now, as you are reading this, if you are secure in Jesus, you're already seated with Jesus in Heaven. Now, of course, this is outside of the physical timeline. We cannot apply this to our physical lives and think we can do whatever we want because it is already done in eternity. We still have free will. We still have a choice. As far as we should be concerned here on earth, our eternal fate is not yet sealed. That occurs at the moment of death and the entrance to eternity. But again, the human language can only bring us so far in attempting to understand the complexities of eternity versus linear time.

Before accepting Jesus' gift of salvation, we lived in sin and death. If we had continued down that path and had never accepted Jesus, we would be already dead spiritually, even though we would still be physically alive. That is what the beginning of the passage in Ephesians is saying. Accepting the gift of salvation takes us out of the spiritual state of death and raises us to life with Jesus Christ outside of knowable time and space. This is what it means to be born again. We're born once into a physical body of death; we must be born again in spirit into a body of incorruptible perfection that can exist in eternity. As the passage suggests, when we accept Jesus, we are lifted into eternity, outside of knowable time and space, to be seated with him where we are now. In a sense, this conveys the idea that we're in two places at once, though we wouldn't normally realize it without revelation from God through the Bible. However, thinking of it as "two places at once" isn't accurate. For example, at the transfiguration, we didn't see a pre-cross a post-cross Jesus side by side. Instead, it was like one became the other, but only briefly and partially. It's because they are both the same Jesus, and ultimately, He occupies a state that is outside of time and space. It's not that He went back in time to meet His former self, it's more that, at that point, future Jesus and present Jesus were the same interchangeably.

Also interesting to note about this passage is that it says we were raised together. This adds to the theory of us already being there. Because God is outside of knowable time (yet also with it), when we are saved, we are raised together, even if we are saved years apart. We are also raised together with the apostle Paul when he accepted Jesus as his Savior.

In linear time, we can point to a specific time when we were saved. However, on the other side, it is all the same and we share in it together. In other words, we are already in Heaven, but not yet. This shows us even more of the sheer beauty and majesty of our Lord Almighty. There is no way any of us will fully understand the depths of this concept until it is time for us to escape our own physical existence. Then, each of us who have found our salvation in Jesus Christ will wake up together, and, like we're coming out of a long and terrifying dream, we will realize with utter relief and joy that we have been with Jesus all along.

How to Prepare for the Afterlife

Some years ago, a friend of ours traveled several hundred miles from his home to a city in another state to attend a small convention. He figured that since his group was so small, he didn't need to make a reservation. Upon his arrival at the host hotel, he was surprised to find that it had no vacancies. Even worse, he found out that his group was attending only one of several conventions taking place in this town, so there wasn't a room to be found within twenty-five miles. The moral of the story is: Make plans ahead of time. We don't know when our appointment with death is scheduled, so we need to make it a priority to have our reservation set as soon as possible. How do we prepare for the afterlife, so that we can enter this beautiful new heavenly city with the Lord on High? Scripture clearly answers this question:

- "Jesus saith unto him, I am the way, the truth, and the life: no man cometh unto the Father, but by me" (John 14:6).
- "That if thou shalt confess with thy mouth the Lord Jesus, and shalt believe in thine heart that God hath raised him from the dead, thou shalt be saved" (Romans 1:9).

As the authors of this book were finalizing its last pages, a funny thing happened that bears mentioning. As coworkers, we texted each other to confirm when the final draft was to be turned in to the editor. During that exchange, an unlikely typo revealed an ironic truth. The conversation, through texting, went like this:

Author #1: When is the last day to turn in afterlife stuff?

Author #2: Last day of life. (This was supposed to say "Last day of July," but the phone's autocorrect changed the word "July" to "life.")

So, although I (Allie) had meant to answer the text in reference to this writing assignment by letting the others know: "the work is due on the last day of July," what I really did was drive home the point of this book: "All afterlife 'stuff' has to be turned in by the last day of life." How true…!

Friedrich Schleiermacher (1768–1834), the man often believed to have fathered modern theology,[276] understood the fear some experienced about the prospects of moving from this life to the next. For many, there is a fear of punishment for deeds done in this life. Others have anxiety regarding which religious deity to place one's faith in. However, for most who experience this uncertainty, the issue stems from an aversion for the unknown. Thus, we focus on the "here and now" aspect of living and ignore eternal implications. As creatures of habit, we make a life for ourselves here on earth, and it's hard to think of leaving it behind for that which seems unfamiliar. This distraction from the spiritual realm deepens in correlation to our worldly comforts. Furthermore, luxuries in this life become a barrier between ourselves and our desire for heavenly things. Consider Schleiermacher's statement regarding this aspect of human nature:

Just as little, I know, do you worship the Deity in sacred retirement, as you visit the forsaken temples. In your ornamented dwellings, the only sacred things to be met with are the sage maxims of our wise men, and the splendid compositions of our poets. Suavity and sociability, art and science have so fully taken possession of your minds, that no room remains for the eternal and holy Being that lies beyond the world. I know how well you have succeeded in making your earthly life so rich and varied, that you no longer stand in need of an eternity.[277]

What a profound statement! However, people who think in the way that Schleiermacher is describing are wrong. Every man and woman "stands in need" of an eternal plan. Those who think they don't are only putting off the inevitable and are at risk of doing so until it's too late.

Yet, those who believe themselves above the need to make eternal preparations have the same dreadful wake-up call awaiting them that the rest of humankind is faces, and avoidance will make things much more dire for those who do not prioritize spiritual matters or humble themselves enough to see their need for God.

Many of us allow this important element of our daily life to influence our view about the necessity of the need for salvation. For some, the injustices and pain of this world become a barrier separating us from the God whose ways we do not understand. For others, success and riches may cloud our perspective on the need to be humble before the Lord. However, when this life is over, and we must—as all humanity eventually does—move into the afterlife, all we take with us is what we built spiritually within this realm. This is a reality that *nobody* escapes.

Karl Barth (1886–1968), a reformed minister in Switzerland in the late 1800s, spoke out against the upsurge of liberal theology during his time. Many of his messages were published, including his influential *Dogmatics*. At one point, after a heated religious debate with one of his contemporaries, Hans Küng, the adversary granted that despite their disagreement on theology, he *at least* perceived Barth to be a man of great faith. Aware of his fragile humanity, Barth responded:

So you allow me good faith. I have never conceded myself good faith. And when once the day comes when I have to appear before my Lord, then I will not come with my deeds, with the volumes of my *Dogmatics* in the basket upon my back. All the angels there would have to laugh. But then shall I also not say, "I have always meant well; I had good faith." No, then I will only say one thing: "Lord, be merciful to me, a poor sinner!"[278]

Ultimately, nobody passing from this life into the next has anything to offer God, yet, He has offered everything to us. All we must do is accept Jesus as our Lord and Savior and ask Him to forgive our sins and lead our lives. It is as simple as the Scriptures outline below:

If we confess our sins, he is faithful and just to forgive us our sins, and to cleanse us from all unrighteousness. (1 John 1:9)

That if thou shalt confess with thy mouth the Lord Jesus, and shalt believe in thine heart that God hath raised him from the dead, thou shalt be saved. (Romans 10:9)

It is our hope that if you have not done so, you will make Jesus Christ the Lord and Savior of your life today. One thing we can all be certain of is that none of us is guaranteed tomorrow. It is easy to allow daily life to pull our attention away from arranging our eternity, yet this life is fleeting in comparison to the time we'll spend at our final destination. To those who would make this extremely important decision today, we invite you to offer the following prayer:

Lord Jesus, I am sorry for my sins. I pray that you would come into my life and be my Savior. Show me daily how to live the abundant life that You have for me, and teach me to follow in

Your footsteps for the rest of this life, so that I can spend eternity with You in the next. Amen.

If you have just rededicated your life to Christ, or have said this prayer for the first time, welcome to the family of God!

Notes

1. "Soul Has Weight, Physician Thinks: Dr. MacDougall of Haverhill Tells of Experiments at Death." Editorial, *New York Times* (New York, NY), March 11, 1907.
2. Ibid.
3. Ibid.
4. Ibid.
5. Ibid.
6. Ibid.
7. Thomas, Ben. "The Man Who Tried to Weigh the Soul." *The Crux.* November 3, 2015. Accessed April 24, 2019. http://blogs.discovermagazine. com/crux/2015/11/03/weight-of-the-soul/#.XMCS0OhKiM8.
8. Ibid.
9. Ibid.
10. "Physician Successfully Measures the Weight of the Human Soul." *Disclose TV.* Accessed April 24, 2019. https://www.disclose.tv/ physician-successfully-measures-the-weight-of-the-human-soul-313942.
11. Thomas, Ben. "The Man Who Tried to Weigh the Soul." *The Crux.* November 3, 2015. Accessed April 24, 2019. http://blogs.discovermagazine. com/crux/2015/11/03/weight-of-the-soul/#.XMCS0OhKiM8.

12. Berk, L. (2018). *Development Through the Lifespan*. (Hoboken, NJ: Pearson Education, Inc.) pp. 648.

13. Paulson, S., Fenwick, P., Neal, M., Nelson, K., Parnia, S. "Experiencing Death: An Insider's Perspective." *Annals of the New York Academy of Sciences: Rethinking Mortality: Exploring the Boundaries Between Life and Death.* Epub. (Nov. 2014). 40–57. Accessed April 25, 2019. https://www.ncbi.nlm.nih.gov/pubmed/25059901. p.42.

14. Parnia, S. "Death and Consciousness—An Overview of the Mental and Cognitive Experience of Death." *Annals of the New York Academy of Sciences: Rethinking Mortality: Exploring the Boundaries Between Life and Death.* (2014): 75–93. Accessed April 26, 2019. https://www.ncbi.nlm.nih.gov/pubmed/25418460.

15. Raymond, Chris. "What Happens to My Body Right After I Die?" March 17, 2019, *Very Well Health*, last accessed April 2, 2019, https://www.verywellhealth.com/what-happens-to-my-body-right-after-i-die-1132498.

16. Ibid.

17. Ibid.

18. Ibid.

19. Ibid.

20. Ibid.

21. Long, Jeffrey & Perry, Paul. (2011), *Evidence of the Afterlife*, (New York, NY) p. 3.

22. Ibid., p. 5.

23. Ibid., p. 2.

24. Ibid., p. 2.

25. Ibid., p. 2.

26. Ibid., p. 2.

27. Perry, Paul (Director, Author, & Filmmaker) & Long, Jeff (Author & Filmmaker). (2011). *Afterlife*. [Documentary]. USA: Sakkara Productions.

28. Long, Jeffrey & Perry, Paul. (2011), *Evidence of the Afterlife*, (New York, NY) p. 8.

29. Freud, Sigmund, "When we attempt to imagine this, we perceive ourselves

as spectators." *Quotefancy.com*, last accessed April 2, 2019.

30. Perry, Paul (Director, Author, & Filmmaker) & Long, Jeff (Author & Filmmaker). (2011). *Afterlife.* [Documentary]. USA: Sakkara Productions.

31. Ibid.

32. Moody, R. "People Can Experience Someone Else's Near-Death Experience." Near-Death.com. Accessed April 10, 2019. https://www.near-death.com/science/evidence/people-can-experience-someone-elses-nde.html.

33. Putnam, Cris. *The Supernatural Worldview.* (Crane, MO: Defender Publishing, 2014).

34. Paranormal Witness, "Haunted Highway," Syfy, http://www.syfy.com/paranormalwitness/episodes/season/1/episode/102/haunted_highway_kentucky_ufo_chase (accessed September 26, 2013).

35. Bill Gorman, "Syfy's New Hit Series 'Paranormal Witness' Spooks 1.63 Million Total Viewers, Up 29% Versus Last Week's Premiere," TV by the Numbers, September 15, 2011 (accessed 09/26/13).

36. Paranormal Witness, season 1, episode 2, "Haunted Highway/Kentucky UFO Chase," Daily Motion, http://www.dailymotion.com/video/xl3oef_paranormal-witness-haunted-highway-kentucky-ufo-chase-s01-e02_shortfilms (5:57–6:09).

37. Personal communication from Karen Nichols to Cris Putnam via Facebook private message, September 26, 2013.

38. Paranormal Witness (8:13–8:20).

39. Personal communication from Karen Nichols to Cris Putnam via Facebook private message, August 23, 2013.

40. Interview transcribed from recorded phone call between Cris Putnam and Nick Skubish, July 19, 2013.

41. Paranormal Witness (15:17–15:54).

42. Associated Press, "Boy, 3, Recovering After 5 Days in Car With Dead Mother," *Los Angeles Times,* June 14,1994, http://articles.latimes.com/1994-06-14/news/mn-3969_1_dead-mother (accessed 02/07/14).

43. Long, Jeffrey & Perry, Paul. (2011), *Evidence of the Afterlife,* (New York, NY) p. 8.

44. Ibid., p. 9.

45. Ibid., p. 10.

46. Paulson, S., Fenwick, P., Neal, M., Nelson, K., Parnia, S. "Experiencing Death: An Insider's Perspective." *Annals of the New York Academy of Sciences: Rethinking Mortality: Exploring the Boundaries Between Life and Death.* Epub. (Nov. 2014). 40–57. Accessed April 25, 2019. https://www.ncbi.nlm.nih.gov/pubmed/25059901. p.47.

47. Ibid., p.47.

48. Long, Jeffrey & Perry, Paul. (2011), *Evidence of the Afterlife*, (New York, NY) p. 12.

49. Ibid., p. 12.

50. Ibid., p. 12.

51. Hinshaw, David, dir., *Seeing the Unseen.* (United States: Beyond Words Publishing, 2019) Dvd, 45 min.

52. Ibid.

53. Long, Jeffrey & Perry, Paul. (2011), *Evidence of the Afterlife*, (New York, NY) p. 13.

54. Ibid., p. 13.

55. Ibid., p. 14–15.

56. Exclusive interview between Allie Anderson of Defender Publishing and Dean Braxton. Tuesday, May 14, 2019, 9 AM ET.

57. Editor's note: Colossians 3:17.

58. Editor's note: Hebrews 8:12, 10:17.

59. Long, Jeffrey & Perry, Paul. (2011), *Evidence of the Afterlife*, (New York, NY) p. 14.

60. "This Was Your Life." (2019). *Chick Publications.* Accessed April 10, 2019. https://www.chick.com/products/tract?stk=0001.

61. Long, Jeffrey & Perry, Paul. (2011), *Evidence of the Afterlife*, (New York, NY) p. 15–16.

62. Horn, Thomas R. *The Boy From El Mirage: A Memoir of Humble Beginnings, Unexpected Miracles, and Why I Have No Idea How I Wound Up Where I Am.* (Crane, MO: Defender Publishing, 2017).

63. Long, Jeffrey & Perry, Paul. (2011), *Evidence of the Afterlife*, (New York, NY) p. 16.

64. Howell, Donna, & Anderson-Henson, Allie. *Encounters: Extraordinary Accounts of Angelic Intervention and What the Bible Actually Says about God's Messengers*. (Crane, MO: Defender Publishing, 2019).

65. Van Natta, Bruce. *A Miraculous Life: True Stories of Supernatural Encounters with God*. (Lake Mary, FL: Charisma House, 2013) 53.

66. Ibid., 55.

67. Ibid., 56.

68. Long, Jeffrey & Perry, Paul. (2011), *Evidence of the Afterlife*, (New York, NY) p. 17.

69. Paulson, S., Fenwick, P., Neal, M., Nelson, K., Parnia, S. "Experiencing Death: An Insider's Perspective." *Annals of the New York Academy of Sciences: Rethinking Mortality: Exploring the Boundaries Between Life and Death*. Epub. (Nov. 2014). 40–57. Accessed April 25, 2019. https://www.ncbi.nlm. nih.gov/pubmed/25059901. p.51.

70. "Stony Brook Professor Leads World's Largest Medical Study on the State of Mind and Consciousness at the Time of Death." *Stony Brook University News Online*. Accessed April 25, 2019.

71. Paulson, S., Fenwick, P., Neal, M., Nelson, K., Parnia, S. "Experiencing Death: An Insider's Perspective." *Annals of the New York Academy of Sciences: Rethinking Mortality: Exploring the Boundaries Between Life and Death*. Epub. (Nov. 2014). 40–57. Accessed April 25, 2019. https://www.ncbi.nlm. nih.gov/pubmed/25059901. p.51.

72. Ibid., p.55.

73. Long, Jeffrey & Perry, Paul. (2011), *Evidence of the Afterlife*, (New York, NY) p. 85.

74. Ibid., p. 89.

75. Putnam, Cris. *The Supernatural Worldview*. (Crane, MO: Defender Publishing, 2014).

76. Kimberly Clark, "Clinical Interventions with Near-Death Experiencers," in Bruce Greyson and Charles P. Flynn, eds., *The Near-Death Experience:*

Problems, Prospects, Perspectives (Springfield, IL: Charles C. Thomas, 1984) p. 243.

77. Ibid., p. 243.

78. Gary R. Habermas and J. P. Moreland, *Beyond Death: Exploring the Evidence for Immortality* (Wheaton, IL: Crossway, 1998) p. 213.

79. Long, Jeffrey. "Frightening NDEs." NDERF.org. Accessed April 10, 2019. https://www.nderf.org/NDERF/EvidenceAfterlife/evidence/Frightening_NDEs.htm.

80. Ibid.

81. Greyson, B. & Bush, N. (1992). "Distressing Near-Death Experiences." *Psychiatry*, 55, 95–110.

82. Long, Jeffrey. "Frightening NDEs." NDERF.org. Accessed April 10, 2019. https://www.nderf.org/NDERF/EvidenceAfterlife/evidence/Frightening_NDEs.htm.

83. "Dr. Barbara Rommer's Negative Near-Death Experience Research." *Near-Death.com*. Accessed April 10, 2019. https://www.near-death.com/science/experts/barbara-rommer.html.

84. Ibid.

85. Ibid.

86. Melvin, Bryan, in a private interview with Josh Peck for Defender Publishing. Emailed Document, January 30, 2019.

87. See 1 Corinthians 13:6.

88. See Ecclesiastes 3:11.

89. See John 3:30.

90. "Stony Brook Professor Leads World's Largest Medical Study on the State of Mind and Consciousness at the Time of Death." *Stony Brook University News Online*. Accessed April 25, 2019. https://news.stonybrook.edu/news/medical/141009Parnia.

91. Ibid.

92. Ibid.

93. Ibid.

94. Ibid.

95. Ibid.

96. Paulson, S., Fenwick, P., Neal, M., Nelson, K., Parnia, S. "Experiencing Death: An Insider's Perspective." *Annals of the New York Academy of Sciences: Rethinking Mortality: Exploring the Boundaries Between Life and Death.* Epub. (Nov. 2014). 40–57. Accessed April 25, 2019. https://www. ncbi.nlm.nih.gov/pubmed/25059901. p.41.

97. Ibid., p.41.

98. Ibid., p.42.

99. Ibid., p.42.

100. Ibid. P.42.

101. Ibid., p.42.

102. This story was shared by Christina Peck, printed with permission, 2019.

103. Cosmology.com, *Journal of Cosmology.* Accessed July 16, 2019. http:// journalofcosmology.com/Consciousness152.html.

104. Ibid.

105. Giulio Fanti, Emanuela Marinelli, and Alessandro Cagnazzo, "Computerized Anthropometric Analysis of the Man of the Turin Shroud," University of Padua, Italy, Department of Mechanical Engineering (1999), 14; last accessed January 18, 2019, https://www.shroud.com/pdfs/marineli. pdf.

106. Ibid., 15.

107. Frederick T. Zugibe, MD, PhD, *The Crucifixion of Jesus: A Forensic Inquiry* (M. Evans and Company, Inc.; New York, NY: Kindle edition, 2005) location 2847.

108. Ibid., location 2834.

109. Ibid., location 2219.

110. Dr. Pierre Barbet, *A Doctor at Calvary: The Passion of Our Lord Jesus Christ as Described by a Surgeon* (originally published 1953: Papamoa Press: Kindle edition, 2017), locations 2198–2203.

111. Frederick T. Zugibe, *The Crucifixion of Jesus*, locations 1319–1342.

112. Ibid 1319–1342.

113. Ibid., location 3779.

114. Ibid., location 4034.

115. Barrie M. Schwortz, "Is the Shroud of Turin a Medieval Photograph? A Critical Examination of the Theory," 2000, *Shroud.com*, last accessed April 3, 2019, https://www.shroud.com/pdfs/orvieto.pdf.

116. Frederick T. Zugibe, *The Crucifixion of Jesus*, location 4219.

117. Ibid., location 4513.

118. Edward Byron Nicholson, M.A., *The Gospel According to the Hebrews: Its Fragments Translated and Annotated with a Critical Analysis of the External and Internal Evidence Relating to It* (C. Kegan Paul & Co.; London: 1879), pp. 62–68. Please note that the passage quoted herein appeared in fragments over six pages as Nicholson's annotations broke it into relevant word studies. To avoid confusion about where the verse began or ended, these authors have inserted the passage as a whole, the way Nicholson had the verse itself set apart in larger text in his original work (without adding ellipses to mark omitted commentary material *by Nicholson,* because doing so would confuse modern readers away from understanding the verse to be a whole).

119. Ibid., 65–66.

120. Frederick T. Zugibe, *The Crucifixion of Jesus*, location 3210.

121. Dr. Alan D. Whanger, "Polarized Image Overlay Technique: A New Image Comparison Method and it's Applications," *Applied Optics*, 1985, Volume 24, Issue 6, 766–772; last accessed online March 25, 2019, https://www.osapublishing.org/ao/viewmedia.cfm?uri=ao-24-6-766&seq=0.

122. "The Second International Conference on the Sudarium of Oviedo," April 13–15, 2007, last accessed March 26, 2019, https://www.shroud.com/pdfs/n65part6.pdf.

123. Dr. Alan Adler, "Updating Recent Studies on the Shroud of Turin," a study in chemistry for Western Connecticut State University in 1996, 226; last accessed online March 26, 2019, http://www.sindone.info/ADLER.PDF.

124. "The Second International Conference on the Sudarium of Oviedo."

125. Dr. Alan Adler, "Updating Recent Studies."

126. *Codex Vossianus Latinus*, Q68; Vatican Library, Codex 5696, fol.35.

Published in Pietro Savio's *Ricerche Storiche Sulla Santa Sindone* in Turin, 1957.

127. Ian Wilson, *The Shroud: The 2,000-Year-Old Mystery Solved* (Bantam Books; London: 2010)p. 224.

128. Ibid., 224.

129. Robert K. Wilcox, *The Truth about the Shroud of Turin: Solving the Mystery* (Regnery Publishing, Inc.; Washington, DC: 2010) p. 109.

130. Ibid., 108.

131. This quote appears in countless Shroud-related research materials. Frederick T. Zugibe quotes it as well, in his *Crucifixion of Jesus*, Kindle location 4943.

132. Frederick T. Zugibe, *The Crucifixion of Jesus*, location 2728.

133. P. E. Damon, D. J. Donahue, B. H. Gore, A. L. Hatheway, A. J. T. Jull, T. W. Linick, P. J. Sercel, L. J. Toolin, C. R. Bronk, E. T. Hall, R. E. M. Hedges, R. Housley, I. A. Law, C. Perry, G. Bonani, S. Trumbore, W. Woefli, J. C. Ambers, S. G. E. Bowman, M. N. Leese, M. S. Tite, "Radiocarbon Dating of the Shroud of Turin," February 16, 1989, *Nature*, Issue 337, 611–615.

134. Frederick T. Zugibe, *The Crucifixion of Jesus*, location 2711.

135. Malcolm W. Browne, "Errors Are Feared in Carbon Dating," May 31, 1990, *The New York Times*, archived online and last accessed April 12, 2019 https://www.nytimes.com/1990/05/31/us/errors-are-feared-in-carbon-dating.html; emphasis added.

136. The discovery of the mummy labeled as "The Younger Lady" has not been confirmed to be Nefertiti. Rather, the currently nameless mummy is confirmed through DNA to be King Tut's biological mother and Pharaoh Amenhotep III's daughter. Considering the nature of the royal Egyptian dynasties' bloodlines and how the family trees interconnect, there remains to be much evidence against the idea that Nefertiti and the "Younger Lady" mummy are one and the same person.

137. William Meacham, *The Rape of the Turin Shroud: How Christianity's Most Precious Relic was Wrongly Condemned, and Violated* (Lulu: 2005, Kindle edition), locations 1139–1156.

138. Ibid., locations 1139–1156.

139. Frederick T. Zugibe, *The Crucifixion of Jesus*, location 5062–5071.

140. Joseph G. Marino and M. Sue Benford, "Evidence for the Skewing of the C-14 Dating of the Shroud of Turin Due to Repairs," August, 2000, last accessed April 24, 2019, https://www.shroud.com/pdfs/marben.pdf, p. 1.

141. Ibid., p. 1.

142. Ibid., p. 2

143. Ibid., p. 2

144. Ibid ., p 2.

145. Frederick T. Zugibe, *Crucifixion of Jesus*, location 5279.

146. Ray Rogers' *curriculum vitae* summary and select commentary, recorded at: Daniel R. Porter, "Carbon 14 Dating and the Shroud of Turin," 2008, *FactsPlusFacts*, last accessed April 25, 2019, http://factsplusfacts.com/shroud-of-turin-carbon-14.htm.

147. Joseph G. Marino and M. Sue Benford, "Evidence for the Skewing…" https://www.shroud.com/pdfs/marben.pdf.

148. Ibid., 5.

149. "Hades: Greek Mythology." *Encyclopædia Britannica Online*. Accessed May 3, 2019. https://www.britannica.com/topic/Hades-Greek-mythology.

150. Romans 1:20: For his invisible attributes, namely, his eternal power and divine nature, have been clearly perceived, ever since the creation of the world, in the things that have been made, so they are without excuse.

151. Witherington, B. (2015). *Reading and Understanding the Bible*. (Oxford University Press, Oxford, NY) p. 11.

152. Ibid. 11–12.

153. Ibid., 12.

154. Gibbs, C. *Principles of Biblical Interpretation: An Independent-Study Textbook,* Fourth Edition, (Springfield, MO: Global University, 2016) p. 131.

155. Gill, N. S. "The Etymology of the Word Pagan." *ThoughtCo.com* August 26, 2018. Accessed July 12, 2019. https://www.thoughtco.com/what-is-pagan-120163.

156. "Who Was Abraham? And Where Did He Come From?" *Bet Yeshurn*

Messianic Assembly Online. 2019. Accessed July 12, 2019. http://www.messianics.us/bible-history/who-was-abraham.html.

157. "Ibid.

158. Gilbert, Derek & Sharon, in a personal, private interview with Defender Publishing agent. April 22, 2019, 11 AM.

159. Ibid.

160. Ibid.

161. Ibid.

162. Ibid.

163. Hester, H. I. *The Heart of Hebrew History: A Study of the Old Testament.* (Liberty, Missouri: William Jewell Press, 1949) p. 53.

164. "Life after Death." *History Museum Online.* Accessed April 15, 2019. https://www.historymuseum.ca/cmc/exhibitions/civil/egypt/egcr04e.html.

165. Hester, H. I. *The Heart of Hebrew History: A Study of the Old Testament.* (Liberty, Missouri: William Jewell Press, 1949) p. 53.

166. "Life after Death." *History Museum Online.* Accessed April 15, 2019. https://www.historymuseum.ca/cmc/exhibitions/civil/egypt/egcr04e.html.

167. "Preparation for Death in Ancient Egypt." *Australian Museum Online.* Accessed April 15, 2019. https://australianmuseum.net.au/learn/cultures/international-collection/ancient-egyptian/preparation-for-death-in-ancient-egypt/.

168. Ibid.

169. Ibid.

170. Ibid.

171. "Life After Death." *History Museum Online.* Accessed April 15, 2019. https://www.historymuseum.ca/cmc/exhibitions/civil/egypt/egcr04e.html.

172. Ibid.

173. Ibid.

174. Ibid.

175. Ibid.

176. Ibid.

177. "Preparation for Death in Ancient Egypt." *Australian Museum Online.* Accessed April 15, 2019. https://australianmuseum.

net.au/learn/cultures/international-collection/ancient-egyptian/
preparation-for-death-in-ancient-egypt/.

178. Ibid.

179. Ibid.

180. Ibid.

181. "Osiris." *Ancient Egypt*. Accessed April 15, 2019. http://www.ancientegypt.
co.uk/gods/explore/osiris.html.

182. Awana, M. "What Did the Ancient Greek Believe Happened ater Death?"
Classroom Synonym. Accessed April 15, 2019. https://classroom.synonym.
com/did-ancient-greek-believe-happened-after-death-13446.html.

183. Roberts, Ivy. "River Styx in Greek Mythology." *Study.com*. Accessed
April 15, 2019. https://study.com/academy/lesson/river-styx-in-greek-
mythology-definition-story.html.

184. "Charon." *Encyclopedia Britannica Online*. Accessed April 15, 2019.
https://www.britannica.com/topic/Charon-Greek-mythology.

185. Awana, M. "What Did the Ancient Greek Believe Happened after Death?"
Classroom Synonym. Accessed April 15, 2019. https://classroom.synonym.
com/did-ancient-greek-believe-happened-after-death-13446.html.

186. Ibid.

187. "Death in Ancient Greece." *My Learning*. Accessed
April 15, 2019. https://www.mylearning.org/stories/
ancient-greeks-everyday-life-beliefs-and-myths/418.

188. Awana, M. "What Did the Ancient Greek Believe Happened after Death?"
Classroom Synonym. Accessed April 15, 2019. https://classroom.synonym.
com/did-ancient-greek-believe-happened-after-death-13446.html.

189. "Death in Ancient Greece." *My Learning*. Accessed
April 15, 2019. https://www.mylearning.org/stories/
ancient-greeks-everyday-life-beliefs-and-myths/418.

190. "Tantalus." *Encyclopedia Britannica Online*. Accessed April 15, 2019.
https://www.britannica.com/topic/Tantalus.

191. "Sisyphus." *Myth Web*. Accessed April 15, 2019. http://www.mythweb.
com/encyc/entries/sisyphus.html.

192. "Death in Ancient Greece." *My Learning*. Accessed April 15, 2019. https://www.mylearning.org/stories/ancient-greeks-everyday-life-beliefs-and-myths/418.

193. Greek, "Afterlife, and Roman Concepts." "Afterlife: Greek and Roman Concepts." Encyclopedia of Religion, 2019. Accessed June 27, 2019. https://www.encyclopedia.com/environment/encyclopedias-almanacs-transcripts-and-maps/afterlife-greek-and-roman-concepts.

194. Price, S. R. F., *Rituals and Power: The Roman Imperial Cult in Asia Minor*, (Cambridge, UK, 1984).

195. Johnston, Patricia A., Virgil, and Virgil. Vergil Aeneid Book 6. (Newburyport, MA: Focus Publishing/R. Pullins Company, 2012).

196. Ibid.

197. DZkmec, Evan. "Roman Beliefs in the Afterlife." Prezi.com. December 13, 2012. Accessed June 27, 2019. https://prezi.com/tuomecxmsi7v/roman-beliefs-in-the-afterlife/.

198. "Strong's H953," As cited on *Blue Letter Bible*, last accessed July 18, 2019, https://www.blueletterbible.org/lang/lexicon/lexicon.cfm?Strongs=H953&t=KJV.

199. Hades: Greek Mythology." *Encyclopædia Britannica Online*. Accessed April 15, 2019. https://www.britannica.com/topic/Hades-Greek-mythology.

200. "The Four Socratic Dialogues of Plato," *Archive.org*, Last impression 1924, made available online 2019, accessed July 18, 2019. https://archive.org/stream/foursocraticdial00platuoft/foursocraticdial00platuoft_djvu.txt.

201. "Hades: Greek Mythology." *Encyclopædia Britannica Online*. Accessed April 15, 2019. https://www.britannica.com/topic/Hades-Greek-mythology.

202. "Strong's G5020," As cited on *Blue Letter Bible*, last accessed July 18, 2019, https://www.blueletterbible.org/lang/lexicon/lexicon.cfm?Strongs=G5020&t=KJV.

203. Metzger, Bruce; Coogan, Michael (1993). *Oxford Companion to the Bible*. (Oxford: Oxford University Press). pp. "Acts of the Apostles", "Luke, The Gospel According to."

204. Strelan, Rick. "*Luke the Priest—The Authority of the Author of the Third Gospel,* "Was Luke a Jew or Gentile?" (Ashgate Publishing, Ltd., May 1, 2013) pp. 102–110.

205. Harris, Stephen L., Understanding the Bible. (Palo Alto: Mayfield. 1985) "The Gospels," pp. 266–268.

206. Merriam-Webster Online Dictionary (Merriam-Webster, Springfield, MA, 2005), s.v. "polemic."

207. Smith, Mark S., and Wayne T. Pitard. The Ugaritic Baal Cycle. (Leiden: E. J. Brill, 1994).

208. "What's Ugaritic Got to Do with Anything?" Logos Bible Software. Accessed June 27, 2019. https://www.logos.com/ugaritic.

209. "Strong's G1067," As cited on *Blue Letter Bible*, last accessed July 18, 2019, https://www.blueletterbible.org/lang/lexicon/lexicon.cfm?Strongs=G1067&t=KJV.

210. Carl Gibbs, *Principles of Biblical Interpretation: An Independent-Study Textbook* (Fourth; Springfield, MO: Global University: 2016) *p.* 133.

211. Ibid., 133.

212. Ibid., 133.

213. Beitzel, B. J. & Lyle, K. A. *Lexham Geographic Commentary on the Gospels.* (2016, Bellingham WA: Lexham Press).

214. Kerr, H. *Readings in Christian Thought* (Nashville, TN: Abingdon Press, 1990) p. 166.

215. Gilbert, Derek & Sharon, personal, private Interview with Defender Publishing agent. April 22, 2019, 11 AM.

216. Ibid.

217. Dickens, Charles. *A Christmas Carol.* Kindle Edition. July 16, 2019, Location 323.

218. Ibid., Location 341.

219. Lane, T. (2006). *A Concise History of Christian Thought* (Grand Rapids, MI: Baker Publishing Group) p. 223–224.

220. Stewart, D. "What Is Purgatory?" *Blue Letter Bible*. Accessed May 2, 2019. https://www.blueletterbible.org/faq/don_stewart/don_stewart_122.cfm.

221. "What is the difference between mortal and venial sin?" *Catholic Straight Answers*. Accessed May 2, 2019. http://catholicstraightanswers.com/what-is-the-difference-between-mortal-and-venial-sin/.

222. "2 Maccabees, Chapter 12." *United States of Conference of Catholic Bishops*. Accessed May 3, 2019. http://www.usccb.org/bible/2maccabees12.

223. Augustine. *City of God*. 21:13, c. AD 413–426.

224. Ibid., 21:42:2.

225. "Visions of Purgatory: St. Gregory the Great." *The Real Presence*. Accessed May 3, 2019. http://www.therealpresence.org/eucharst/misc/PHP/purg_sg_great.pdf.

226. Ibid.

227. Ibid.

228. Ibid.

229. Brom, R. and Carr, B. "Purgatory." *Catholic Answers*. Accessed May 2, 2019. https://www.catholic.com/tract/purgatory.

230. Ibid.

231. Ikram, Salima (2003). *Death and Burial in Ancient Egypt*. (Longman, ISBN 978-0582772168).

232. *A Concise History of Christian Thought* (Grand Rapids, MI: Baker Publishing Group, 2006) p. 9.

233. Lane, T. *Concise History of Christian Thought*. (Grand Rapids, MI: Baker Publishing Group, 2006) p. 289.

234. "Strong's H4578," As cited on *Blue Letter Bible*, last accessed July 17, 2019, https://www.blueletterbible.org/lang/lexicon/lexicon.cfm?Strongs=H4578&t=KJV.

235. "Strong's H990," As cited on *Blue Letter Bible*, last accessed July 17, 2019, https://www.blueletterbible.org/lang/lexicon/lexicon.cfm?Strongs=H990&t=KJV.

236. "Strong's H7585," As cited on *Blue Letter Bible*, last accessed July 17, 2019, https://www.blueletterbible.org/lang/lexicon/lexicon.cfm?Strongs=H7585&t=KJV.

237. "Strong's H776, H1280, & H5769," As cited on *Blue Letter Bible*,

last accessed July 17, 2019, at the following sources: https://www.blueletterbible.org/lang/lexicon/lexicon.cfm?Strongs=H776&t=KJV; https://www.blueletterbible.org/lang/lexicon/lexicon.cfm?Strongs=H1280&t=KJV; https://www.blueletterbible.org/lang/lexicon/lexicon.cfm?Strongs=H5769&t=KJV.

238. Homily on Our Lord IV, *Christian Classics Ethereal Library*, accessed July 30, 2019. http://www.ccel.org/ccel/schaff/npnf213.iii.viii.ii.html.

239. "The Epistle of Ignatius to the Trallians," as cited by *Bible Study Tools Online*: Ante-Nicene Fathers, Vol. 1, Ignatius—Epistle to the Trallians, Chap. IX, Last accessed July 23, 2019, https://www.biblestudytools.com/history/early-church-fathers/ante-nicene/vol-1-apostolic-with-justin-martyr-irenaeus/ignatius/epistle-of-ignatius-trallians.html.

240. "Fragments from the Lost Writings of Irenaeus," as cited by *Bible Study Tools Online*: Ante-Nicene Fathers, Vol. 1, Fragments from the Lost Writings of Irenaeus XXVIII, Last accessed July 23, 2019, https://www.biblestudytools.com/history/early-church-fathers/ante-nicene/vol-1-apostolic-with-justin-martyr-irenaeus/irenaeus/fragments-from-lost-writings-of-irenaeus.html.

241. Ante-Nicene Fathers, Vol. II, Clement—Stromata, Book 6, Chap. VI., 1869.

242. Kerr, H. T. (1990). *Readings in Christian Thought* (Nashville, TN: Abingdon Press, 1990) P. 82.

243. Ibid., 83.

244. Although no direct quotation occurs, the concepts presented within this section are presented by Michael Heiser. More information is available at: Houseform Apologetics. "Naked Bible Podcast 090—The Lake of Fire." December 2, 2017. YouTube Video: 50:20. https://www.youtube.com/watch?v=FnhO0Vp6BHY&t=2118s.

245. For more information regarding angels, theologically sound information on this subject can be found in the book *Encounters: Extraordinary Accounts of Angelic Intervention and What the Bible Actually Says about God's Messengers*, by Howell, Donna, & Anderson-Henson, Allie. (Crane, MO: Defender Publishing, 2019).

246. "Muslims and Islam: Key Findings in the U.S. and Around the World," *Pew Research Center*, August 9, 2017, accessed July 30, 2019, https://www.pewresearch.org/fact-tank/2017/08/09/muslims-and-islam-key-findings-in-the-u-s-and-around-the-world/.

247. "Number of Buddhists World-Wide," *Buddhanet.net*, accessed July 30, 2019, https://www.buddhanet.net/e-learning/history/bud_statwrld.htm.

248. "Karma," *Merriam-Webster's OnlineDictionary*, accessed July 30, 2019, https://www.merriam-webster.com/dictionary/karma.

249. Corbett-Hemeyer J., (2005). Inter-religious Perspectives on Hope and Limits in Cancer Treatment: On Buddhist Chaplain's Response to the Case. *Journal of Clinical Oncology* 23(31): 8140–8141. Doi: 10.1200/JCO.2005.03.5725

250. "How Different Religions View the Afterlife." Accessed July 23, 2019. http://www.victorzammit.com/articles/religions3.html.

251. Ibid.

252. Editors, History.com. "History of Ghost Stories." History.com. October 29, 2009. Accessed July 23, 2019. https://www.history.com/topics/halloween/historical-ghost-stories.

253. Flavius Josephus and William Whiston, *The Works of Josephus: Complete and Unabridged* (Peabody: Hendrickson, 1996, c1987), Ant. 6.330.

254. *The Academy: A Weekly Review of Literature, Science, and Art*, Vol. L, 1986, p. 519.

255. Sunim, Hwansan, and Hwansan Sunim. "A Quantum Theory of Consciousness." HuffPost, July 19, 2017. Accessed July 23, 2019. https://www.huffpost.com/entry/a-quantum-theory-of-consciousness_b_596fb782e4b04dcf308d29bb.

256. Chandel, Payal Kanwar. "Religious Interpretations of Reincarnation," *Indian Journal of Health and Wellbeing*, 2015, 6(7) 737–740, ISSN-p-2229-5356.c-2321-3698.

257. "Article: Liberation." JAINpedia Themes Principles Liberation. Accessed July 23, 2019. http://www.jainpedia.org/themes/principles/jain-beliefs/liberation.html.

258. "Religions—Jainism: The Soul." BBC. September 10, 2009. Accessed July 23, 2019. https://www.bbc.co.uk/religion/religions/jainism/beliefs/soul.shtml.

259. The Internet Classics Archive | On Metaphysics by Aristotle, classics.mit.edu/Aristotle/metaphysics.html.

260. Siegel, Ethan. "What Is the Physics of Nothing?" *Forbes*, 22 Sept. 2016, www.forbes.com/sites/startswithabang/2016/09/22/what-is-the-physics-of-nothing/#13580ad075f8.

261. Exodus 3:14.

262. Feser, Edward. *Five Proofs of the Existence of God*,p. 27.

263. Inwagen, Peter Van. "The Possibility of Resurrection" and Other Essays in Christian Apologetics. (Boulder, CO: Westview Press, 1999).

264. Ibid., 51.

265. "Doppelgänger," Encyclopædia Britannica. Accessed July 24, 2019. https://www.britannica.com/art/doppelganger.

266. *Introduction to Islam,* 5th ed. (Global University) p. 129.

267. Ibid.

268. Barry, J. D., Mangum, D., Brown, D. R., Heiser, M. S., Custis, M., Ritzema, E., ... Bomar, D. (2012, 2016). Faithlife Study Bible (Ac 12:15). (Bellingham, WA: Lexham Press).

269. Gangel, K. O. (1998). Acts (Vol. 5, p. 196). (Nashville, TN: Broadman & Holman Publishers).

270. Renegade, Daily. "Dr. Michael Heiser | Angels & 'Doppelgänger' Divine Doubles | Peck Underground Church." YouTube. February 15, 2019. Accessed July 24, 2019. https://www.youtube.com/watch?v=zyfAPiRTsvs.

271. Stang, Charles M. *Our Divine Double*. (Cambridge: Harvard University Press, 2016).

272. M. Whittaker, trans., *Tatian: Oratio ad Graecos and Fragments* (Oxford: Clarendon, 1984), Oratio 7.30 (14).

273. Oratio 12.18–22(22).

274. Oratio 14.21–15.7 (26–28)

275. "Greek G4891." Greek Lexicon, as quoted by *Blue Letter Bible*, accessed

July 24, 2019, http://www.blueletterbible.org/lang/Lexicon/Lexicon. cfm?Strongs=G4891&t=KJV.

276. Kerr, H. T. (1990). *Readings in Christian Thought*. (Nashville, TN: Abingdon Press) p. 212.

277. http://www.blueletterbible.org/lang/Lexicon/Lexicon. cfm?Strongs=G4891&t=KJV. P. 213.

278. Lane, Anthony. *Justifiication by Faith*, (Bloomsbury Publishing: London, 2006) 206.